D0936890

PRAISE FOR
IN THE SHADOW OF THE IVORY TOWER

"Davarian Baldwin is one of the most important urban historians and cultural critics we have today. In his new book, *In the Shadow of the Ivory Tower: How Universities Are Plundering Our Cities*, Baldwin brings his incisive insights and analysis to bear in a devastating critique of our dated and quaint notions of universities and colleges as egalitarian sites of learning and cultural production. Baldwin unmasks 'UniverCities' as growth machines, unleashing gentrification, stewarding large police forces, cheating tax coffers while exploiting low wage Black and Brown labor throughout the campus. Deeply researched and forcefully written, Baldwin cracks open new debates about the complicated roles of these institutions of higher education and the cities they call home."

—Keeanga-Yamahtta Taylor, author of *Race for Profit: How Banks and the Real Estate Industry Undermined Black Homeownership*

"An unflinching and comprehensive look at how capital has reached its talons into every facet of our lives, from the halls of our elite universities to the street corners of our local communities. A good read for anyone interested in the depressing reality of universities today, a must-read for anyone interested in envisioning a more equitable future for education and city life."

—P. E. Moskowitz, author of *How to Kill a City*

"Insightful, compelling, and timely. *In the Shadow of the Ivory Tower* unveils a widely neglected aspect of American history: the role of higher education in shaping American cities. This book lays the groundwork for the role of universities in creating equitable and just cities."

—Ibram X. Kendi, National Book Award–winning author of
Stamped from the Beginning and *How to Be an Antiracist*

"Classes with professors and students are now a minor side business on college and university campuses with the economic and political power to reshape cities. One of the nation's foremost urban historians, Davarian Baldwin reveals how these institutions have acquired massive financial and real estate holdings and leveraged them to displace vulnerable communities, control public access to essential services, define progress, and, even, command their own police forces. This brilliant study shows that higher education continues to thrive off the injustices that plague our society."

—Craig Steven Wilder, author of *Ebony & Ivy: Race, Slavery,
and the Troubled History of America's Universities*

DAVARIAN L. BALDWIN

IN THE SHADOW OF THE IVORY TOWER

HOW UNIVERSITIES ARE PLUNDERING OUR CITIES

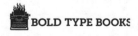

BOLD TYPE BOOKS

New York

Copyright © 2021 by Davarian L. Baldwin

Cover design by Pete Garceau
Cover image copyright © Shutterstock
Cover copyright © 2021 by Hachette Book Group, Inc.

Hachette Book Group supports the right to free expression and the value of copyright. The purpose of copyright is to encourage writers and artists to produce the creative works that enrich our culture.

The scanning, uploading, and distribution of this book without permission is a theft of the author's intellectual property. If you would like permission to use material from the book (other than for review purposes), please contact permissions@hbgusa.com. Thank you for your support of the author's rights.

Bold Type Books
116 East 16th Street, 8th Floor, New York, NY 10003
www.boldtypebooks.org
@BoldTypeBooks

Printed in the United States of America

First Edition: March 2021

Published by Bold Type Books, an imprint of Perseus Books, LLC, a subsidiary of Hachette Book Group, Inc. Bold Type Books is a co-publishing venture of the Type Media Center and Perseus Books.

The Hachette Speakers Bureau provides a wide range of authors for speaking events. To find out more, go to www.hachettespeakersbureau.com or call (866) 376-6591.

The publisher is not responsible for websites (or their content) that are not owned by the publisher.

Print book interior design by Amy Quinn.

Library of Congress Cataloging-in-Publication Data

Names: Baldwin, Davarian L., author.
Title: In the shadow of the ivory tower : how universities are plundering our cities /
    Davarian L. Baldwin.
Description: First edition. | New York, NY : Bold Type Books, [2021] | Includes
    bibliographical references and index.
Identifiers: LCCN 2020045203 | ISBN 9781568588926 (hardcover) | ISBN
    9781568588919 (ebook)
Subjects: LCSH: Community and college—United States. | Universities and colleges—
    United States—Economic aspects. | Universities and colleges—United States—Social
    aspects. | Education, Higher—United States—Economic aspects. | Community
    development, Urban—United States.
Classification: LCC LC238 .B35 2021 | DDC 378.1/03—dc23
LC record available at https://lccn.loc.gov/2020045203

ISBNs: 978-1-56858-892-6 (hardcover), 978-1-56858-891-9 (e-book)

LSC-C

Printing 1, 2021

For Nylan, Noah, Ellison, and Bridgette
Always reminding me it's the grace of life, not the pace of life

CONTENTS

CHESS MOVES ON A CHECKERBOARD

I never thought a university would foretell the future of our cities. But there I was, on a December afternoon in 2003, stepping out into the brisk South Side air after hours holed away in the University of Chicago's Regenstein Library. I immediately heard chants of protest and saw people buzzing about. So I followed the sound over to the main quadrangle, just outside the university's administration building. There I saw a crowd of about fifty people surrounded by media crews and onlookers. On one side stood residents from the historic Black neighborhood of Bronzeville, alongside students and others chanting "U of C, look at your history!" while holding signs that read "Support the Checkerboard Lounge in Bronzeville."[1] And on the other side, university officials listened, mostly playing defense, with a silent chorus of furrowed brows.

The famed Checkerboard Lounge had been a cultural mainstay of Bronzeville, a "blues shrine" that had stood on 43rd Street since 1972. The lounge needed restoring, but instead of providing funding the university put together a plan to relocate the lounge from its original spot to a university-owned building inside the Hyde Park neighborhood's Harper Court shopping district. Outraged, Restoring Bronzeville advocates immediately charged UChicago with "cultural piracy."[2] For decades the city had turned its back on Bronzeville, but things were slowly changing, largely because of the sweat equity of local advocates working to turn things around.

Renovated hundred-year-old graystones, newly built condominium developments, and small shops slowly began to fill in the spaces between vacant lots and run-down storefronts. And many saw the Checkerboard as central to the economic revitalization of Bronzeville as "a heritage tourist destination."[3] But just when momentum started building around a modest neighborhood comeback, the university swept in and bought up one of the area's best cultural assets. And UChicago's backdoor deal resuscitated almost a century of local stories in which the school had either demolished Black neighborhood blocks or built institutional walls to keep Black residents away from campus. Here we go again, activists thought.

The "old" Checkerboard Lounge, 423 East 43rd Street, Chicago, Illinois, 2003. Photo by discosour, Flickr.

Of course, the university had a much different take on the story. School administrators and local stakeholders for the Hyde Park campus neighborhood argued that the Checkerboard acquisition was a simple economic transaction between owner and buyer. UChicago officials also explained that the relocation was an act of Black historic preservation.[4] At the time, Sonya Malunda was the senior associate vice president for Civic Engagement at the university. She rejected any suggestion that UChicago did anything wrong in the acquisition. In fact, the lounge owner, L. C. Thurman, got on a bullhorn at the December rally and told the protestors to go home. "A lot of myths surrounding the Checkerboard became the narrative," Malunda explained. School officials were responding to the closing of the lounge because of building code violations and considered the relocation a mutual benefit to the university and the community. She still looks back with frustration on that chapter in her life: "We wanted to do the right thing, but it seems no good deed goes unpunished."

"I think that's complete bullshit" is how Bernard Loyd responded to Malunda's account. As he saw it, the university identified the Checkerboard Lounge as a key attraction for the Hyde Park campus neighborhood . . . and for no one else. He pointed out that the Harper Court shopping and entertainment district, where the Checkerboard would sit, was being renovated because there was hardly anything to do in Hyde Park. "Students were coming to the Checkerboard," he exclaimed. In 2003 Loyd was working as a high-end consultant at the downtown business-management firm McKinsey and Company. And there was one moment during the December protest when things got tense and he and Malunda squared off in a testy shouting match.[5] As Loyd told me the story, I wondered how this corporate executive became such a feisty Bronzeville community activist waging battle with the university.

Loyd didn't even grow up on the South Side, but he brought his broad perspective to the Checkerboard controversy. He was born to a white German mother and an African American military vet from Chicago, by way of Louisiana. I could still hear a German inflection in his voice while he explained why the Checkerboard meant so much to him. Loyd had lived with his mother in Liberia before going to school at MIT. After graduation he served on the school's board of trustees while living in the neighborhoods that Harvard and MIT targeted for campus expansion. "Town-gown friction is not new to me," he explained. Loyd saw how higher education institutions worked from the inside. This knowledge of town-gown—or the city and its schools—proved critical when he moved to Chicago's South Side.

Very few corporate executives working for white-shoe firms like McKinsey look for housing on the South Side and definitely not in the hardscrabble blocks of Bronzeville. But Loyd went there anyway, and in 1993 he purchased what he described as a "shell of a home" on 43rd and King Drive. He said one of the things that kept him in the neighborhood was the Checkerboard Lounge. Just two hundred feet from Loyd's porch steps stood the place known as "Home of the Blues." Blues great Buddy Guy and local small-business owner L. C. Thurman opened the Checkerboard in 1972. And its "nicotine-hued wall of fame" held many stories about impromptu jam sessions that included Muddy Waters, the Rolling Stones, Eric Clapton, Junior Walker, and KoKo Taylor, just to name a few. Long after blues' popular appeal faded, university students, suburbanites, and both local and international tourists still came to pray at the altar of this "blues shrine."[6] As Loyd told me, "Anybody and everybody would trickle into the Checkerboard . . . and I was one of them."

The city shut down the lounge for what was essentially a problem with the roof. And Loyd had even met with Thurman to address what he considered an easy fix. But he couldn't believe how quickly the public story became "the University of Chicago is going to 'save' the Checkerboard by moving it south to Hyde Park." Loyd knew something else was going on. When he met with UChicago officials, such as Vice President of Community and Government Affairs Hank Webber, they told him the university was very interested in preserving a community landmark by finding a "mutually agreeable location." And Loyd believed the best solution was to save the Checkerboard in its original location, within its historic cultural context. But when asked about that solution, Webber told the press, "We don't make grants to for-profit institutions."[7]

As a business consultant, Loyd then wondered why UChicago was willing to renovate a building for free and rent space to the Checkerboard at less than half the market rate in Hyde Park. He certainly didn't blame

The "new" Checkerboard Lounge, 5201 South Harper Court, Chicago, Illinois, 2013. Photo by author.

Thurman for taking such a sweetheart deal. But if the university was so invested in preserving a historic landmark, why not do it in Bronzeville? He believed that UChicago saw the steady stream of students and faculty going to the lounge and wanted that kind of magnetic pull for its own "entertainment district" in Hyde Park.[8] A thriving campus neighborhood draws students and faculty while redirecting investment dollars and new residents to the city. Loyd saw that grabbing the Checkerboard "helped the university increase the allure of Hyde Park as a profitable destination." But what about Bronzeville?

＝

UChicago's chess moves on the Checkerboard Lounge were about much more than a simple neighborhood squabble. The Checkerboard controversy points to a new reality affecting anyone who cares about urban America. Higher education exerts an increasingly powerful hold over our cities and those who struggle to survive in its shadows. Schools have become the dominant employers, real estate holders, health-care providers, and even policing agents in major cities across the country. And the lower-income neighborhoods and communities of color that stand in the immediate path of campus expansion, while in deep need of new investments, are left the most vulnerable. These residents face increased housing costs or even displacement amid university land developments. Many of the same Black and brown urbanites also toil in the low-wage sectors of the higher education workforce as groundskeepers and food service staff. And they often endure violence and surveillance from campus police forces.

Those in the immediate shadow of the ivory towers have long been the first to experience the consequences of the entangled relationship between higher education and urban life, or what I call the rise of UniverCities. But the story here is bigger than campus neighborhoods. The growing influence of these schools on entire cities solidifies their political authority over housing costs, labor conditions, and policing practices for everyone living in urban America.[9]

In times of meager state funding, colleges and universities have had to find new ways to shore up their fiscal stability. Urban development is higher education's latest economic growth strategy. And building profitable UniverCities helps schools offset a drop in state funding. Campus-expansion projects meet the increased demands for upscale housing, high-tech laboratories, and plentiful retail options that will attract world-class students, faculty, and researchers. These university developments also reorganize their host cities for new private investments in the bioscience and information-technology industries. As urban campuses continue to grow, all city residents will be living in the shadows of ivory towers.

Indeed, urban universities and their medical centers—the "meds and eds"—stand as one of the most central yet least examined social forces shaping today's cities.[10] In today's knowledge economy, universities have become the new companies, and our major cities serve as their company towns. But unlike Amazon, Microsoft, and other info-tech industries, higher education claims responsibility for our public good. It's time we investigated that promise, asking whether a school's increased for-profit ambitions can undermine the interests of the public. In fact, the presumption that higher education is a public good has for too long distracted critics and urban residents from getting to the heart of the matter: what makes universities good for our cities? We need fewer assumptions and more analysis.

When most of the United States had abandoned cities in the mid-twentieth century, higher education was one of the only institutions that remained. A core group of colleges and universities used public urban renewal money to bunker themselves behind the walls of campus buildings or demolished city blocks—and away from the growing "invasion" of Black and Latinx residents. But starting in the 1990s, young professionals, empty nesters, and the children of suburban sprawl began to seek a more urbane lifestyle. And municipal politicians and real estate developers from different cities started competing with one another to capture the potentially lucrative new tax base and its consumer dollars. At the same time, colleges and universities were looking for new revenue streams in the face of tight state budgets. The interests of university and city leaders converged when the college campus was reimaged as the palatable and profitable version of a safe urban experience.[11]

The university has shifted from being one small, noble part of the city to serving as a model for the city itself. It is precisely the commercial amenities associated with "university life"—concerts, coffee shops, foot traffic congestion, fully wired networking, and high-tech research—that are sold today as a desirable urban lifestyle. Residents have flocked back to cities looking for these university-style urban experiences. And city schools are finding ways to generate new revenue in the for-profit realms of low-wage labor management, health care, applied science, and real estate.

The urban planning model of UniverCities is celebrated for providing needed capital to institutions of higher education and for generating a vibrant kind of urban life with cultural activities, sporting events, and student energy that can entice nonstudent residents to resettle in once-struggling cities. Social scientist and "prosperity" expert Richard Florida used the term *creative city* to describe these enlivened urban locales that attract wealth-building entrepreneurs and the workers they employ. A 2009 article discussing the economic development of Ithaca, New York, celebrated higher education as a key weapon for countering what it called the "bright flight" of the creative class.[12] This racially charged allusion to "white flight" was left for the reader to interpret.

But no matter the dangerous implications, everyone wants to build a UniverCity. Places ranging from New York City to Mesa, Arizona, have

recruited schools from across the country to build a campus in their backyard.[13] Former New York City mayor Michael Bloomberg issued an international call for a school to establish a tech campus in exchange for land
on New York City's Roosevelt Island and up to $100 million toward infra-
structure improvements. The partnership between Cornell University and
Technicon–Israel Institute of Technology won the 2011 Applied Sciences
NYC competition. During a waning third mayoral term of worker layoffs
and budget cuts in the city, Bloomberg sought to reenergize confidence in
New York's capacity to generate prosperity. In a July 2011 speech he openly
lamented that during "the 1980s and 90s, Silicon Valley—not New York—
became the world capital of technology start-ups."[14]

    Colleges and universities are celebrated for sparking neighborhood vi-
tality when they provide museums, lectures, and public safety protections
while also creating new economic opportunities. The most successful of
these efforts often arise when city leaders and higher education administrators come together in resourceful ways to navigate the changing economy.[15] In Pittsburgh, for example, the University of Pittsburgh, Carnegie
Mellon University, and the city government collaborated to transform the
dangerous brownfields from an abandoned steel mill into the Pittsburgh

The Pittsburgh Technology Center on the site of a former steel mill, 2018. Photo by
author.

Technology Center in 1994, an office park for advanced academic and corporate technology research. Saint Louis University instituted the Hometown SLU mortgage-loan-forgiveness program for employees and in 2011 opened the boutique-style Hotel Ignacio as part of its multimillion-dollar investment into the revitalized Midtown Alley district.[16]

There is no question that higher education institutions can deliver positive community outcomes for their cities. But a central question remains: what are the costs when colleges and universities exercise significant power over a city's financial resources, policing priorities, labor relations, and land values? Despite all of the triumphalist rhetoric surrounding higher education's expansive reach across US cities, Black and Latinx communities that largely surround campuses don't experience the same levels of prosperity. These neighboring communities of color frequently sit in zones of relatively cheap and sometimes divested land, while holding little political influence.

By the 1970s, many urban schools had become islands of wealth amid a sea of poverty. But in the 2000s, this uneven geography rapidly gave way to an extension of the campus as a planning model for larger swaths of the city. The result? Poorer neighbors are pushed farther to the periphery of "meds and eds" prosperity. Large-scale university acquisitions of now prime real estate—in cities such as Philadelphia, New York City, Chicago, and Los Angeles—lead to housing and land values that skyrocket beyond the reach of local community members. In 2017 the University of Southern California demolished a decaying shopping center to make way for its upscale $900 million residential and commercial complex, USC Village. But with a design derided as "Disneyland meets Hogwarts," the new complex also pushed out community-friendly stores while doing little to prevent student-related rent spikes in the impoverished South-Central neighborhoods around the school.[17]

In the 2000s, Johns Hopkins University and the city of Baltimore joined forces to create the East Baltimore Development Initiative (EBDI) and take control of eighty acres of the city. This partnership invoked the power of eminent domain to displace 742 Black families and make way for a biotechnology park. Residents first learned of their own forced removal from news reports. According to EBDI officials, residents were given funds for a comparable replacement home minus appraisal costs, as mandated by the

USC Village, 2020. Photo by Shana Skelton.

Department of Housing and Urban Development. But activists and residents counter it was only after they formed the Save Middle East Action Committee that homes were purchased at fair-market value and relocation funds were included. In 2011 Lorna Alexander was one of many displaced residents angry about what she saw as the broken promises that they would have jobs and housing to return to in the mixed-use development area. "They came in and tore up the community," she said. It wasn't until 2018 that housing, laboratories, and biotech incubators began taking root.[18]

Johns Hopkins points to a portion of construction jobs made available to residents of East Baltimore and the hefty housing subsidy of $36,000 for some of the school's employees to settle in new townhouses on the development site. But one professor told me the housing program "represents one of the signal examples of how gentrification is packaged at Hopkins." The subsidy underwrites inflated housing costs for its employees in the new development but at prices above the means of previous residents. At the same time, subsidies are not accessible to the lower-wage workers employed by the university subcontractor, Broadway Services. Former residents have found few pathways of return to their original homes.

Many of the excluded residents return only through the low-wage sectors of higher education labor, as ivory tower janitors, cooks, groundskeepers, and other support staff. At the University of Virginia, African Americans and women from the city of Charlottesville make up a large portion of the school's low-income employees. Black workers continue to endure clear racial inequalities in salary, promotions, and disciplinary sanctions. Since the 1960s, a core group of students has been organizing around these disparities; in 2006 UVA's living-wage supporters staged a three-day sit-in at the president's office, in solidarity with local workers, until they were arrested by the police.[19]

On another battlefront, roughly twenty-six thousand low-wage workers throughout the University of California system went on strike in November 2019 to protest unfair labor practices. Workers charged the university with outsourcing a significant number of jobs to subcontractors to avoid paying negotiated wages and benefits. AFSCME's local 329, the university's largest employee union, supplied the *Mercury News* with two sets of pay stubs for one food service worker at rates well below the $15-per-hour minimum. The union alleged that this worker was paid under two names to avoid providing overtime pay. UC has since amended its outsourcing and competitive bidding protocols, and spokesperson Claire Doan insisted that the worker might have been employed with a company under a contract that predated the new minimum wage. Still, both workers and organizers remain suspicious of the contract loopholes that seem to remain.[20]

At the same time, residents near city schools are subjected to racial disparities in policing. Residents in Black and brown neighborhoods that surround predominantly white schools grow especially weary when university police have jurisdiction to patrol their blocks but are driven by a mandate to protect the campus. A 2003 University of Pennsylvania Police report found that the department stopped Black people in a car or on foot more than any other racial group. And between 2012 and 2015, seven cases involving excessive force and violation of civil rights were filed against the same police force. Four of these cases were settled out of court and dismissed. Penn officials also point to the "Municipal Police Officers' Education and Training" required for all police officers in the state of Pennsylvania. But the training fails to curtail the broad discretion that campus officers are given when making arrests and determining the appropriate amount of force.[21]

Students and staff of color face similar kinds of surveillance. Tahj Blow, the son of *New York Times* columnist Charles Blow, got forced to the ground at gunpoint by Yale police in 2015. Reportedly, the officer let Blow get up after learning he was a Yale student, as if that kind of rough treatment would have been acceptable for a mere New Haven resident. Ultimately, Yale conducted an internal investigation and found that the police officer did nothing wrong while also oddly acknowledging that "the student [Tahj Blow] who was detained endured a deeply troubling experience."[22]

The long-simmering racial injustice of urban policing came to a boil in the summer of 2020, when the coronavirus pandemic forced the world to confront a series of killings that included George Floyd, Breonna Taylor, Tony McDade, and Rayshard Brooks on a digital feedback loop. The terror was unrelenting. Yet these deaths galvanized years of grassroots organizing into a social movement that called for the abolition of the current policing apparatus as a state-sanctioned expression of white supremacy. Both community and student activists have also reignited long-standing critiques of campus police. But this time policing, for many, became a window into a deeper analysis of higher education's broad political and economic impact.

As this critical moment forces us to reckon with higher education's wide-ranging influence over our cities, we can't keep discussing colleges and universities in purely educational terms. UniverCities are all around us, yet we fail to examine the consequences of schools embracing an increasingly for-profit approach to their urban surroundings. Our blind spot to this shift largely comes from the assumption that higher education is an inherent public good, most clearly marked by its tax-exempt status for providing services that would otherwise come from the government.

But it's here that a critical paradox has emerged. Nonprofit status is precisely what allows for an easier transfer of public dollars into higher education's private developments with little public oversight or scrutiny. City colleges and universities pay virtually no taxes on their increasingly prominent real estate footprint. Even public universities, which are in fact government entities, use their public-good status to shelter their own interests in for-profit research or even the financial security of private developers and investors that sit on their campus land. Schools also reap the benefits of police and fire protections, snow and trash removal, road maintenance, and other municipal services while shouldering little financial burden. Homeowners and small-business owners take on the weight of inflated property taxes caused by urban campuses while the cost of rental properties skyrocket.

Such unfair taxing rates compelled Princeton to pay more than $18 million to settle a 2016 lawsuit with residents of the historically Black New Jersey neighborhood of Witherspoon-Jackson.[23] Residents argued that while local property taxes increased, the university still received tax exemption for buildings where research had generated millions of dollars in commercial royalties. The unqualified belief in higher education's public good creates a lucrative "shelter" economy where tax-exempt status helps generate significant private profits for schools without public discussion and with little public benefit. Donor gifts to endowments are tax deductible. The investment income earned by endowments is tax free.[24] And higher education institutions have a competitive edge over similar industries, whether biotech or property management, that still pay property taxes.

One plaintiff in the Princeton case described the university as "a hedge fund that conducts classes."[25] It's an insult often lobbed at today's higher education institutions. Colleges and universities have become city managers that, along with producing educational services, also discuss students as consumers, see alumni as shareholders, and imagine the world beyond the campus walls as either prime real estate or a dangerous threat to the brand.

This corporate mode includes the financially predatory relationship between universities and their own students. Although many colleges have recently banned this practice, it wasn't long ago that fliers for preapproved credit cards were stuffed into the mailbox of every college student at the start of each school year.

At one point, Catherine Reynolds was heavily scrutinized for what some perceived as a conflict of interest because she served on NYU's Board of Trustees while also owning Servus International, which made high-interest loans to students who maxed out of the federal loan market. Reynolds has continually explained that she followed standard business practices. But the optics of a company Gulfstream jet and million-dollar salaries, acquired from the interest rates charged to high-risk borrowers, simply exposed another exploitative market in the world of nonprofit higher education.[26] And when campuses expand across cities, they often choose to bank land and await its appreciation rather than invest in services and infrastructure that would aid the existing community. Higher education is central to the growth of capital in today's cities. These institutions have been given the keys to drive the urban economy forward by reorganizing urban space to best service their institutional desires, as much or more than any public interest.

$$\equiv$$

It is time for a broad examination of higher education's growing for-profit influence on our cities. And this conversation must take place now, before it's too late and America's cities have fully ceded our public resources and public control to these tax-exempt "hedge fund[s] that conduct classes." Urban colleges and universities are increasingly setting the wage ceiling for workers, determining the use and value of our land, directing the priorities of our police, and dictating the distribution of our public funds in cities all over the country. We regularly rail against the high price tag and diminished value of higher education. But public discourse remains overwhelmingly silent about the consequences of turning the US city into one big campus.

To be clear, the growing faith in higher education as an urban growth engine has also gone global. The provocatively named Education City in Doha, Qatar, and the controversies surrounding NYU's franchising of its university brand in Shanghai and Abu Dhabi help demonstrate the worldwide reach of the city-as-campus model.[27]

In the last two decades a growing body of work has examined what is being called "the university as corporation." Soaring tuition costs, corporate-funded research, and the for-profit push of online learning seem to signal the death of the university as we knew it.[28] The "university-as-corporation" scholarship is insightful for highlighting the shift in higher education policy from public good to private profits. However, we must move beyond campus walls to understand the full impact of universities.

A much smaller group of thinkers and activists has started to detail the recent history of universities as engines of "smart growth," driving the urban economy.[29] But it's time to bring this story to the present and explore university-driven city building on a national scale, from the small private liberal arts college to the large public research university.

When Richard Florida introduced us to the "creative class," many dying cities could finally see a future after the fall of factories. Florida prophesied that innovations produced in hospitals, laboratories, tech start-ups, and design studios would power the economic rebirth of cities. He explained that in order to attract creative types, cities must redesign their landscape around a "street level culture" that blurs the lines between work and play.[30] Florida has recently pulled back on his grand claims about the creative city, admitting that the increased settlement of creative types can actually heighten inequalities. But all across the country, urban stakeholders are still scrambling to build a creative city with a dynamic array of lofts and workstations adorned in glass and steel facades that spill out onto a teeming blend of cafés, galleries, bookstores, and street life.[31]

Not surprisingly, this creative landscape sounds a lot like a campus. In fact, Florida marked urban universities as a "central hub institution of the knowledge economy" that can help revitalize cities and attract the creative class.[32] But again, the urban realities of town-gown relations mean that many people are left out of the "public" that benefits when the private interests of colleges, universities, and their medical centers chart the course of struggling cities. We must rethink the uncritical celebration of "creative cities" by prioritizing desperate urban issues, from affordable housing and health care to equitable policing and living wages. *In the Shadow of the Ivory Tower* is a call for greater public oversight as universities take control of urban America.

Drawn from more than one hundred interviews, *In the Shadow of the Ivory Tower* takes readers into the heart of an urban transformation unfolding right before us. We get to see the world of UniverCities shaped by the aims of municipal leaders, the ambitions of higher education administrators, the anxieties of long-term residents, and the ambivalence of newcomers trying to grapple with the evolving terms of urban living.

Chapter 1 traces the central threads that answer this question: How did we get here? What were the historical conditions that breathed life into the UniverCity? The chapters that follow then offer a deep dive into four present-day urban experiences, each challenging simple celebrations of the city as a campus. Chapter 2 explores the elite liberal arts world of Trinity College and the school's ambivalent relationship with its location in the largely poor, brown capital city of Hartford, Connecticut. The biggest college town in the country anchors chapter 3, as Columbia and NYU manipulate the levers of city governance to reshape New York City. We then travel to the Midwestern metropolis of Chicago for chapter 4, to focus on UChicago's dominion over South Side neighborhoods through a dual power of campus policing and campus building. Chapter 5 moves to the Southwest and charts Arizona State University's rise as one of the most powerful real estate developers in greater Phoenix. The epilogue centers on the University of Winnipeg, offering a vision for equitable and just partnerships between cities and their schools.

Because I am a professor seated behind the walls of a campus, it may seem quite the hypocrisy for me to offer this critique of universities. However, it is precisely my place in higher education that compels me to push this conversation forward. I am hard on city schools because I expect colleges and universities to be a source of public good, which requires being honest about the full reach and implications of our actions. We often see caricatures of colleges and universities as ivory tower bastions for tenured radicals and young "snowflakes," both out of touch with reality.

But higher education's footprint across the nation's cities tells a different story. How do flourishing urban colleges and universities act in the public good when the very people we pass on campus (and pass on the way to campus) are paying the cost of the school's prosperity? The very notion of a university's public good has been used as justification to underwrite multimillion-dollar tax-exempt endowments. Higher education has made way for a massive contingent of low-wage labor, increased racial profiling, and the elimination of affordable housing, retail, and health care in campus neighborhoods. But that's not the only story. Activists, residents, and students have fought hard against these changes and pulled progressive university administrators along to model alternative ways of relating to their cities. It is my hope that readers, whether they are part of the ivory tower or in its shadows, will grapple with these new challenges. The future of urban America depends on it.

CHAPTER ONE

WHEN UNIVERSITIES SWALLOW CITIES

Yale University often gets credit for "saving" the once beat-down city of New Haven, making it safer while attracting new industry and development. But the truth is much more complicated. In March 2016, New Haven was struggling to balance its shrinking budget. And then-mayor Toni Harp joined local politicians and labor unions to set their sights on Yale. They called for a state senate bill to help fine-tune the university's property tax-exempt status, an area where the school's prosperity was directly tied to the city's despair.

Universities and their medical centers are registered with the Internal Revenue Service as 501(c)(3) charitable nonprofits. Because of the public services that higher education institutions ostensibly provide to surrounding communities, their property holdings are exempt from taxation in all fifty states. But New Haven officials said Yale's multimillion-dollar tax exemption actually contributed to the budget deficit of the city. The

Connecticut bill, SB 414, would have allowed the state to tax university properties that generate $6,000 or more in annual income.[1]

At a city hall press conference, Harp immediately acknowledged the need to uphold the tax protections for nonprofit organizations, including Yale. She celebrated the university's undeniable role "in the city's transformation." Over the past forty years, Yale had become the single largest commercial power in New Haven. But Harp also warned that although cities rely "more and more on eds and meds," New Haven leaders must "be clear . . . about the fiscal impact of this transition." The mayor reminded listeners that "we still have to run a city." Yale offered, as a compromise, an annual $8 million "payment in lieu of taxes," or PILOT. By 2019, that payment jumped to more than $12 million. These contributions are voluntary, however, and are a fraction of the taxes Yale would pay based on the assessed value of its properties. But Yale didn't have to worry; SB 414 did not pass, and the city of New Haven still struggles while its largest local economic entity remains exempt from property taxes.[2]

Yale's financial dominance in New Haven is tied to the meteoric ascendancy of the knowledge economy. Here, academic research is used to create profitable, commercial goods or patents in a range of fields, from the pharmaceutical industries and software products to military defense weaponry.[3] Yale, in particular, has cultivated relationships with a number of biotech firms to produce new jobs and draw commercial revenue to the university and its host city. But this partnership between private industry and academic research has also created a property-tax "gray area" where profitable research produced for private companies is conducted in educational buildings that are not on the tax rolls.

Yale's revenues from patent licenses grew from just more than $5 million in 1996 to more than $45 million in 2000.[4] And it has also been difficult for New Haven to attract investors to this unlevel playing field. New businesses must pay taxes, and they struggle to coexist with competitors in the same market that are affiliated with the tax-exempt behemoth of Yale. Local politicians such as Harp simply wanted the university to contribute its fair share to the broader community.

But Yale's financial position in New Haven is the result of more than just biotech. The school also oversees a lucrative portfolio of commercial and residential assets managed by its University Properties. Both students and alumni marvel at the transformation of the area from what was once dingy and even a bit dangerous. Now, when walking through the blocks surrounding the campus, they enjoy a new range of restaurants, shops, and housing options. By 2014, Yale's more than four hundred downtown properties totaled roughly $2.44 billion in value.

However, the city sees only a small portion of the estimated $102 million in property taxes that, if Yale wasn't tax-exempt, would come from the school or the additional $31 million that would come from Yale–New Haven Hospital (YNHH). The combined assessed value of properties held by the school and hospital reached $8.47 billion in 2019. Yale's focus on student rentals has also driven housing prices far above the means of local residents. And commercial tenants have been pushed out in favor of more trendy shops to satisfy the desires of students, such as Abercrombie & Fitch and Shake Shack.[5]

Yale's overwhelming footprint not only makes the university one of the city's largest landlords but, with fourteen hundred employees, also its largest single employer. New Haven was a factory town in the 1960s, most known for the rifle maker Winchester Repeating Arms. The steady relocation of manufacturing to the "global South" in the 1980s helped create a hollowed-out urban core, except for Yale. Even now, one in four New Haven residents lives at or below the poverty line. The city has struggled, in some part because the state failed on its promise to compensate New Haven for the taxes lost to large nonprofits such as Yale. By 1995, there were almost twice as many jobs at Yale as at all of the city's factories combined.[6] But hardly any of the well-paying jobs went to the increasingly brown and poor neighborhoods that surround the campus.

A number of political alliances took shape to fight against the unjust conditions for those living in the shadows of Yale's ivory towers. New Haven Rising emerged in 2012 to help temper what it considered the heavy hand of Yale–New Haven Hospital. Administrators at the medical center, which built a moneymaking cancer center, blocked union drives and aggressively pursued debt collection on low-income, local patients, which included pursuing liens on homes. Yale never conceded to all of these charges, but New Haven Rising activists pushed the university to enter an agreement for youth programs, a local hiring mandate, and the lowering of medical debt, especially because the hospital's tax-exempt status was predicated on providing care to indigent patients.[7]

In 2014 Unidad Latina en Accion (ULA) rallied against Gourmet Heaven, a deli and convenience store located on Yale property, where workers toiled for long hours and made less than minimum wage with no overtime pay. Although that store is no longer in business, the owner was charged with wage theft and had to pay back workers. And local activism forced Yale to say it would not renew the lease of any tenant that failed to comply with labor laws.[8] In August 2019, after years of local organizing and protest, Yale signed a new agreement to create job training and apprenticeship programs for residents of New Haven. The university also agreed to hire three hundred new full-time employees from local "neighborhoods of need," the largely working-class, Black, and Latinx areas of the city.[9] The walls of the ivory tower were slowly coming down.

Still, even for those well-placed behind Yale's formidable campus walls, membership can come with a high cost. Consider the story of Brian. He wasn't a low-wage university worker. Brian wasn't even a New Haven local. He came to Yale on scholarship in its prestigious Graduate School of Nursing. But Brian also suffered from severe clinical depression, a condition that he did not want to make public at a university that was notorious for what many perceived as a draconian forced-withdrawal policy for medical reasons. If the university ever pushed him out, Brian would lose his nursing scholarship.

Yale students sometimes refuse to seek out help with mental-health issues precisely because they fear they will be forced to withdraw or will be hospitalized. According to Yale regulations, students can be withdrawn if they pose "a danger to self or others because of a serious medical problem."[10] In a recent study, Yale scored an *F* for its policies regarding students with mental illness.[11] While on a clinical rotation, Brian saw a student who refused to take medication. He believed that this student was then forced into compliance by the threat of informing the academic program, despite state and federal laws protecting patient privacy. And, of course, there was the devastating 2015 case of a Yale student jumping from the Golden Gate Bridge to her death after posting a Facebook status describing her fear of seeking treatment because it might trigger a forced withdrawal.[12] Still, the consequences of Yale's forced withdrawal remained pretty theoretical for Brian, until October 2018.

One evening Brian went to the Emergency Department at Yale–New Haven Hospital after feeling urges to overdose on prescribed sleep medication. It was in that moment that he experienced, firsthand, the overwhelming dominance of Yale in the region. As a health-care professional in training, Brian had watched Yale take over health treatment services along the Connecticut shoreline. Now that Brian sought help with his own depression, where would he go without running into a colleague or instructor? And how would his privacy be maintained? Yale Psychiatric Health was Brian's outpatient provider, YaleHealth was the insurance provider *and* pharmacy, and Yale School of Nursing was his academic home. Brian said that he was finally admitted to Yale Psychiatric against his own wishes: "I cringed as I was pushed through a hallway where former supervisors were stationed." He felt forced to sign "release of information" forms for his nursing faculty. One of his own professors/clinical coordinators was assigned to him as a provider. Yale Psychiatric Health reached out to Brian's academic advisor to assess his academic and clinical performance. He says that whenever he disagreed with treatment, they suggested an involuntary leave with what Brian saw as the cryptic threat that "it wouldn't look good" to the university if he didn't comply.

Brian ultimately returned to classes and finished the program but calls himself "lucky" because of his comprehensive understanding of the mental-health system. Still, he was left totally disillusioned by Yale's forced-withdrawal policy coupled with the university's monopoly on health-care services in New Haven and throughout the region, which, in his mind, allowed the school to flout standard medical practices. For Brian, the hospital constantly coerced his consent by threatening his academic standing. As a student, patient, and employee, "the conflicts of interest are staggering," he said. And Brian believed that the university cared more about depressed students as a threat to Yale's image than his well-being or even his consent: "My privacy was doomed from the start. This is avoidable if other facilities are available but not when your school owns them all."

Yale's relentless control of New Haven doesn't stop at health care, land, and labor. The growing campus footprint is secured by a private police force extending its influence across the entire city. On April 16, 2019, Stephanie Washington and Paul Witherspoon, who are Black, were parked near the Yale campus. Cell-phone footage showed them singing love songs to each other. Then, Hampden (a suburb of New Haven) Police Officer Devin Eaton and Yale Police Officer Terrance Pollock approached the car and shot more than fifteen rounds at the couple. Washington suffered a nonfatal bullet wound to the face; remarkably, Witherspoon was unharmed. This unarmed Black couple posed no threat, but police had received a false report that their red Honda Civic had been involved in an attempted armed robbery.[13] The shooting infuriated Black residents who had endured decades of racial profiling in the city and especially around the campus.

Pollock was not arrested or charged because the Yale officer fired in response to Eaton's actions and because none of his bullets caused injury. He was suspended without pay for thirty days, and after a university review, Pollock returned to the force in a position that does not require a gun or a uniform.[14]

But Pollock's presence on the scene raised a critical question: Why was a campus police officer firing his weapon a mile away from campus? Immediately following the shooting, students and residents stormed the streets. With chants of "Who do you protect? Who do you serve?" protestors called for the disarming of all Yale police officers, a restricted police jurisdiction around the campus area, and changes to the university's labor practices. The university has announced it will partner with the consulting firm 21CP Solutions to improve police services. But many residents of New Haven believe that piecemeal reforms fail to address the scope of the university's power. Yale PD is seen as the front line that protects the elite, white, billion-dollar ivory tower from the poor brown poverty that surrounds it on all sides. Some even call the area "Yale Haven."[15]

Yale's supremacy over New Haven might seem extreme, but this story illuminates the growing and multilayered points of influence that higher education institutions exert on our cities across the country. How did colleges and universities come to significantly dictate the terms of urban living, from a city's housing costs and wage ceilings to its health-care standards and even policing practices? The growing dominance of higher education has been transformative for cities. And the roots of this story can be traced to social and economic conditions that have been taking shape for at least the past century.

=====

The profit motive driving higher education goes as far back as the Atlantic slave trade, as historian Craig Steven Wilder has illustrated in his book *Ebony and Ivy*. History students at UChicago recently discovered that their school's massive $7 billion endowment derived from an initial ten acres of land donated by the politician Stephen Douglas, land that was purchased with his slave plantation profits. The university denies any explicit financial or legal relationship between today's University of Chicago and the "first" University of Chicago, which collapsed in a state of debt and foreclosure in 1886. However, activists point to the work of university historian John Boyer, who argues that an overlapping network of donors and faculty cements a clear inheritance between the two campuses. Even in controversy, universities across the country are being forced to reckon with their varying but unavoidable role in facilitating the country's dominant economic systems, including slavery.[16]

During the Civil War the federal government explicitly turned to universities as a key driver of economic growth and urban development. The Morrill Land Grant Acts of 1862 and 1890 helped fund public universities to support agricultural research; the applied sciences, such as engineering; and general education for a growing population. Most accounts have celebrated the Morrill Act for democratizing higher education but have downplayed its true economic focus: to retrain workers for a new urban industrial economy. And until recently there was no discussion of the policy's origins in American colonialism or its role in reinforcing Jim Crow segregation.[17]

The Morrill Act first distributed public-domain lands to states that could then be used or sold to build the financial endowments of universities. However, the 10.7 million acres for this project were actually indigenous lands, confiscated through seizure or suspect land treaties. The money made from land sales still sit on the books of these universities, and at least twelve states continue to hold title to unsold acres and profit from associated mineral rights. Most land-grant institutions are in rural areas or small towns, but even city schools, from Massachusetts Institute of Technology to the University of Minnesota, built their endowments on this seizure of indigenous land. We have failed to fully engage with what education studies scholar Sharon Stein calls "the material entanglement of higher education with colonialism."[18]

The 1890 version of the act extended land grants to the former Confederate states but through direct cash payments. To their credit, lawmakers included a clause prohibiting racial discrimination in admissions. However, instead of enforcing the integration of land-grant schools, the act provided additional monies to southern states so they could build separate and underfunded historically Black colleges and universities (HBCUs). With that decision, the federal government used higher education policy to help reinforce racial segregation, even through city schools in Tallahassee, New Orleans, and Dover, Delaware. And this government-funded Jim Crow university system emerged six years before the "separate but equal doctrine" of *Plessy v. Ferguson* became the law of the land.[19] But higher education's impact on urban segregation didn't stop at the Mason-Dixon Line.

Since American colonial times, the placement and design of college campuses reflected a clear antagonism toward urban life and the kind of social diversity that cities engendered.[20] In fact, higher education acquired greater value as a pastoral retreat when city life continued to take hold. The word *campus* even means "field" in Latin. These lush, green campuses were further ensconced in at least quasi-rural environments, where the fresh air and open space were meant to serve as a balm from the foul smell and so-called dangerous ethnic amalgams found in cities. Many of today's urban schools sat on what once were the fringes of their cities, including Harvard (Cambridge), Columbia (Harlem), and UChicago (Hyde Park).

Trinity first moved from its original downtown Hartford "Capitol Hill" campus to relocate atop Gallows Hill in 1878. This new rural location, outside the city, gave the school a physical profile that reinforced its place alongside other prestigious New England colleges. Trinity existed among a cohort of schools that were later nicknamed the "Little Ivies" and included

Amherst, Williams, Bowdoin, and Colby. Like students at traditional Ivy League colleges and universities, the young men at Trinity didn't enroll to learn a trade or acquire professional development. Higher education was a sort of "finishing school," meant to develop the character and enhance the networks of male students already well-positioned in families of power and influence.[21] The campus setting of rural retreat helped reinforce a status of racial and class distinction.

If Trinity's rural location wasn't enough to signal retreat, the college also modeled its architecture on the Victorian design of Oxford University and Trinity College in Scotland. Renderings depict opulent campus quadrangles surrounded by brick facades on all sides with spires atop tall towers on each corner of the quads. Visitors had to breach imposing outer walls on Summit Street to even witness campus life. The architecture screamed exclusivity and prestige. Trinity never finalized all of the walls needed to complete this design, but its plans became the model for UChicago's notorious quadrangle fortress dressed in stone gargoyles.[22]

Beyond the explicit fortress imagery of the quadrangle, UChicago grounded its vision of affluent retreat in an economic strategy of land

Burges's Plan of Trinity College (1874), William Burges Drawings, Watkinson Library, Trinity College.

control. Before the first building cornerstone was laid on its second campus in 1892, UChicago raised a large portion of its start-up capital through real estate donations to the school in the surrounding Hyde Park neighborhood. Residential development generated revenue, especially during the economic recession of 1890, when university donors could more easily offer property rather than liquid assets.[23] This growing portfolio of real estate assets encouraged the university to manage land development in Hyde Park.

Rising property values on or around university holdings translated into a bigger endowment. Securing this financial wealth in property turned UChicago into a major landlord in the area. The university razed many of the World's Fair–related tenements that housed commercial laborers from the then "undesirable" races of Irish, Swede, Greek, and German origins. Many of these buildings were replaced with new structures rented out to faculty, students, and other professionals in the neighborhood. By subsidizing rents for its employees, UChicago inflated the property values that served as a primary economic base for the university. This economic boundary of high land value also provided a virtual wall from the slowly encroaching city.[24]

By the 1920s, these colleges and universities, which once rested on the urban margins, were awash in the striking transformations that came with urbanization. Even in the small capital of Hartford, city growth advanced toward Trinity's "Rocky Ridge" campus in ways that threatened to compromise the pastoral ethos of this elite, small liberal arts college. The school now sat in the middle of an immigrant city. Hartford was home to industrial giants, including Colt's firearms, Pope's bicycles, and Weed's sewing machines before the city became an international capital of insurance and finance. These factories beckoned working-class immigrants warehoused in dense, poorly built tenements just blocks from campus.[25]

As the city changed, Trinity also attracted local students. By 1918, about 50 percent of the student body came from Hartford. This demographic shift posed a direct challenge to the more "gentleman's country club" profile of the college. Becoming a commuter school endangered Trinity's desire to maintain the prestige of its liberal arts peers. Some were especially alarmed by the 15 percent Jewish population in the 1920s, believing that these students undermined college culture and could even corrupt the curriculum with "foreign" socialist ideas.[26] Especially for students and alumni, the college had to do something.

The student senate marked the college's one-hundredth anniversary with a resolution that it called the "Student Movement for Americanization at Trinity." This new edict required all undergraduates to live in buildings "owned or controlled by the college." A residency requirement seems rather innocuous on the surface, but it was specifically designed to protect the pastoral campus from urban influences. This requirement served a dual purpose: it created an economic barrier for the working-class families who couldn't afford to attend school *and* live on campus. And for the immigrants who could still come, the policy separated them from their local environment. A coalition of students, faculty, alumni, and trustees called this approach a "necessity" for Trinity to "Americanize the country's foreign-born population." The alumni also established a 20 percent cap on Hartford students.[27] Trinity's Americanization policy lasted only two years, but it reflected higher education's continued desire to maintain an elite status by keeping the changing city at arm's length.

During the first wave of the Great Migration in Chicago, African Americans moved to the near northwest of the UChicago campus in the 1920s and 1930s. The actions of university administrators suggested that these new arrivals posed a significant threat to property values in the campus neighborhood. In fact, scholars from the famed "Chicago School" of social science helped provide a pseudoscientific justification for Jim Crow zoning policies across the country with academic theories that described racial segregation in cities as a product of nature. UChicago administrators followed suit by underwriting racially restrictive housing covenants for the notorious Hyde Park and Kenwood neighborhood associations. These were legally binding agreements to prevent the sale, lease, or occupation of property to a targeted racial group. In this case it was African Americans. The university has never officially acknowledged its role in racial segregation. But Black Chicagoans called these covenants "the University of Chicago Agreement to get rid of Negroes."[28]

The migration filled the South Side's segregated "Black Belt" neighborhood beyond capacity in the 1930s and 1940s. And citywide covenants

prevented African Americans from living anywhere else. But the local decision of *Hansberry v. Lee* (1940) set the tone for the landmark 1948 *Shelly
v. Kramer* case, which rendered restrictive covenants unenforceable by law.
This decision opened the proverbial floodgates on Black community expansion south into the Hyde Park campus neighborhood. The plaintiff in
the Chicago case was the father of writer Lorraine Hansberry, who would
dramatize this time of her childhood in the award-winning 1959 Broadway
play *A Raisin in the Sun*.[29] These legal cases weakened the ability of the
university to sponsor neighborhood groups that upheld residential segregation. UChicago responded to this setback by purchasing and demolishing
buildings that could potentially face racial integration. The school also increased the rent levels of subsidized faculty and employee housing to help
"maintain the white population" around the campus.[30] But such strategies
failed to deter African Americans who could still afford to purchase or rent
Hyde Park properties.

By the 1950s, the Hyde Park–Kenwood Community Conference
shifted its strategy from complete racial exclusion to "community preservation." With the growing threat of Black neighbors, the conference pushed
to build an "interracial community of high standards."[31] Hyde Park boosters began to focus on the economic status of potential middle-class Black
residents as a way to control property values. But such efforts failed to stave
off panic selling by white residents.

The South East Chicago Commission (SECC) stepped in as "the political action arm of the University."[32] UChicago officials and alumni took full
control of urban development on the South Side. They helped to write the
Urban Community Conservation Act of 1953, where any areas that were
simply close to Black neighborhood expansion were targeted for eminent
domain and slum clearance. Ultimately, white-occupied Hyde Park blocks
that were physically deteriorating got marked for rehabilitation. At the
same time, majority-Black areas (from 55th to 56th between Cottage Grove
and Woodlawn Avenues) became the sites targeted for clearance and university acquisition, even if the homes and streets were well-maintained. The
Hyde Park–Kenwood Urban Renewal Plan of 1958 coordinated the massive displacement of African Americans and rezoned 80 percent of Hyde
Park's commercial districts for residential use, in the process securing land

values for the campus community. Instead of urban renewal, local African American residents renamed this process "Negro Removal."[33]

The ability to target well-kept Black neighborhoods for urban renewal is rooted in the politics of eminent domain and the racially charged urban designation of "blight." Eminent domain signals the legal right of a government to compensate a private owner after seizing the land for public use, such as roads and public utilities. However, a property or neighborhood must be deemed "blighted" before a state authority can invoke eminent domain for urban renewal. The term *blight*, which has its origins in the study of plant disease, is now vaguely used to describe any perceived decay that may turn what are deemed healthy neighborhoods into slums. The *perception* of decay, as urban historians have shown, is often tied to an area's racial or ethnic composition. African American neighborhoods, regardless of their physical conditions, were often the ones deemed blighted to justify the demolition of areas that made way for highways, hospitals, public housing, etc.[34] Universities couldn't profit from this designation on their own. UChicago worked with the city of Chicago to wield the racially charged weapon of blight in ways that further bolstered the school's dominance over the late-twentieth-century city.

The Hyde Park efforts to uphold residential segregation would set a national urban trend where universities served the function of a "parastate"—a proxy role of governance—in the areas of policy making and economic development.[35] They also benefited from the federal government's infusion of capital and resources into Cold War universities that supplied academic research for military applications. UChicago's Met Lab, for instance, conducted research for the Manhattan Project. Since World War II, the Massachusetts Institute of Technology has generated millions as the largest university defense contractor in the country. Stanford used the defense contract system to propel itself from a regional school into a science and technology powerhouse.[36] In 1967 Senator J. William Fulbright delivered two speeches at Stanford railing against the new intimacy between the government, the defense industry, and university life, or what he called the "Military-Industrial-Academic Complex."[37]

Beyond military research, the federal government standardized higher education's power to manage the economic development of increasingly multiracial cities. Historian Arnold Hirsch points out that the US shared a similar approach to cold war threats on the world stage and the home front: containment.[38] Millions of African Americans continued to flood into cities during the second postwar phase of the Great Migration, and Latinx migrants soon followed. They were forced into already cramped neighborhoods filled with deteriorating buildings, what most called slums. At the same time, white residents fled the cities following industry and a massive government infusion of capital into what became the suburbs. The twin forces of brown poverty and so-called "white flight" signaled a nationwide "urban crisis."[39] Landlocked city colleges and universities believed that they had to stand and fight, working with both local and federal authorities to keep brown residents out and white students and faculty coming onto campus. As one of the few major institutions forced to remain in struggling cities, universities fought to hold the line on neighborhood integration and helped shape the future of urban life.[40]

Universities became the friendly face of urban renewal, masking ruthless policies that bolstered racial segregation. In Chicago, Executive Director of the South East Chicago Commission (SECC) Julian Levi saw slums surrounding the Hyde Park campus. He wanted to clear away conditions that "will attract lower class Whites and Negroes." Levi gained a national reputation as "Slum Fighter Levi" when he joined forces with UChicago Chancellor and SECC President Lawrence Kimpton.[41] Kimpton sat on the boards of the American Council of Education and the Association of American Universities. In 1959 Kimpton and Levi coordinated fourteen urban universities into a lobbying force that successfully pushed for a significant change in the Federal Housing Act of 1949.

Dubbed the "Section 112 credits program," this initiative triggered a two-to-one federal matching grant for any urban renewal project on or near a college or university up to five years before the project even began. Moreover, the aid was "transferrable to urban renewal projects anywhere in the city."[42] Municipal leaders clamored to make their schools the showpiece of an urban renewal scheme that could generate so much federal aid. Of course, colleges and universities were happy to let city and federal governments pay for development that kept the growing urban poor at bay. The double barrel of eminent domain and the Section 112 credits helped city schools such as Case Western Reserve and the University of Alabama at Birmingham turn their campuses into largely barricaded zones of learning to stem the tide of African American and Latinx residents living nearby.[43] By 1964, there were 154 projects supported by the 112 credits program that involved 120 colleges and universities and 75 hospitals.[44]

However, not everyone agreed with the consequences of this university-related urban renewal. Some even resisted. Outraged students became urban activists and joined residents to protest how the renewal efforts of their schools helped modernize racial segregation. In the battles over university-based development, New York City stood at the center.

=

Karla Spurlock-Evans came to Barnard—Columbia University's women's college—as a freshman in 1968. That April, she went to hear a student band called the Soul Syndicate on the Columbia campus across the street. Spurlock-Evans ended up occupying that building for a week as part of a student uprising that drew attention from all over the world. The Students for a Democratic Society and the Student Afro-American Society joined forces to protest Columbia's involvement in military weapons research. But what really drew the attention of Black students such as Spurlock-Evans was the university's efforts to place a private gymnasium in the middle of nearby Morningside Park.

Both students and residents would be able to use the facility, but protestors charged "Gym Crow" when they learned that the building would have separate entrances for the largely white school at the top of the hill and the predominantly Black Harlem down below, with limited hours of community access.[45] Spurlock-Evans quickly shifted from partying to protest on behalf of those Black people who didn't share her privileges of sitting behind Columbia's gates: "I wanted to have a voice and stand on the right side of history regarding Columbia's encroachment on community property."

The student occupation of Columbia erupted within a perfect storm of larger events. Students were angered by the US war effort in Vietnam and inspired by a recent student takeover of Howard University in Washington, D.C. Many worried that Harlem would explode after the assassination of Martin Luther King Jr. just three weeks earlier. Nearly a thousand

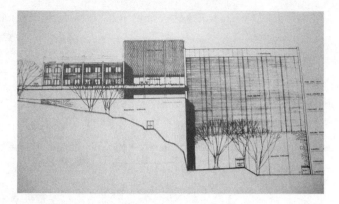

Plan for Morningside Park Gym, 1968. Photo by Tao Tan, Wikimedia Commons.

students occupied five buildings on campus. But Hamilton Hall remained the center of the world, especially for Black students and the surrounding Harlem community. Spurlock-Evans remembers a stream of people entering through the week, churches picketing outside, and plates of soul food handed through the windows while messages went out to worried parents. Black militant leaders H. Rap Brown and Stokely Carmichael visited the protestors. Even China's Chairman Mao sent a telegram pledging solidarity with the Black students of Hamilton Hall. Ultimately, police removed protestors in one of the largest mass arrests in New York City history. Still, Columbia canceled all weapons research, plans for the gym came to a screeching halt, and the world was forced to confront the broader implications when universities become selfish agents of urban development.[46] Spurlock-Evans remains transformed: "Cute guys brought me into the building, but cute guys didn't keep me."

In 1960s Morningside Heights, like Chicago's Hyde Park, Columbia had sought ways to contain the influx of Black and brown residents before they encroached on the campus. Instead of investing in the surrounding community, the university purchased properties and displaced residents, most of whom were African American or Puerto Rican.[47] In 1961 the New York City Commission on Human Rights issued a letter to Columbia, calling on the school to end its "reliance on tenant removal as a solution to social problems in the neighborhood." Columbia responded that its first responsibility is to create a desirable neighborhood where its students will feel safe.[48] Not much had changed by the time Spurlock-Evans came to campus. In fact, the efforts at building Gym Crow can be seen as the logical extension of the school's forced evictions from years before.

Just a year after the dust settled at Columbia, the University of Pennsylvania (UPenn) announced its desire to build a massive science center in West Philadelphia. Administrators argued that such a complex would instigate residential, retail, and school improvements, and attract the research units of major technology industries to "University City." UPenn students followed the lead of Columbia with their own six-day sit-in to protest. But the university moved forward, using the funding power of the 112 credits urban renewal program to build its University City Science Center. It became the nation's first inner-city urban research park. The University Archives & Records Center commissioned a 1999 exhibit confirming that approximately six hundred low-income and African American families were displaced in the process.[49]

Peter Dougherty saw the entire UPenn drama unfold from his family's bar at South 40th, right near the university. Although he is white, Dougherty also maintained an ambivalent relationship to the university, where he said the town-gown distinctions were stark. Dougherty lamented what he saw as UPenn's wide-ranging actions to level most of West Philadelphia: neighborhoods, schools, homes, and small businesses. Dougherty said the messaging from the university was simple: "We don't want you!" Working-class whites rode the early white-flight wave out to the suburbs while his Black neighbors got corralled into public housing at 46th and Market.

Even city leaders in Denver used the 112 credits program to build their Auraria campus by displacing 250 businesses and 330 households from an African American and largely Latinx community. It was only because of historic-preservation activists and neighborhood residents that developers provided relocation funds and repurposed important community landmarks for educational purposes. Community opposition couldn't stop the campus from opening in 1974, but it sparked a robust Chicano movement around the broader issues of housing rights, health care, and police violence.[50]

The displacement caused by elite universities helped spark critical student and community-led activism, but nothing compared to the role that local city colleges played in creating new relationships between town and gown in a changing urban landscape. Urban junior or community colleges largely hearken back to the Progressive Era, as a public-good effort of spreading the liberal arts to working-class children in rapidly industrializing cities. The idea was to place educational outposts in white ethnic communities as a form of public service. These schools were also meant to instill the conventional values of American culture or "civilization" in the children of immigrants.[51]

UChicago President William Raney Harper, who served from 1891 to 1906, became one of the most vocal advocates for the community college. But his motives weren't altruistic. Harper believed that by placing the first two years of basic undergraduate education (junior college) in the high schools or by creating two-year preliminary schools, he could preserve the university as a place of advanced instruction and research. Chicago's Joliet High School first adopted the new model in 1901; by 1917, there were 170 junior colleges across the country.[52] Despite Harper's gatekeeping ambitions, urban community colleges helped democratize higher education and cultivate civic engagement. The four-year City College of New York was dubbed "Harvard of the Proletariat" in the 1930s, a hotbed of intellectual debate and political agitation for working-class, urban youths.

After World War II, the very notion of the "community" described by the community college model underwent drastic transformation when African American and Latinx migrants occupied the neighborhoods once held by white ethnic families. The now largely Black and brown student bodies demanded that city schools serve the new community. Merritt College became an educational extension of North Oakland's Black community: reading groups, cafeteria conversations, street speaking, and sponsored tours to Cuba helped lay the groundwork for what became the Black Panther Party for Self Defense in 1966. Black students on Chicago's West Side seized control of Crane Junior College and renamed it Malcolm X Community College in 1968. What was once a school that failed to transition its Black students to four-year colleges became an institution of community service with increased student aid programs and a "prison annex" to educate incarcerated residents. Students also helped rethink campus safety by pushing to hire unarmed workers from a Black-owned security firm in place of Chicago Police Department officers.[53]

In 1969 Black students led their Puerto Rican and white allies in a massive protest at New York's Brooklyn College and City College, demanding the admission of more students of color. These students insisted the city's tuition-free colleges should help correct for a segregated and inferior school system by providing the bridge instruction to prepare a broader range of taxpaying citizens for social mobility. This political action set the stage for a landmark 1970 open-admissions policy, with support services, for the next three decades. But then the early forays into neoliberal urban policy instigated a wholesale shift of public resources into private accounts. We now look askance at the dysfunction of public services without talking about the full-scale divestment and retreat from a community-controlled public good. But the history of community colleges is a valuable, if forgotten, model for building a people-powered relationship between cities and their schools.[54]

By the 1970s, most elite universities had become islands of wealth amid a sea of poverty. Outside of investing in private research schools, it seemed America had turned its back on cities, instead embracing suburban sprawl as the future. With a massive influx of Black and brown migrants, along with the exodus of not only white people but also public resources and private industry, cities were left to die. Then, starting in the 1990s, young professionals and empty nesters grew weary of suburban homogeneity and isolation, gradually electing to seek out a more urbane lifestyle. They were especially drawn to cities because municipal leaders reorganized urban areas to make them more attractive, advertising the shorter commutes and cultural amenities that came with urban living. But the real pull came from the public subsidies that underwrote higher-paying knowledge, tech, and creative industries while clearing out the poor from prime real estate with ruthless eviction and policing tactics.[55]

The back-to-the-city movement found municipal politicians and real estate developers scrambling to prepare a table for the potential economic windfall brought by a renewed urban interest. These "growth coalitions" in different cities began competing with one another to capture the lucrative tax base from new residents, shoppers, and investors. And with the decline in manufacturing, the "bell towers" of higher education were targeted as the new "smokestacks": the signals of a thriving urban economy after the fall of factories.[56]

A trendy catchphrase emerged to describe city schools. They were deemed "anchor institutions," perfectly placed to help bring economic stabilization to urban areas and possibly even rebuild successful communities. Revived campus rebellions around a broad range of issues and the fight for scarce public resources found higher education looking for new ways to explain its value as a public good. University presidents created Campus Compact to solidify an institutional commitment to civic education and community outreach. The Coalition of Urban and Metropolitan Universities touted the university as an "anchor" for rebuilding communities. Finally, in 1994 the Department of Housing and Urban Development (HUD) created the Office of University Partnerships to provide grants and sponsored research that encouraged a better integration between schools and their cities.[57]

Henry Taylor and Ira Harkavy were both early advocates in the struggle for the anchor idea. Taylor was an urban planner and community activist who moved to the State University of New York at Buffalo (SUNY Buffalo) to lead community engagement efforts in 1987. Harkavy started as a student activist at UPenn in the 1960s, eventually steering the school's community partnership projects throughout the 1980s and 1990s. They, like many others at the time, shared a desire for neighborhood revitalization; they differed only in what they emphasized. An older cadre of activists and educators looked to urban schools as a beacon for enlivening the values of civic engagement. The classroom and the research center, they believed, could be reoriented to address the needs of the city. Meanwhile, a growing class of administrators, coming out of the corporate world, identified universities as central command posts for generating needed profits in new research and real estate markets.

Both groups used the language of anchor institutions and shared interests in crime reduction and neighborhood improvement. However, fissures began to fester even within the same university about whose interests should dictate community partnerships. A school's chief financial officer doesn't discuss real estate investments with the Office of Community

Learning. Yet both groups are engaging with the same urban neighborhood. And the failure to reconcile what have become parallel approaches to revitalization continues to shape how university-driven development is done in our cities.

SUNY Buffalo recruited Taylor from Ohio State in 1987 to build stronger connections between the school and the city. But the university had moved its undergraduate education to the suburban town of Amherst in the early 1970s, and its "South campus" now looked abandoned. They asked Taylor to develop a comprehensive plan using the school's original urban location to help stimulate the deteriorating University Heights neighborhood. The area was in the middle of transition with a still largely white population, a small Black middle class, and a growing spate of unkempt predatory rental facilities packing in as many students as possible to increase profits.

But Taylor made sure to remind me that this campus neighborhood had not faced the crisis that rocked many urban universities. Still, SUNY Buffalo needed to service a broader public good. As he explained, "The university was beginning to understand they had to prove to the legislature that they could have positive impacts in urban areas to generate funding and support." The main campus was in the suburbs, so the immediate survival of the university wasn't at stake. Urban engagement became an opportunity to brand SUNY Buffalo as a school interested in helping a largely industrial city struggling with massive out-migration to the suburbs. The workforce that remained scrambled for fewer jobs while lacking the training for a world without factories. University Heights became the laboratory for proving the school's worth in changing times.

Taylor dove headfirst into the task, working closely with the president, meeting with local politicians, and developing more than ten research designs to bolster the university's community initiative. His vision was broad and bold. Taylor imagined turning the entire South campus into a "commons," a porous space where the university serviced the needs of the city. Anyone living in the area could get an ID card and access all university resources. SUNY Buffalo would also create mixed housing for faculty and staff to meet different income levels and revitalize the commercial corridor.

The goal was to build institutions that broke down racial and class barriers. "For the university, that was a bit much," he laughed. Taylor said administrators immediately bought into the cosmetic labors of landscaping and partnering with developers on the residential and retail pieces. But they drastically scaled down the plan and only focused on faculty housing, higher-end shopping, and community access to university gym memberships. Administrators quickly discarded the broader commons plan: "It just gradually became a nice little neighborhood to live in and invest in. I try to separate myself from it now." Taylor laments how these celebrated bits and pieces were extracted from his larger vision of community development.

The impasse over building out the South campus made Taylor confront a fundamental difference in his approach to university community partnerships: "I made choices without regard for university interests. I placed Black people's interests first, and that was incompatible with how the university wanted to operate." He eventually broke ties with such top-down university projects and moved directly into community work to better serve Buffalo's Black neighborhoods. But no matter where he went in the city, the university was always nearby . . . and always building.

Taylor also looks back at that time with a profound sense of dismay about his inability to see the university as a mechanism of power within the city's political economy, as a function of urban capitalism.[58] As he says, "They were always with outside consultants helping them plot. There were all of these shadowy relationships with industry and land development." The university celebrated faculty activities in the community while the real work was taking place in the cover of night. Taylor described the disparity like a watch: "We were the shit on top that everybody got excited about. While the invisible mechanisms were doing other things in a different way." He chuckles now, but the role that his urban outreach played in serving the university's economic interests stays with Taylor: "You know, I'm a Black Marxist. I'm looking for all this shit. And the stuff is right under my nose, and I didn't see it. That's how good these people are."

Harkavy was not a Black Marxist, yet he knew exactly what he was dealing with at the University of Pennsylvania (UPenn). A year after the Columbia protests against the Morningside gym, there was young Ira serving as what he describes as a "moderate" student voice, contesting the

University City Science Center project in West Philadelphia. Fast-forward twenty years, and the predominantly Black neighborhoods surrounding UPenn were rocked by crime and poverty. The headlines were filled with stories of rapes and robberies. A graduate student and an instructor were murdered in the street. Still, UPenn didn't want to become Columbia. It refused to shut the gates.

Activists had lost the Science Center battle, but Harkavy continued to believe that from inside the university he could grow the networks cultivated from his student days to serve the neighborhoods around UPenn. He remained a strategic player between school and city, compelling university leaders to embrace civic engagement as an institutional imperative. With all of the crime tarnishing the UPenn brand, Harkavy leveraged the importance of "enlightened self-interest." The fates of the city and school were linked.

Always the broker, Harkavy and his civic engagement efforts at UPenn also helped guide early national conversations about anchor institutions. In the 1990s he worked with Housing and Urban Development Secretary Henry Cisneros and other higher education leaders to shape public conversations, and he later served as one of the cofounders of the National Anchor Institute Task Force after the 2008 election of President Barack Obama. Harkavy's years of work around urban engagement culminated into his appointment as director of UPenn's Netter Center for Community Partnerships in 2007. The center has become the national model for university-based civic engagement.

Harkavy shares Taylor's strong insistence that urban institutions must be evaluated by the health of the neighborhoods that surround them. And he is not satisfied with the current realities: "I believe firmly that overall universities are not yet part of the solution to the tragic and inexcusable conditions in the poorer communities that are near them or have been moved out and remain relatively close. They contribute more to privilege and to sustaining the current situation than they do to change it." Unlike Taylor, Harkavy leaned in to the university's power to influence urban renewal. His Netter Center has made some amazing advances, but as a UPenn center for community partnerships, its initiatives are heavily shaped by trying to improve the university on its own terms.

With references to Sir Francis Bacon and John Dewey, the Netter Center appeals to the "service" roots of the research university. Harkavy endorses a relatively conventional understanding of higher education as a center of teaching and learning. According to this thinking, something like the Science Center represents a "betrayal" of the university's core values because it prizes corporate research over community engagement through teaching. The Netter Center then becomes UPenn's moral compass, built around a broad menu of credit-bearing service-learning courses and outreach projects. For Harkavy, the service-learning work of the Netter Center induces the university to be its best self: a cultivator of democratic citizenship.

Community engagement encourages status-hungry faculty to think beyond pure research. Students break down the false divides between the ivory tower and what's been called the "real world." The Netter Center works intimately with underserved neighborhood schools. It has even pushed UPenn to more seriously consider local residents for their employment databases and procurement programs when subcontracting for suppliers and services. Medical students conduct screenings at community centers; small businesses are incubated on campus; schoolteachers receive professional-development training in their specialty areas.

Harkavy is emphatic that all of his service-learning initiatives must cultivate "activities that benefit the community." However, the narrative of revival or return to the true university, represented by the Netter Center and other groups like it at elite institutions, fails to grapple with the multifaceted history of what universities have always done in cities beyond their educational mandate. Think about Henry Taylor's simile of the watch and all the things we don't see. In fact, urban planning scholar Harley Etienne takes UPenn to task precisely because of the dual nature of its revitalization efforts. University administrators were using Harkavy's language of civic engagement to bolster its profiteering in the neighborhoods. Etienne argues that the Netter Center couldn't have predicted how "various university-based stakeholders would adopt, and in some cases, adapt those principles for their own purposes."[59]

Etienne uses interviews with university employees to support his observation that the Netter Center was "deployed" to provide moral cover for UPenn's real estate office. The center encourages the university to serve as a good neighbor. In the realm of land management, however, being a "good neighbor" meant creating an investment environment to bank land for future research labs that will make lifesaving discoveries, building upscale retail on Fortieth Street, and underwriting employee home-ownership programs. These efforts all seem to help stabilize a struggling neighborhood. But they also raise both shopping and housing costs above the means of low-income residents while catering to the needs of students, faculty, and their families. Who becomes "the community" for university community partnerships amid this upscaling of the neighborhood?

Harkavy has primarily focused on getting the university to see the legitimacy of civic engagement so that it continues supporting his broad vision of service learning. It's better to have a moderate voice at UPenn than no voice at all. Therefore, he sees being deployed as part of "acceptable compromises" to preserve the greater good. Harkavy concedes that not everything went his way. But he remains committed to the integrity of community service, which, for him, means the Netter Center had to stay separate from what went on in the real estate office: "There were things that may have happened in real estate that I am not on top of. Well, I can only do so much. But we are now part of the conversation with those entities."

Well-meaning civic engagement programs talked about campus neighborhoods as sites of democratic citizenship. At the same time, city leaders and universities discussed the same places as investment environments. Higher education has advertised to the world its skill set as a developer as much or more than its service as an educational resource. Amid growing interests in urban life, universities became a powerful axis point for parceling and repackaging "blighted" areas into "destinations," and not just for the students. Along with a tax-exempt status, local and state authorities infused higher education with additional capital and governmental authority to help manage the renewed attraction to city life. But when the "the campus" becomes a planning model for the rest of the city, it's less clear where long-term urban residents fit in.

═══

As UPenn and even SUNY Buffalo display, city schools offer far more than just classes. Universities and municipal leaders broker land deals, manage labor relations, provide health care, and dictate policing in the build-out of "university districts" that power the political economy of today's cities.

And in the last two decades, colleges and universities have witnessed an explosive rise in the salaries for a growing administrative class running divisions tasked with accelerating campus expansion. Whether it's the real estate department, the university foundation, campus security, the development office, or the office of technology transfer, beefed-up executive units have grown to outsized proportions. These noneducational divisions are responsible for creating "anchor strategies" that turn urban planning into a key pathway for higher education's growing influence over land, labor, and commercial development.[60] For example, today's schools often cultivate tech communities or innovation districts, which have become dominant models for both the economic development and physical planning of cities.[61] The formerly suburban industrial parks and research parks are now the centerpiece of urban revitalization. These are often tax-free zones, and it's here that academic research and corporate partnerships meet real estate and retail.

Real estate developers like Wexford: Science + Technology, a group with projects across the US, focus exclusively on what they call "knowledge communities." Urban neighborhoods are being transformed to optimize "value capture," the conversion of city blocks into tech profits. Local governments, developers, and universities reap economic rewards by dressing spaces of academic/industry collaboration within a mix of luxury housing, storefronts, classrooms, and laboratories. Wexford has built a monied portfolio of university-affiliated projects such as Philadelphia's UCity Square, Converge Miami, and Cortex in St. Louis. Here, students, researchers, and other contingent workers perform labors that can secure lucrative patents or product licenses for the school and the corporate sponsor, while drawing new residents and investors to the city. Universities have received millions in gross royalty revenue from products that began as research in their laboratories, including Gatorade at the University of Florida, the antiepilepsy drug Lyrica at Northwestern, and Google at Stanford.[62]

Before the Bayh-Dole act passed in 1980, the patents for any research sponsored by federal funding were placed in the public domain and remained freely available to the public. The rise of the "technology-transfer" movement pushed to commercialize academic research by making its licensing available to the private sector. Seven universities created the Society of University Patent Administrators, a private lobbying group that advised lawmakers to craft a bill allowing schools and their researchers to obtain the intellectual property rights for scientific academic discoveries that came from federal grant money.[63]

After passing Bayh-Dole, research universities jumped at the chance to secure patent and licensing arrangements with corporate sponsors. Schools such as Stanford, MIT, and Yale immediately created technology-transfer offices as important mechanisms for privatizing and profiting from tax-exempt, sponsored research. For example, Arizona State (ASU) has nurtured a voracious appetite for capturing the profits that might come from commercializing academic research. And the university's SkySong Innovation facility is its mission-command center for monetizing research.

The primary goal at SkySong is to generate profits by connecting global business partners with ASU for a range of services from leasing office space and licensing research technology to providing student labor. I sat down with Todd Hardy and Julia Rosen when they both worked as executives at the center, in the affluent haven of Scottsdale, where SkySong is located. Even this location was a moneymaking venture for ASU. They told me Scottsdale bought the land in a struggling part of town and rented it to the ASU foundation for ninety-eight years at one dollar per year.[64] In exchange, the Scottsdale City Council and the university use office space for free; there is a fee for the mostly modest businesses that rent out units in the complex. SkySong is especially profitable for ASU to incubate student-run entrepreneurship ventures and spin out patents from faculty research, of which the university gets 60 percent.

SkySong is wide-ranging in the ways it attempts to profit from controlling the intellectual property of faculty and student research. The Edge Program aids "industry-sponsored research," where ASU faculty offer their expertise on applied research with existing companies such as Honeywell. On capstone projects, students work on ventures brought to the university by private industry. In exchange for their labors, students receive academic credit but must sign over their rights to the intellectual property.

Hardy and Rosen told me during our conversation these various arrangements have been quite lucrative for the university, especially through partnerships in the battery-storage, security, and defense industries. Although ASU's intellectual property provisions may have changed in the years since, SkySong reveals the extent of the school's use of academic research (and researchers) to maximize financial profits. Even still, ASU's innovation center lags far behind other metropolitan hubs that have fully reorganized cities to best capture the profits that come from partnerships between higher education and private industry. For that story, consider Pittsburgh.

Pittsburgh is in the middle of a renaissance. Local stakeholders are happy to tell the story of their new "Tech Town" rising from the ashes of the once-dominant Steel City. In the last three decades of the twentieth century, the mills became hulking gravestones to commemorate a formerly great industrial past. Forty percent of the city's residents fled the city. Pittsburgh seemed all but dead. But now an old Nabisco cookie factory has been repurposed with Google's colorful logo, and self-driving vehicle prototypes are seen on local highways as part of Pittsburgh's broader shift toward the high-tech world. The University of Pittsburgh Medical Center is the largest employer in the area. Yet people love to celebrate "Roboburgh"—despite how awkward it sounds—to remind the world that Pittsburgh is still the place where things get made.[65] It was in Pittsburgh where Richard Florida first worked out his thesis regarding the creative class. If a steel-addicted company town like Pittsburgh could rise above the fog of its own comeback delusions and forge a new economic path, any deindustrialized city could.

Carnegie Mellon is a beacon in the new Pittsburgh. Because CMU's School of Computer Science began "churning out" top young talent and pathbreaking research, tech companies such as Apple, Facebook, Google, and Uber all opened up offices in Pittsburgh. CMU Professor Luis von Ahn embodies what's possible when academic research meets an entrepreneurial spirit. This MacArthur "Genius" Award winner helped create the reCAPTCHA software to identify a human user online, as well as the language-learning platform Duolingo. The city got mentioned alongside Brooklyn and Portland as an urban hotspot for millennial creatives. Two decades ago, the unemployment rate was worse than in Detroit, but now Pittsburgh is being touted as one of the cities that can legitimately claim the title "Silicon Valley of the East."[66]

Yet Pittsburgh also foreshadows the pitfalls when higher education's profit motive takes such a dominant hand in rebuilding US cities. Pittsburgh reveals who got lost in the tech rush. And this UniverCity brings to light the dirty secrets of deep exploitation that underwrite prosperity in the new economy.

Steve was one of the millennials immediately drawn to this new Pittsburgh. In 2011 he was a PhD candidate in CMU's Electrical and Computer Engineering Department. Steve started working on the campus even before classes began. He specialized in high-end software engineering for the control systems on vehicles and other power networks. Steve received funding from Bombardier Transportation to work on self-driving vehicle research. It was clear that CMU recruited him to advance research that had potentially lucrative commercial applications.

The campus still buzzed with excitement because CMU had just settled a $750 million lawsuit for alleged patent infringement against Marvell Technology Group. A CMU professor and his graduate student had developed algorithms that allowed devices to sort through errors when retrieving digital data from increasingly smaller storage spaces. Marvell had made a fortune selling its products to data-storage giants like Seagate and Western Digital. Half of one of the largest patent infringements ever paid went to the inventors and the other half to the university.[67] This court settlement announced that CMU researchers were open for business and ready to license their research for technology innovations.

The lawsuit unfolded, and Steve knew that CMU had presented his expertise to Bombardier in the hopes that their graduate students could make more high-tech magic. After being immersed in the tech-transfer world, Steve saw the advantages for the industry sponsor and a potential windfall for the university. An industry sponsor such as General Motors or Bombardier makes gifts to CMU. Out of that fund the university buys equipment, pays the salary of the research principal investigator, and pays for the graduate fellowships of research students. Also, according to Steve, a huge chunk of money gets dumped into the murky category of "overhead" or "administrative costs" for the university. The industry sponsor benefits from getting important preliminary research from a deep talent pool of cheap and hardworking students while its financial contributions are a tax write-off because the money is supporting education. Steve describes this arrangement as a "big-business transaction" under the cover of an educational partnership. He said for both the university and the industry sponsor, it's a "cheap way to make things happen." But what about the students?

Steve tells me that he could have gone directly to Bombardier with his bachelor's degree and earned about $60,000, and after a couple years of good research he could have earned up to $110,000: "But at CMU I am effectively a full-time researcher that gets $30,000 a year." Steve said it would be one thing if he worked twenty hours a week on graduate duties and twenty on sponsored research, but that is never the case: "In reality, a student works thirty hours a week on graduate stuff and thirty or forty hours a week on research stuff for their sponsor. And they still receive the same $30,000 stipend." Steve called these working conditions exploitative and explained that if he was producing graduate student research that might have a commercial application and could be sold, he would stop all development: "I am leaving."

He told me a story about a friend at CMU who was working on his own research while also a student. This friend worked up individual pieces of the research for different class projects, and then in his spare time he connected the dots. Right before the work became a cohesive product that could be sold, he left for California. Steve makes clear that this kind of clandestine work is extremely dangerous. Students can get kicked out of school or, worse, blacklisted within the high-tech community. But he also believes that students lose when they fail to see the school and industry sponsors as their adversaries.

Steve pointed out that it had been only five years since graduate students received maternity leave and could apply for a stipend continuation. In the past, if a woman gave birth and lost research time, she didn't officially get a break for that and would still be expected to complete her degree in the same number of years.[68] Steve disclosed that life is just as bad for international students. They come to CMU because the name is so prestigious, but if they find conditions to be unfair, they can't protest or leave and create a start-up in California. International students have to work for the university that arranged their visa: "They are starting off in a tremendous position of weakness." Steve understands that it is a huge privilege to study at an elite institution like CMU. But the university and its industry sponsors hide behind the category of education and apprenticeship to exploit extremely talented student workers: "This is the city of unions, and one of the big demographics in Pittsburgh, as far as labor goes, is graduate students. And there is no union." The profound exploitation of student labor is a critical warning sign about what can happen when profit-driven higher education propels economic development in our cities.

=

A discussion of labor in the knowledge economy can be terrifying and also revealing. But a focus on graduate employees or faculty exploitation can blind us to the vast and varied ivory tower workforce that powers not just American higher education but our cities more broadly. Many of the residents who struggle to maintain their lives in the campus neighborhoods that become knowledge communities are also shunted into the low-wage sectors of the ivory tower labor force. Baltimore follows the patterns of so many deindustrialized cities, with growing enclaves of returning white wealth dotted among waves of Black and brown poverty. In the middle sits Johns Hopkins University as the largest private employer in a Baltimore economy that ranks among the worst in the nation for its poverty rate, median annual income, and job loss.

Kiva Robbins worked as an environmental services employee at Baltimore's Johns Hopkins Hospital, toiling away daily, cleaning rooms and mopping floors. By 2014, she had been there for twelve years but lost her apartment when rent kept rising, yet her salary wouldn't budge past $12.20 an hour. Kiva already relied on food stamps and other forms of public assistance just to scrape together a life for her and her two sons. Even with a full-time job, she ended up sharing a tiny apartment with a relative.[69] To make matters worse, Hopkins had just rejected health-care workers' demands for a $14 minimum wage. The hospital pointed to economic instability for its hesitance to raise wages. But a year earlier the CEO of the Johns Hopkins Health System Corporation earned a salary of $1.7 million.[70] All across the country, former manufacturing centers are now dominated by "meds and eds." In Baltimore, like cities from Pittsburgh to Los Angeles, universities and their medical schools are the largest employers in the area. But this doesn't mean well-paying jobs with good benefits.

Usually, faculty, researchers, and administrators come to mind when we think about workers in today's knowledge economy. But knowledge-economy labor is in fact dominated by lower-wage workers like Kiva. It is the nurse's aides, custodians, clerical and security staff, and maintenance workers who largely keep colleges and universities running. And with such an outsized economic influence, higher education sets the nonprofessional wage ceiling for most cities in America. If Johns Hopkins offered Kiva a living wage—perhaps out of its reported $145 million operating surplus—other employers would have to be just as competitive to recruit and keep their workers in Baltimore.[71] Unfortunately, the gap is only widening between university endowments and administrative payouts on one hand and employee wages and health benefits on the other.

Just in terms of salary, most nonprofessional jobs in the "meds and eds" market pay below $50,000 annually in cities where it costs much more to live, especially with a family. At the same time, the salary doesn't even account for the range of ways that higher education maintains the gap between living and surviving for its most-marginalized workers. Most low-wage workers have to find another job in the summer, when campus operations are significantly scaled back. Seasonal downsizing can drastically affect the health benefits for workers and their families. Higher education labor is also increasingly outsourced to corporate subcontractors such as Aramark or Wolf.[72] Therefore, workers may receive lower wages or might be excluded from housing subsidies they would otherwise receive if directly employed by the university.

But university workers have begun to unionize, engage in work stoppages, and join community-based coalitions like New Haven Rising in order to rethink the terms of urban revitalization in their increasingly expensive cities. Harvard's food service workers went on strike in October 2016 to protest low wages and rising health-care costs at the same time that the university wielded a $38 billion endowment to continue rapid campus growth into the Allston Brighton neighborhood across the Charles River.

The food service workers won a new contract that includes summer pay while halting increased employee co-pays for health insurance.[73]

≡

The new economy is firmly rooted in cities like Pittsburgh. But part of this success story evades the fact that good-paying union jobs that once existed there will not come back, at least not in the same form. The industrial working class has not been invited to the knowledge and high-tech boom party. At the same time, residents are struggling to hold on in university districts now overrun by pressed-juice bars, custom bike shops, and tech office buildings.[74] We are left wondering how these knowledge economies can attract talented new workers that will help revitalize our cities without pushing low-income residents out of the revitalized parts of urban America. The answers lie with deep and hard investigations into specific urban experiences where higher education takes control.

The history of higher education's role in cities has meant that more and more people are part of a university's ecosystem: people like Kiva, whose work foretells the labor conditions for us all. Or Brian, whose struggles for fair and adequate medical service at Yale could have threatened his career. Or Steve, who says he won't fully benefit from the work he put in on Carnegie Mellon's profitable scientific discoveries. Or, most urgently, people like Stephanie, whose very lives are at risk in the name of policing urban growth. Higher education sits at the center of our cities and their future. And it's the communities living in the shadows of these ivory towers, it's *their* stories, that must guide us on the path moving forward.

CHAPTER TWO

RURAL COLLEGE IN A CAPITAL CITY

I n April 1994 it seemed all hell was breaking loose in the small capital city of Hartford, Connecticut. The Latin Kings and Los Solidos brought their heated gang rivalry right to the doorsteps of the Trinity College campus. According to reports, a car chase between the gangs traversed the immediate border streets of the campus with gunshots blazing. Two vehicles flew east down New Britain Avenue, turned left and drove along Summit Street, and then barreled down Vernon Street. They headed directly for one of the main points of entrance to the campus at the intersection of Vernon and Broad. Once the chase reached Broad, one of the drivers lost control and drove onto a sidewalk, where he hit an empty Campus Safety cruiser. But the chase didn't end there.

Passengers in both cars jumped out and continued the pursuit on foot. Two Campus Safety officers, who had watched the events unfold, jumped into the fray. When the officers finally caught up to the runners, one of the men hit an officer in the head several times while another tried to

HARTFORD

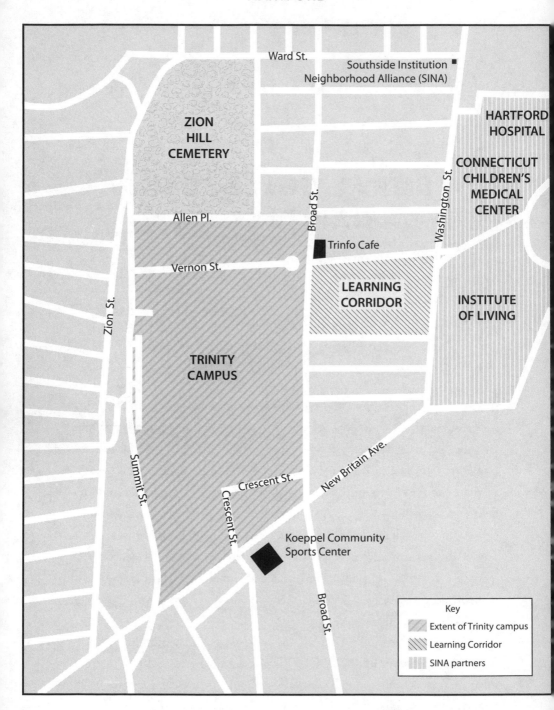

Ward St.

Southside Institution
Neighborhood Alliance (SINA)

ZION
HILL
CEMETERY

HARTFORD
HOSPITAL

CONNECTICUT
CHILDREN'S
MEDICAL
CENTER

Allen Pl.

Broad St.

Trinfo Cafe

Washington St.

Vernon St.

LEARNING
CORRIDOR

INSTITUTE
OF LIVING

Zion St.

TRINITY
CAMPUS

Summit St.

New Britain Ave.

Crescent St.

Crescent St.

Koeppel Community
Sports Center

Broad St.

Key

Extent of Trinity campus

Learning Corridor

SINA partners

barricade himself in the hallway of a campus building. Finally, six Hartford Police squad cars reached the scene and placed the attackers under arrest.[1]

This car chase took place on a Hartford public street, but Vernon also runs right through the heart of student life on the Trinity campus. The car chase and its implications enraptured this elite liberal arts college set atop a hill in the middle of Hartford's impoverished Latinx and Black neighborhood of Frog Hollow. In an interview for the *Tripod* student newspaper, Trinity's Campus Safety director, Brian Kelley, went to great lengths to assure everyone that "the gangs are only angry at each other and they are not interested in Trinity students."[2] Official statements about the incident continued to focus on "safety," but then the discussion took an unexpected turn, shifting from gang violence to an ostensible concern with traffic problems. Trinity administrators concentrated on the dangers of the Vernon and Broad intersection, or what Director of Community Relations and eventual Hartford mayor Eddie Perez described as "an accident waiting to happen."[3] The college proposed to take the existing fence that separated the campus from Broad Street and extend it across the Vernon Street entrance, effectively closing Trinity off from Hartford.

Because Vernon is a public street, Trinity had to submit a proposal before the Hartford City Council, again couching the street closing in the language of traffic safety. But many in the city understood that fencing off Vernon was about closing the doors to the surrounding poverty and crime that threatened to damage Trinity's enrollment and overall school brand. One article in the *Hartford Courant* argued that "eliminating through traffic on Vernon will discourage criminals from using the street where about 500 college students live." Councilman Anthony DiPentima described how closing off Vernon would help the school rebound while "enrollment is down because of crime and perceptions of crime."[4] It was true; Trinity faced a dip in applications. But the link between crime and traffic control was dubious at best.

Others were more explicit about the way a street closing aided the college's effort to separate itself from the struggling city. One alumnus described this privatization of a public street as "another example of Trinity trying to isolate itself more." Council Majority Leader John B. O'Connell, who was the only one to vote against the street closing in a seven-to-one decision, chided, "We all do not have the option to turn our neighborhood into a secure enclave."[5] In a letter to the editor of the school newspaper, a student added that the traffic safety claim sounded more like a "plausible and acceptable excuse to close the road for ulterior motives rather than a justifiable necessity." No matter the motive, just four months after the car chase, Trinity ran a wrought-iron fence across Vernon Street.[6] It remains there today.

Closing off public access to campus from Vernon Street sent a clear message: Trinity is a world apart. This act of enclosure was, in many ways, reflective of the college's century-long ambivalence, its mixed feelings about being stuck in the city and the limited resources to do much about it. Like its elite New England peers, including Williams and Bowdoin, Trinity originally positioned itself as a pastoral retreat from urban life, a place of reflection and renewal. The difference is that unlike other liberal arts colleges, Trinity faced the public relations nightmare of being located in a poor and increasingly nonwhite city. The liberal arts aura of learned refuge became a polite way of signaling exclusivity and safety. And yet that branding

Trinity gate on Broad Street, 2020. Photo by VisionMerge Productions.

goes only so far. Trinity's fate was increasingly linked to the struggles of Hartford. Unlike other elite universities, the school didn't sit in a sleepy college town or wield the economic means to exert powerful influence over its host city. Trinity had to exist as a college in, if not for, Hartford.

Trinity's story illustrates how a small, elite college with limited leverage finds ways to use the language of community partnership in order to prioritize its interests. It's a tale of big dreams, broken promises, and brokered concessions. In many ways, Trinity has been forced to work with Hartford because of its modest resources; it has tried to turn the liability of its location into a unique asset in the higher education marketplace. Through it all, Trinity's fluctuations between calculated outreach and knee-jerk enclosure reveal a profound ambivalence about its location in this second-tier capital city.

=

In the mid-twentieth century, Hartford, like cities across the country, went through the urban crisis of industrial divestment and growing poverty. Trinity had long fortified its gates and ignored the factories that employed a largely immigrant workforce. But when the college finally looked up in the late 1960s, it faced a city ravaged by neglect and decay. White ethnic residents started following factories to the suburbs, only looking back to attend church or maybe a Hartford Whalers hockey game. And when enrollment numbers dipped, the college could no longer afford to bury its head in the sand. The campus ideal of pastoral retreat seemed to be withering on the vine as the state of the city increasingly shaped the fate of the college.

Trinity invited a world-renowned urban planner, Constantinos Doxiadis, to campus in 1966 with hopes that he could inspire a new relationship between campus and city. Doxiadis had made his name supervising the Marshall Plan during the recovery of European cities after World War II.[7] Bringing an expert on postwar recovery to address its concerns about Hartford signaled that Trinity saw the city in a state of emergency.

While in Hartford, Doxiadis proposed that the best way to save Trinity was by adopting a suburban vision of social control, turning nearby city blocks into a controlled campus cul-de-sac. The school needed to implement his vision of "dynopolis," which called for limiting population growth to grid-like neighborhoods where streets were closed off and parks served as barriers.[8] In his report, "The Trinity Community," Doxiadis implored the school to collaborate with nearby anchor institutions—Hartford Hospital and the residential psychiatric facility, the Institute of Living—to purchase properties that sat between the three institutions. He called it a "town within the city." It sounded a lot like turning parts of the city into a campus. The corridor would serve as a revitalized residential and recreational space for faculty, students, and other employees: "The goal of these studies is to provide the means by which a desirable living environment may be created in this confused area."[9]

Trinity didn't have the political power or economic means to bulldoze city blocks. And the college couldn't get the necessary cooperation from its institutional partners in the neighborhood. So the college purchased some of the properties on its immediate Allen Place northern border and on the interior Vernon Street because it cut through campus. Trinity sought to "stabilize" the area by modestly extending the campus borders, which pushed the neighborhood further back.[10] For Doxiadis, residents living in the surrounding communities represented a "confused area" and therefore had to be driven to the perimeter of this expanded new campus community. One of those residents was Carlos Espinosa.

Espinosa grew up in the shadows of Trinity's Gothic spires. His family lived on Hillside Avenue, just six blocks from campus. In 1972 Espinosa's father came to Hartford from Miami by way of New York City. He joined an existing enclave of Cuban families attracted by the city's union-based factory jobs serving the military-industrial complex. Espinosa's dad started at the Fafnir ball bearing company, working on helicopter rotors until the factory followed the growing trend of moving south. And Espinosa remembers a friendly relationship with Trinity. At the old arcade, "Students gave us quarters to play," he recalled. But the flight of industry changed everything: "I think it was emblematic of a lot of what happened; either the factories closed or picked up and moved away." His father continued to bounce around from job to job; he lived the phrase "last one hired, first one fired." Job loss put Espinosa's home life in turmoil. His parents divorced. Espinosa describes this part of his childhood as "a personal story on a larger narrative that was going on in the city, in terms of the crazy flux and disequilibrium."[11]

In elementary school, Espinosa got immersed in a dynamic mix of French Canadians, Italians, Irish, and Puerto Ricans. But he called that "the last chapter of white dominance." By the time he reached middle school, white residents had taken advantage of federally subsidized mortgages to follow industry out to the suburbs. He said his neighbors moved to Wethersfield, Rocky Hill, and other areas covered by racially restrictive covenants. At the same time, more upwardly mobile Latinx residents filled in the blocks around him. By the time Espinosa got to high school, "white flight had smashed the accelerator pedal," and Puerto Ricans had become the biggest subgroup. "Even the few white kids that remained had flavor, listened to Latin Freestyle music, and could pop off with some Spanish if they got into a heated quarrel with someone," Espinosa laughed.

But there were few jobs, and, of course, even the poorest people will still find ways to make money. As factories left, the drug trade became a dominant economy. Various youth gangs fought for wider swaths of the city where they could control the market. Espinosa remembers the early 1990s as the height of the gang wars: "It was lit." He described the Savage Nomads gang as "a vertically integrated conglomerate" that got too big, which brought increased attention from the police, ultimately breaking the gang up. Its demise opened the door for upstart rivalries and violent battles for market share. The two largest challengers for the throne were the Latin Kings, who were exclusively Latinx, and the multiracial Los Solidos. The wars began to ramp up until all the blocks surrounding Trinity were hot.

In 1992 Espinosa went from looking at Trinity as this prestigious educational institution up on the hill to entering its freshman class. Even though he left Hartford down on Hillside Avenue, some of the city still managed to creep through the gates. During his second year at Trinity, Espinosa joined friends to watch a women's rugby game right along the Broad Street fence line on the border of campus. It was a beautiful day on the idyllic campus: "And then BOOM! You just hear this huge gunshot." Out of instinct, Espinosa dropped to the ground until police swarmed the area.

Turns out a member of Los Solidos had killed Hector Santiago, a twenty-three-year-old leader of the Latin Kings, just on the other side of Trinity's wrought-iron fence.[12]

Trinity had done little to address the conditions facing the city struggling for survival just beyond its campus borders. As early as 1977, the college finally persuaded leaders of Hartford Hospital and the Institute of Living to join in creating the Southside Institutions Neighborhood Alliance (SINA). SINA most notably focused on providing mortgage and down-payment assistance for employees to buy homes and help stabilize the area.[13] Individual home mortgages served as a small-scale attempt to complete the Doxiadis plan.

In 1986 Art Feltman issued the award-winning report, "Tax Exemption of Private Colleges and Hospitals: A Hartford Case Study." In it, Feltman noted the valiant efforts of SINA's Ivan Backer to address local issues with limited resources. But the report also levied a harsh condemnation of Trinity's tax-exempt status while failing to serve students of Hartford and the residents of color who now surrounded the campus. A small public outcry erupted when the report circulated around the city. Yet Trinity President James English remained unmoved: "[We] are just not in the business of being real estate developers."[14] Trinity had barely managed to keep Hartford's decline at the campus border. But the college could no longer afford to play the violin while the *Titanic* sank.

Santiago's murder signaled a much broader shift in the blocks surrounding Trinity. Between the 1980 and 1990 census, Frog Hollow's white population dropped in half while the Latinx community almost doubled in size. And 40 percent of the fifteen thousand residents lived below the poverty line. At the same time, Trinity's reputation declined with the city. The school was losing students. The national pool of college eligible students had shrunk, and the country faced an economic recession. But families also kept their kids away because of the perceptions and reality of crime and poverty near campus. Trinity had to become less selective. In 1987 it had almost 3,500 applicants and accepted 39.7 percent. By 1991, applications dropped to just under 2,800 while the acceptance rate jumped to 61.5 percent. Trinity came to be known by some as a "good school in a bad neighborhood."[15] Administrators couldn't afford to fully implement the Doxiadis plan of building a suburban fortress. And they weren't necessarily concerned with any robust urban engagement. But school leaders had to engage the city enough to at least change perceptions about Hartford's impact on this liberal arts college.

Trinity worked to transform its location from a liability into an asset. In 1989 the college hired Tom Gerety as the next president. He was a bit unconventional; he had a limited résumé of administrative experience. But Gerety had served in the Peace Corps in Peru and spoke reasonable Spanish, and he also made a ten-year pledge to both the college and the city. Then all of a sudden, the college got blindsided by what insiders coined "The Betrayal." Gerety bolted for greener pastures, to go lead Amherst College after only a few years on the job. Trinity leaders were devastated, and many wanted to turn back toward a more traditional president.[16] But then came Evan Dobelle.

Dobelle arrived at his final interview for the Trinity presidency in a New York City penthouse owned by one of the trustees. He immediately let the search committee know that he had already made a quiet visit to campus and walked the neighborhood. They said Dobelle was the first one to ever do that. And then he told the committee what Trinity must do to turn things around and why he was the man to do it. Administrators and alumni wanted to believe that Trinity's "Little Ivy" status transcended its location, but Dobelle understood that the college reputation was tied to the quality of life in Hartford. These scions of the New England elite were certainly turned off by Dobelle's brash style, but also intrigued. A few weeks later, they offered him the job.

In the words of one trustee, Dobelle was "an outlandishly unconventional choice." More politician than academic, he had served as a Republican mayor of Pittsfield, Massachusetts, and worked as Democratic president Jimmy Carter's chief of protocol. His only experience in academia was serving as president at a pair of two-year colleges. He did not receive his bachelor's degree until the age of thirty-eight. Dobelle also placed results over tradition in ways that unsettled many. He refused a contract and tenure, calling them "inappropriate and irrelevant."[17] His job was to revitalize the community and raise the status of the college. And Dobelle had the political connections that just might get the job done.

Dario Eraque joined Trinity's History Department in 1990, just a few years before Dobelle came. When he arrived, people were talking about packing up the campus and moving to the suburbs. Eraque was one of a very few faculty members of color on campus, and he loved cities. He was born in Tegucigalpa, the capital of Honduras, and spent ten years of his childhood in New Orleans, where he learned English. So during his first visit Eraque grew confused when Trinity colleagues never showed him any housing options near campus. His family owned just one car, and he wanted to walk to work. But at the same time, an urban neighborhood appealed to him.

Eraque didn't know anything about Hartford, but he jumped out on his own and found a place on Brownell Street, just steps away from the gates. He said the neighborhood was certainly dangerous. Eraque and his wife had to duck when they heard gunshots: "But to me, you know, I grew up in inner city New Orleans on Iberville. . . . Did I enjoy it? No, but it was part of living in a diverse city." Eraque joined up with a student, Eddie Perez, who had been gang affiliated and would eventually become a Trinity administrator and then mayor of Hartford. They went around and talked with gang members, tried to organize tenants and connect with the police. But when Eraque reached out to colleagues in his department about partnering with the community, most were dismissive: "They told me Trinity College is not a social agency."

In 1994 Eraque mobilized with other sympathetic faculty and students, such as Espinosa, to protest the closing of Vernon Street. First, they directly contested the idea that street danger was caused solely by local residents. Eraque used to walk up Vernon Street to his office and witnessed the locals drive through there: "But I also saw Trinity kids with their big, different kinds of cars that the locals didn't have." The fence wouldn't stop reckless students. Second, the street closing served as a huge signal to the residents about boundaries.[18]

Eraque got up in faculty meetings and said, "I don't speak from just logic and sociological theories. I live on Brownell. My mother goes to a little Seventh Day Adventist Church in Frog Hollow. I am one of 'those people.'" And then he said that something bizarre kept happening. Colleagues constantly responded with the quip "Well, this is a liberal arts college." Eraque

said he had heard the phrase before, but the street-closing controversy finally helped clarify what Trinity folks really meant. They were associating
"liberal arts" with an education removed from the messiness of everyday
life, or what Eraque called "the mambo." He concluded that a significant
cohort of the faculty and alums "wanted Trinity College to be a citadel,"
closed off from the city. So for Eraque, Dobelle was a breath of fresh air.

When it came to the new president, Eraque pointed out that there were
strong divisions among the trustees and the faculty from the start. He didn't
have the right academic pedigree; he talked too fast; he was a politician—
but the city burned all around Trinity. Dobelle was what Eraque described
as "a doer," and something needed to be done. One day Eraque asked a white
colleague if they ever heard of the Latin jazz superstar Tito Puente. And
when they said no, Eraque explained, "That's a problem because you're surrounded by a community where if you say Tito Puente, everyone knows." In
a bold move, Eraque and his colleague went to Dobelle and asked the president if he might bring Puente to Hartford. But they didn't want him to just
come to the city; they wanted to have a concert directly on campus. Dobelle
said it'd be a lot of money, but he agreed. Not only would they invite Puente
to play on campus, but the whole community would be invited. "That was a
trip," Eraque recalled with a sparkle in his eyes.

Puente played a free concert at Trinity in 1996. Hundreds of people
came, residents brought food, and it was a festive success. Many students
holed up in their dorms, scared of the locals. But the concert helped transform the community's relationship to Trinity.[19] For Eraque, the concert also
reflected a more profound quality about Dobelle. He said that although
Gerety knew Spanish and walked the streets presenting himself as "Pres-
idente en Trinity College," there was no deeper connection. Dobelle was
different: "Dobelle didn't speak a word of Spanish, and he didn't know who
Tito Puente was. But he listened to the people who knew." Eraque did not
agree with everything put forward by the new president, but he respected
that Dobelle made his intentions clear about establishing real connections
with the city that surrounded him. Still, nobody could have prepared for
the magnitude of the proposal the new president unveiled in 1996.

That January, Dobelle announced Trinity was "coming down off the
mountain" to lead a $175 million investment into a fifteen-square-block

section of the neighborhood just east of campus. A former city bus garage, sitting on top of a dangerous brownfield, would become a thriving center where people could "live, work, and learn." Dobelle asked everyone to imagine an "urban Shangri-La" of quality, affordable housing and job opportunities. Residents would walk tree-lined streets to a "learning corridor" of buildings with education available from day care to college and even adult-learning classes.[20] A neighborhood child could sit in a class with kids from the suburbs or play basketball and use computer labs at night.

Welcome to what Dobelle called "Trinity Heights." This building project would generate his vision of "geographic affirmative action." The site was to include three new public schools, a health and technology center, and a Boys and Girls Club run by Trinity student volunteers and interns. "This is not about gentrification but rather about the difficult task of community-building," Dobelle said. A neighborhood ravaged by crime, drugs, and poverty would become a hub for education and opportunity. He wanted to avoid past development strategies of building high walls around campus, or demolishing blocks, or filling neighborhoods with college employees, "as if the people there aren't worthy to live there."[21]

A total of $75 million from Fannie Mae would allow Trinity's partners in the Southside Institutions Neighborhood Alliance (SINA) to buy, rehabilitate, and offer reduced mortgage financing to low-income buyers. Dobelle wanted owners to sign contracts of commitment to education on the Learning Corridor, where, whether with a GED or a college degree, graduates received job assistance. Everyone loves a comeback story, and both the local and national media ate it up.

Dobelle remained the consummate political strategist, and the Trinity Heights project allowed him to position the college as a model for liberal arts. The *Hartford Courant* trumpeted the plan almost daily while Trinity received notable press in the *New York Times*, the *Washington Post*, and *Time*. Outgoing US Department of Housing and Urban Development secretary Henry Cisneros also gave vocal support to his friend Dobelle and his plan. Retired general Colin Powell named Trinity a "College of Promise." The Aetna Foundation added a $1 million donation to help build and run the Center for Families and Children. Dobelle was in his element, often regaling the "origins story" of Trinity Heights to anyone who would

Learning Corridor, to the east of Trinity campus, 2020. Photo by David Tatem.

listen. He said that on his first visit to Hartford before meeting with the board, he sat on the football field bleachers at dusk and stared out beyond the campus. "I always believe that if I can see it, I can do it," Dobelle declared. "I could see it that day." In his telling, the Learning Corridor was providential.[22]

I asked Jackie Mandyck about Dobelle's story. Mandyck was director of Community and Institutional Relations when Trinity built the Learning Corridor. She paused, looked at me, and said, "Do you want me to make it up, or do you want me to tell you the honest-to-God truth about what happened?"

Mandyck had come to Connecticut from upstate New York in 1996, when her husband got a job at United Technologies Corporation. She had worked in public policy for the state legislature and asked around about the most exciting thing happening in Hartford. People kept mentioning this guy Dobelle over at Trinity, so she got a job there. Mandyck first worked as a consultant at Trinity for a year and then headed up community relations at the college. She said there were almost sixteen full-time people working on some aspect of community engagement, from curriculum that took students into the neighborhood to college partnerships with community groups. Dobelle had "amazing ideas," but, Mandyck suggested, they had no idea what they were doing.

At one point, Trinity started negotiations to bring the Connecticut Science Center to campus, and then it looked at incorporating an aerospace center to make connections with private partners such as Pratt & Whitney. A team even went out to California to meet with Frank Gehry about designing a new Connecticut Historical Society building in a nearby park, until they got push-back from local residents who wanted to keep the green space. At the same time, Trinity had a relatively modest endowment of $177 million (compared to Yale's $3.2 billion). The school's limited resources forced it to engage in what Dobelle called "enlightened self-interest," or, as Mandyck explained in plainer language, "it forced us to work with our neighbors."[23]

Mandyck said that open-bond authorizations to build Hartford public schools are what gave the Learning Corridor its shape. These open bonds are funds issued by the state to sponsor large-scale projects; in this case it was the construction of schools. There were three pockets of money: for building a middle school as a magnet school, for the renovation of an old Montessori school, and for the relocation of the arts academy from a former funeral home. New legislation also provided money for an additional math and science center. All the schools got state funding because technically they were marketed as magnets, just as school boards were trying to get out in front of the *Sheff v. O'Neill* case coming down the path.[24]

Sheff v. O'Neill was a landmark desegregation case ordering the region to integrate its schools. And magnet schools became a popular tool to "integrate" white suburban students into better-quality city schools organized around a core area of study. Building magnet schools was one of the only ways that neglected urban districts could get new educational amenities built. And integration would force the state to improve local facilities in order to draw consumer-conscious suburban and white families. This approach to integration was also attractive to suburban families because it staved off a massive influx of Black and brown children into their school districts.[25] The magnet strategy proved key to funding the Learning Corridor.

As SINA members, both Trinity and Hartford Hospital added $5 million each from their endowments to the corridor. Private donations then followed. For example, Loctite, a company that produced industrial adhesives and sealants, was founded in a Trinity basement, and it donated

$1 million to the math and science academy. The Kellogg Foundation, whose chairman was a Trinity alum, added more than $6 million. "We were one of the first to create what's now called a public/private partnership," Mandyck said. Dobelle was certainly a visionary, but the project got built by chasing the money: "It was never designed to be what it was."

Mandyck loved her time at Trinity but also remembers that "the gas pedal was down all the time." She described Dobelle as an entrepreneur more than an academic. Mandyck thinks that all institutions need a "change agent" but that you also have to slow down and breathe. Dobelle couldn't scale back in the end, which resulted in what many described as a glaring overreach. His grand claims never matched up with Trinity's limited resources or completely aligned with the aloof liberal arts traditions of the college.

By this time, Espinosa had moved from protesting the Vernon Street gate to working on his master's degree at Trinity. He saw so much. I asked Espinosa about Dobelle. His response? "Oh, slick Willie!" Espinosa told me that as a student, he was among a small cohort that Dobelle took on "the road show to go around and meet with donors, trustees, and alums to go hustle up some dough." Espinosa described himself as the perfect case study: someone born and raised in Hartford who excelled at Trinity. He called the president a slick salesman but also a man who "thoroughly rebranded Trinity as the liberal arts college in the city." And then Perez moved from gang-affiliated neighborhood kid to Trinity graduate and administrator and finally the chairman of SINA. He and Dobelle became a perfect pair. "It was a hand-in-glove moment right there," recalls Espinosa.

However, residents ended up paying heavy costs for all of the public pronouncements about community partnerships. On too many occasions, the benefits promised from Trinity Heights got lost in the details. Dobelle shined in the press as the white knight saving the 'hood, while Perez worked in the shadows, closing deals. When houses needed to be demolished to complete the project, Perez used the third-party Lemquil Realty or bought them through SINA so that owners wouldn't jack up prices after realizing the properties were for Trinity.

Dobelle and Perez promised the community that 50 percent of the slots at the middle school would be reserved for kids from the 06106 and 06114 zip codes. It never happened. The student split ended up being 50 percent from the suburbs and the other half from Hartford more broadly. Espinosa was the community organizer in Frog Hollow for the community group Hartford Areas Rally Together (HART) at the time. He believed that it was truly demoralizing for local kids to live next to a shiny new school that they could not attend: "They lied to us repeatedly." He witnessed architects and construction representatives come to several community meetings to discuss the project, making many promises that they didn't keep. Ultimately, the glossy brochures got way out in front of the reality. But Trinity stood on the cutting edge with smaller-scale projects like service learning, where students learn by tackling real-life problems in the surrounding communities. Double-talk was far less possible on curricular issues because of committed faculty and the belief among community groups, such as HART, that research could be a tool for political change.

Alta Lash joined HART at its 1975 founding as the first chairwoman and Frog Hollow leader. She was actually in the convent when fliers circulated around Frog Hollow about the neighborhood's giant-rat problem. Turns out there was an open sewage line, and the rodents were feasting away. When the city failed to do anything, Lash joined a group that stormed a swanky medical event and continued embarrassing officials out in public until the hole got plugged. Lash recalls, "I was shaking in my shoes." But she learned that being "right" doesn't always matter and that victories come only from understanding how power works. That's where HART was born. It became known for aggressive direct-action protest based on Saul Alinsky's organizing tradition in Chicago.

Lash eventually left the convent and helped the group shift focus from rats to redlining when they realized that banks and realtors were steering particular racial groups to certain parts of town. HART organized residents block by block and protested at the homes of realtors until Hartford passed an ordinance to remove all city funds from any bank found guilty of redlining. Over the decades, HART joined with Trinity on various campaigns where their interests converged. Together they advocated for community policing, early home-ownership support, and, in 1993, helped push through a state law allowing police to seize the cars of any men soliciting sex workers in the neighborhoods.[26]

Trinity benefited from the direct action of this community group as
the low-cost front line for pushing crime reduction and neighborhood stabilization. HART, meanwhile, used the institutional leverage of an elite
liberal arts college in the city to help shift power to the neighborhood.
Then Lash saw an opportunity to work with Trinity more directly. She
helped turn the campus into a new command center for HART's community interests.

Just before Dobelle came, Lash went to Perez with an advertisement for
grant money to support university/community partnerships through the
Department of Housing and Urban Development (HUD). This is the time
when "anchor" solutions were in vogue. She joined with a group of faculty
to write the proposal for HUD; Trinity was awarded in the first round, the
only liberal arts college to do so. With the grant, Lash helped create the
Trinity Center for Neighborhoods (TCN). She said that when Dobelle arrived, he wanted to get on the cover of *Time* by constructing buildings: "But
our agenda at Trinity Center for Neighborhoods wasn't to invest in bricks
and mortar. It was to invest in community." Her community-organizing
experiences with HART kept Lash sober about the possibilities and the
limits of getting into bed with Trinity. The college and its neighborhoods
shared a mutual self-interest to clean up the streets and neutralize the violence, but she wanted to make sure that "urban engagement" would address
the needs of residents as much as bolster Trinity's brand. Their mutual interests best converged in the curriculum.

Above all, Lash saw the college as an intellectual resource. Students and
faculty could provide technical assistance by pursuing questions the community needed answering when developing political strategies. She talked
about using the research of an economics professor to pass state legislation
so that the families of senior citizens received financial assistance as care-
givers. Lash sent out a student to neighborhood pharmacies, and he tracked
the varying prices for the same drugs in support of a subsidy program for
low-income seniors. The student ended up on NPR and in the *Wall Street
Journal*. TCN also established a training program for staff of color in local
organizations to help them pursue management and executive positions.
It had a community mobilization course where students conducted background research at city hall on buildings out of compliance with housing

codes and then reported back to the neighborhood.[27] Lash said that Hartford's community court came out of such partnerships.

These curricular developments also helped bolster Trinity's Community Learning Initiative. Faculty were able to take the classrooms out into the city and bring the city into their courses. These early partnerships set the tone for service-learning efforts across the country. But again, Dobelle's branding of the "liberal arts college in the city" failed to align with the school's capacity to create and run the programs. The neighborhood got excited, and then the money ran out.

To this day, Dobelle and Perez are either loved or hated. Many residents thought they were both a lot of talk, but the neglected parts of Hartford appreciated that these two unconventional Trinity leaders could hustle and flow in the city streets, even if it was mostly game. The Learning Corridor was real. It still exists. But Trinity never did build a neighborhood school.[28] Lash said that Dobelle created the space to do good things but "spent money like a drunken sailor." Others confirmed that the president spread the cash around for high-profile media events and lavish trips to the Middle East, for example, all of which ultimately led to his departure in 2000.[29]

Dobelle would go on to overspend at multiple schools, as if no one ever checked his references. His beloved partner in crime, Perez, became the mayor and CEO of Hartford and in 2017 ended up pleading guilty to receiving bribes and a criminal attempt to commit larceny in the first degree by extortion. Dobelle and Perez were also easy scapegoats for a snobbish college that never held sure footing in this urban-engagement dance with its impoverished and multiracial host city. Community advocates and interested faculty soldiered on, scrambling to maintain what they considered the best parts of the Dobelle years.

The vision of Dobelle's Trinity Heights held lots of promise for the future of university/community partnerships. It sought to establish a comprehensive project of educational enrichment, surrounded by a range of wraparound services of affordable housing and job training that would allow for development without displacement. However, Trinity's limited resources required a piecemeal approach to fund-raising that created a gap between the stated ambitions and the ultimate outcomes. State resources for magnet schools prioritized integrating suburban families over local students. Large-scale building projects raised the college profile but did little to meet the needs for community programs.

Still, Trinity Heights leaves us with an expanded vision of what a small liberal arts college could imagine for its surrounding neighborhood. Even with administrative missteps, it remains an important legacy for what is possible. But for those who saw Dobelle's project as a betrayal of the liberal arts mission, his overreach became an opportunity to reclaim the elitist tradition of enclosure. Even when Trinity did engage with the neighborhood after Dobelle, administrators raised the idea of "community" to primarily serve the college's interests above anything else.

=====

By 2004, Espinosa returned to Trinity from Washington, D.C. He had spent some time on Capitol Hill, trying to find job training and health care for people getting pushed off welfare after Bill Clinton's punitive "workfare" reforms. Espinosa wanted to take part in change on the local level. He came home and ultimately became the director of Trinfo Café in Hartford. Trinity had received an initial $5 million grant from the Kellogg Foundation in 1998, and part of the money went toward addressing the "digital divide" in poor urban communities.[30] Under Dobelle, the college had already partnered with the Hartford Public Housing Authority to extend the campus dial-up access to residents. The Kellogg money allowed the school to ramp up all urban-engagement efforts.

Trinity renovated a building on Broad Street that, between moments of abandonment, had been everything from a Friendly's restaurant and a Pentecostal church to a construction staging ground for the Learning Corridor. In 1999 Trinfo Café was born. Espinosa joined a team of advocates spreading computer literacy throughout the neighborhoods. Even at this relatively late period in the digital gold rush, underserved communities were still clamoring just to get internet access.[31] "They wanted to take a ride on the information superhighway," he laughed. Trinfo taught free classes on basic instruction, software applications, and web design. At its height, five full-time staff serviced more than eighteen thousand visits per year. Trinfo Café joined the school's innovations in service learning. But at a small school, with an even smaller endowment, messaging from the leadership matters a great deal.

The next significant president, Jimmy Jones, arrived in 2004. The city looked different than it had in the 1990s. Violence had declined in urban areas all across the country. Hartford was no different. But the city was even more impoverished, with wealth concentrated in the surrounding towns. And images of urban divestment didn't help Trinity's brand when potential students conflated poverty with crime. Trinity became the insulated party school for the preppy set, where wealthy students went when they didn't get into Yale.

Jones came in to upgrade the academic reputation of the college. He made gestures toward the still-struggling city, but his actions signaled a pronounced retreat back to Trinity's traditional liberal arts roots. Under Jones, the Trinfo staff shrank to two, and the budget collapsed from half a million a year to $170,000. The additional burden of the recession forced Trinfo to start charging for classes from community organizations that depended on the free or subsidized staff training that had come from this Trinity institution. Espinosa called Jones's presidency "the storm that never ended."

"Jimmy is the Donald Trump to Barack Obama" is how Espinosa described Jones's efforts to roll back Dobelle's vision of a liberal arts college in the city.[32] Many people on campus agreed that Jones was not interested in wasting his political capital on anything his predecessors had done. But at the same time, the new president came with his own ambitions to craft a legacy. The trustees brought him from Kalamazoo College to rebuild the endowment. For Jones, and many of the trustees that backed him, the liberal arts should focus on curricular innovations and other student-centered needs. Urban engagement was social work.

Jones created the Cornerstone Project to centralize budget allocation, which ultimately resulted in divesting from community-based projects. He also came with a noted pedigree for increasing study-abroad opportunities. Jones pushed money into ramping up global sites rather than more-local urban initiatives already in place.[33] He did build the Center for Urban and Global Studies. But many believed that even with this new center, the college placed more emphasis on classroom instruction within the campus or at their global sites beyond Hartford. As Lash said, "Jimmy had no interest in this [urban engagement] at all." To be fair, he did wage battle against Trinity's elitism by trying to diversify an exclusive and very white student life of fraternities and clubs, against much protest. But again, these efforts prioritized the campus experience. In the few instances when Jones did reach out to the city, "community" outreach seemed to be a polite catch-phrase that masked Trinity's self-interest.

The $13 million ice rink and community center was one such flash point. In 2004 Trinity joined SINA and a number of other public and private partners to build the rink. However, the Connecticut First Coalition complained that the college failed to hire enough local and minority-owned businesses for the construction. This collection of area contractors, community leaders, and local business owners rallied to make the project inclusive. "We pay taxes. Why aren't we partaking in these projects? We should not be excluded," said Jocelyn Chance, owner of JFC Construction.[34] Community activist Hyacinth Yennie, who is also the parent of Trinity alums, helped President Jones acquire the property. She assumed that the school would do the right thing: "We figured that's a given that they would want to hire Hartford people to do the job. So it was built, and after that, everything is history." She believed that Trinity's acquiring and demolishing of two abandoned buildings was a good thing but that the planners did not think about other consequences.

People started to smell something fishy when Trinity began talking about the ice rink as a community benefit to a primarily Latinx neighborhood. Lash pointed out that calling the ice rink a community asset helped the school secure a $3 million state bond toward finishing what became the Koeppel Community Sports Center.[35] And Yennie looks back with regret: "They need to take that 'community' part out; that rink is for Trinity." The memorandum of understanding between Trinity and area residents guaranteed fifteen hours per week for community use. But the language is vague.[36] The residents who were actually interested in learning to skate couldn't even get in because the community hours were scheduled in the middle of school days or on the weekends. Espinosa pointed out that the additional revenue generated from weekend youth hockey tournaments and adult leagues became a priority to help cover the massive annual costs of maintaining the facility.

A weak reference to community appeared to serve as cover so Trinity could secure public funds to finish this state-of-the-art rink and help the school attract better recruits for its collegiate hockey teams. "Talk about incongruences: ice hockey and today's Hartford," Espinosa shrugged. On August 1, 2005, several hundred people marched to campus from the SINA headquarters at Washington and Ward streets to protest the way the project had been handled. It didn't change the outcome. The ice rink drama was the last straw for Lash. She quit the college after looking out at a massive "community" complex that seemed most effective at creating an additional brick-and-mortar boundary between Trinity and Hartford.

But the boundary got further extended with the Crescent Street townhouses. In 2010 Trinity announced a $25 million plan to add new housing that connected the campus with the city.[37] The Crescent Street townhouses would be reserved primarily for "upper-class" or more-senior students and would come with higher housing fees to generate additional revenue for the college. It took a long time for officials to see the irony of calling more costly housing "upper class" at a school filled with elite families. The administration eventually started offering additional aid so that lower-income students could have the privilege of living on Crescent Street.

These prefabricated units offered stainless-steel appliances, central air, and lawn care. They put Trinity back in what has been called "the amenities arms race" with other schools.[38] The townhouses became one of the first stops on admissions tours. But in a neighborhood still known for its crime and poverty, the new housing and its design also signaled safety to students and their parents, a space of campus enclosure.

Trinity alum Hunter Drews pointed out that the design of this new housing corridor actually revived the original master plan from the 1870s, of enclosed quadrangles keeping the city at bay. But with the townhouses, leafy green courtyards were replaced with an internal parking lot while the backs of the buildings still face exterior city streets.[39] Their cookie-cutter suburban design also created a wall of delineation between the campus and the city. Campus Safety Office Assistant Jorge Lugo said the previous amalgam of students and residents in the area "proved unsafe," although he couldn't point to any incidents where residents put students in harm's way.[40]

Crescent Street Townhouses, 2019. Photo by VisionMerge Productions.

The campus also seemed to downplay that Trinity built the townhouses on a controversial wave of evictions. Eraque remembers going to parties in the Crescent Street area when it was a mix of student dorms, faculty offices, and Hartford residences. Lugo had called this urban environment unsafe, but Eraque called it a "bridge" between the campus and the community. Safety apparently required the forced eviction of Hartford tenants from Trinity-owned properties to make way for homogeneous rows of townhouses. But Aurice Barlow, a Crescent Street resident of thirteen years, told a different story. She pointed out that area tenants provided a "stabilizing influence." They put up with noisy parties, picked up trash behind students, and maintained area homes, unlike their college neighbors. Paul Mutone, former treasurer and vice president for Finance and Operations at the college, said that he understood the frustration: "We're picking them up and telling them they have to move."[41] But he added that relocations were an opportunity to put residents in a better living situation.

Some residents were happy with the management company that Trinity hired to help them relocate. Others believed that the school didn't provide the required ninety-day notice.[42] Joe Barber is the director of the Office of Community Service and Civic Engagement. One of his employees, who lived on Crescent, said she had to translate eviction notices because Trinity didn't even think to send out information in Spanish. From the outside, the townhouses seemed to indicate that Trinity had literally turned its back on the surrounding community. But many countered that fortifying the campus was justified after a brutal and high-profile assault on a student. The attack helped revive highbrow ideas about the sacred place that monied alums still called "Camp Trin-Trin." But the old elitist desire to patrol boundaries between "us" and "them" got rebranded as a new security model necessary for practical urban engagement.

In the early hours of March 4, 2012, a small group of assailants left Chris Kenny bloody and beaten on the sidewalk of Allen Place, while he was returning from a party on the outskirts of campus. After some student consternation about the school's lack of detail concerning the incident, the dean's office sent out an email which, above all, notified the campus that "the assailants were not Trinity students."[43] However, a *Hartford Courant* article later reported that although Kenny and his friends described a mix of males and females who were "Spanish," a witness reported seeing two "preppy-looking white males" and three college-age females. Patrol officers added that the car full of attackers never passed them on Summit Street, which meant the vehicle would have turned down an enclosed Vernon Street and into a campus parking lot.[44] This evidence further suggested that students played a role in the attack. But to the broader Trinity community it was unthinkable that the danger came from within. Parents immediately complained about "community crime problems." And one student exclaimed, "It could never be one of us."[45]

On May 7 more than seven hundred students stormed the campus green in a "Rally for Chris Kenny." With signs reading "We deserve a safe campus," rally-goers called for increased security measures, from additional lighting and cameras to shuttle bus and escort services. Students of the 1 percent had become an oppressed minority. And a Facebook petition further clarified where students identified the source of their oppression: the surrounding community. The authors called for a "secured campus policy," which included a gate to surround the campus with entrances patrolled by Campus Safety officers. Anyone entering would have to show a school ID

Student rally for Chris Kenny, 2012. Photo by author.

card or what they called a "Trinity Pass" for guests with legitimate reasons to be on the grounds.[46]

These student demands were not pursued. But Hartford police increased patrols, and ten new private security officers were hired specifically to patrol the exterior streets around campus. Former Yale University director of Security Operations James Perrotti, known for keeping New Haven at bay, briefly served as Trinity's director of Campus Safety. Three years later, two area residents were charged with the Kenny assault, and both parents and administrators celebrated a moment of "closure."[47] But the arrests failed to put an end to the controversy.

The student militancy during the Chris Kenny protest brought to the surface long-simmering tensions between "us and them." President Jones had pushed to revive the self-contained liberal arts experience. His turn inward encouraged a predominantly white and elite student body to associate crime and danger with the largely brown and poor blocks just on the outside of campus. Lash, after forty years of community activism, had no time for demonizing residents: "Any time they would accuse the people in the community of causing the problem, we'd just laugh at them because we all knew the rich kids on campus were in fact the problem."

After twenty-five years of living in the neighborhood, Community Service Director Joe Barber said the campus climate had never been worse after the assault. Administrators on campus had shifted drastically toward fearmongering and questionable uses of the word *safety*. "I mean who would be against safety? But what people were really talking about, after Chris Kenny, was race and class. We just need to really admit that and deal with our problems. You're scared of people who don't look like you," he said. Barber added that even if someone from the neighborhood was guilty, Trinity couldn't blame an entire community and become a fortress.

The *Hartford Courant* continued to follow the inconsistencies of the case after Pedro Carillo and Veronica Marquez were charged for the assault of Kenny. Marquez had been interviewed shortly after the assault and denied any involvement, but then in 2013 she admitted lying in the original statement and said that she was in the car while others, including Carillo, assaulted Kenny, according to the warrant. Court documents also mention that Marquez told police she came forward hoping that her cooperation would help a current boyfriend, who had been arrested. It also seems that Carillo was an easy target because he was already in custody on unrelated charges. Rumors wouldn't go away that Carillo was offered a lesser sentence for the other case if he admitted to an involvement in the Kenny assault. In 2016 Marquez pled guilty to making a false statement to police as part of a plea agreement, and Carillo served a two-year sentence for the assault on Kenny.[48]

No matter the truth, both Trinity and the police got their "Hartford local," and all seemed well on campus. But almost everyone I spoke with in the surrounding neighborhood said the Kenny incident never stood up to "'hood logic." Even if the blocks surrounding campus were filled with criminals, it would be stupid to attack a Trinity student because these students' lives matter the most in the area. And any assault could bring undue attention to whatever else might be going on in the area. Perhaps, most importantly, why would drug dealers and boosters mess with Trinity students, who are some of their best customers? All the new security measures had successfully fortified the border, but what about the dangers from within?

For some students the false narrative—that all dangers came from the city—left them even more vulnerable to the actual criminals who lurked on campus. The incongruity between perception and reality was too much. Chiarra Davis grew up in the northern California Bay Area's elite world of prep-school culture. And like most students who can afford the $70,000-plus tuition, she saw Trinity as an extension of the social networks she had experienced her whole life. Davis identified as African American or mixed race, but her light complexion led many to misidentify her as white. The combination of appearance and pedigree allowed Davis to navigate Trinity's very insular social life, often difficult to penetrate for those who did not fit the elite, prep-school, and white profile of an "insider." Like most college-age young people, she found drugs, sex, and alcohol use to be hardly scandalous. Still, Davis was shocked by what she saw at Trinity.

In March 2016, Campus Safety issued three emails in eleven days ringing the alarm about "boys on bikes" roaming the campus slapping female students on the buttocks. Considering the racial demographics of the area, everyone knew that "boys" was code for African American and Latinx youths and "female students" were white girls.[49] Davis noticed that around the same time, *NBC Connecticut* detailed three reports of student-on-student sexual assault within two weeks at Trinity. But sources told NBC that the school failed to notify the campus community.[50]

Considering the alarm around "boys on bikes," Davis wondered why the school remained silent about sexual assaults on campus. She couldn't believe the implications. "The racial disparity in the college reportage is staggering," she realized.[51] Davis began to look around the campus with new eyes. What she saw was a place where the majority elite, white student body engaged in sexual assault and drug use and sales without much criminal prosecution at all. She had just missed the Kenny controversy but saw how negative perceptions of poor, brown Hartford—as the source of crime—allowed white criminal activity to thrive on campus. She called it "criminal amnesty."[52]

In her senior thesis, Davis uncovered a pervasive code of silence around sexual assault and a lucrative drug market that pervaded campus culture. She fully acknowledged that colleges and universities across the nation are faced with combating these same ills. But Trinity's "racial geography" allowed white student criminals to move freely in the gap between what she marked as "assumptions about the purity of the campus and the speculation about the dangers of the city."[53] Under President Jones, Trinity attempted to address both its fiscal deficit and its drop in the rankings. The college tried to bolster its brand by distinguishing the bucolic liberal arts campus life from the reputation of its Hartford surroundings and by also admitting as many full payers as possible. The turn inward became a recipe for disaster.

Pushing an image of campus innocence left many students vulnerable, including women sexually assaulted on campus and Black and brown youths profiled as dangerous threats, whether students or local residents. Alerts about boys on bikes were issued immediately, while students' drug use and instances of sexual assault got buried in one annual report as mandated by the Cleary Act.

Espinosa points out that one long report of incidents versus the immediate announcements of outside threats reinforced the perception that the most-urgent dangers were external to campus life. But as one female student said, "I am more worried about the guys sitting in class next to me than a few kids on bikes." Admissions policies reinforced this student's fears. A senior admissions officer acknowledged that in order to capture more full payers, Trinity lowered its academic standards for acceptance. This officer told Davis that Trinity even welcomed rich students with poor disciplinary records, including those with sexual-assault and rape charges. Another administrator reluctantly confirmed, "Trinity really prized tuition-paying students."[54]

At the same time, brand management kept the campus silent about an expansive drug market of marijuana, cocaine, and prescription pills such as Xanax, Adderall, and Valium. One Campus Safety officer told Davis that, based on his recollections, when drugs were found on students, they didn't even confiscate them. Nor did campus police keep a log on repeat offenders. They certainly didn't call Hartford police. A largely white drug market of sales and consumption hid in plain sight, without criminal prosecution. Because of the racial assumptions about crime and danger, students of color talked about always wearing Trinity apparel to avoid undue harassment. At the same time, white drug dealers allegedly ran a lucrative cocaine trade with no fear of arrest or censure. As the officer commented, "It's like the Wild West out here."[55]

In fall 2014, Joanne Berger-Sweeney became the new sheriff in town. She became the first woman and first African American president of Trinity. Of course, Berger-Sweeney had to tread lightly on a campus steeped in traditions of race and class exclusivity. Trinity didn't admit its first women students until 1969. But she immediately firmed up the school's protocols on sexual-assault claims and expanded recruitment efforts beyond the traditional network of elite prep schools. The new admissions team even made Trinity test-optional for college admissions. But Espinosa said he was especially excited when the new president started talking about the city again: "In the first minute of her speech, Joanne talked about Hartford as an asset; we need to embrace it. We need to figure out how to be better neighbors to the people around us." Espinosa proudly served on a new subcommittee called "The Partnership with Hartford." And perhaps the biggest symbol of a renewed urban commitment that came out of this committee was the new downtown campus.

≡

With Berger-Sweeney, Trinity had turned back toward Hartford. But her approach to community engagement was very different than what had been tried earlier. People still remembered the failed promise of Trinity Heights. And what many saw as Dobelle's overspending made it very difficult to get alums and trustees behind far-ranging projects that included affordable housing or any other initiatives that reached beyond the liberal arts identity of teaching and learning.

At the same time, Trinity had been known as the Wall Street feeder school among the Little Ivies, and although the recession destroyed that pipeline, an entrepreneurial culture still pervaded the school. The new downtown campus at Constitution Plaza would put Trinity in contact with corporate partners at a time when career development became an effective branding strategy for schools struggling over a shrinking pool of wealthy families. Moving downtown worked as a savvy real estate move that used the language of urban outreach to secure a potentially lucrative business investment for the college.

Trinity's push for a downtown campus endured many fits and starts. Reminiscent of the Dobelle years, announcements of a new urban campus made a big splash. But at first, few people were clear about what was actually going on. In 2014 an alum brought an investment deal to the college. He recommended that Trinity buy the building at 200 Constitution Plaza on auction for "the steal" of $2 million. Suddenly, a school strapped for cash got the deal done. Trinity became a downtown landlord in a complex many deemed a horrible remnant of urban-renewal development from the 1960s.

The entire plaza is elevated above street level with little parking and is also difficult to access by public transportation. Moreover, this downtown campus is in the central business district, nowhere near the communities that could most benefit from partnerships with Trinity. The financial team thought the college could use the first floor and lease the rest. When the property failed to attract tenants, Trinity sold the building to a NYC real estate group for a small profit. Then the college turned around and spent more money leasing two spaces on the plaza at 1 and 10 Constitution Plaza.[56] What was really going on?

When I talked to the president, she admitted their strategy wasn't fully developed. But it was important for Trinity to make a big statement. Berger-Sweeney pointed out that for decades, Trinity was the only residential college in the city but that now it had been left behind. When the college finally looked back toward Hartford, other schools had surpassed Trinity as engines of urban revitalization. Saint Joseph and the University of Connecticut both stretched beyond their suburban outposts to stake a claim in the city. The former opened a pharmacy school downtown in 2010. And in 2017, UConn unveiled a full campus where students move from renovated historic buildings to shared space in the Hartford Public Library and the 170-year-old Wadsworth Atheneum Museum of Art.[57] Espinosa described the hasty Constitution Plaza purchase as a higher education "rush to the Arctic," when Trinity followed behind other schools planting their flag in downtown Hartford.

Trinity had made a bold land move. And then, in December 2017, the college opened its innovative Liberal Arts Action Lab as the centerpiece of its return to the city.[58] Sort of a nod to the old Trinity Center for

Neighborhoods, the lab became a partnership with Capital Community College. This community college is the biggest public undergraduate institution in the city and one of the most diverse campuses in New England, with almost 70 percent of the students identifying as African American or Latinx. Teams of students and faculty, from both schools, work at the downtown campus with community partners to study and solve problems facing the city. In a short period the lab has engaged a range of issues, from absentee landlords and neighborhood blight to urban food policy. By offering research data to help community partners create policy, the Liberal Arts Action Lab has been touted as a cutting-edge civic and educational endeavor.

The Action Lab signaled an important moment in university-community relations. But it wasn't the only Trinity project at Constitution Plaza. Being downtown allowed the college to package its forays into unchartered corporate partnerships and new student markets, as if they were initiatives of urban engagement. For example, occupying space in the central business district established stronger relationships between Trinity and the financial sector, helping to secure internships and signal a broader capacity for career development. Beyond community outreach, the downtown footprint strengthened the college's brand in the higher education marketplace.

Espinosa explained that under Jones the one division that went from nonexistent to being "pumped full of steroids" was the career development office. He said the board of trustees had experienced a fundamental shift from old blue-blood types to Wall Street interests. They worked to remake the college in their image: as a preprofessional training ground for industry and finance. At the same time, liberal arts education was under fire, in general, as parents spending hundreds of thousands of dollars wanted to see a greater connection between the curriculum and job training. So career-development projects at the downtown campus became a way to redefine urban engagement and bolster Trinity's brand among other liberal arts schools.

Another member of the downtown campus design committee, who asked to remain anonymous, was even more candid. This person said that when Trinity turned back to the city, administrators never even thought to secure a foothold in the neighborhoods where the community

organizations existed. They pointed out that Eraque and others had proposed renovating a historic theater right on Broad and Park, in the Latinx
neighborhood near the college. But that was never going to happen. Trinity
had always focused on the central business district to secure internships
and also to gain a foothold in the lucrative graduate certificate market used
by adult professionals. The school was losing adult students in Hartford
to programs as far away as Brown University and its executive leadership
curriculum. And as the pool of college-ready students able to pay $70,000
rapidly shrank, the Action Lab partnership with a community college also
tapped into a new pool of low-income students carrying federal aid that
could be shuttled into Trinity programs.

This administrator said money was always the priority, whether through
leasing property, securing a new student pool, or bolstering the school
brand around career development: "The Liberal Arts Action Lab is political cover." Everyone I spoke to agreed that the work of the lab is exciting,
no matter how it got started. But the biggest concern rests with the broader
shift in the meaning of urban engagement under President Berger-Sweeney.
They wonder whether Trinity's revived outreach into Hartford is about equitable community partnerships or primarily a brand-management strategy for financial gain. The latest Trinity program to occupy the downtown
campus seems to suggest the latter.

In fall 2018, Infosys, a multinational corporation providing business
consulting, information technology, and outsourcing services, announced
its exclusive partnership with Trinity. This applied-learning initiative is
housed on the downtown campus and promises to develop new educational
programs that prepare liberal arts students and Infosys employees for the
changing digital workplace. Infosys President Ravi Kumar has been on a
world tour touting the "soft skills" that liberal arts students bring to the
tech workforce. He explains that, along with skill-specific training, we need
workers who can best adapt technology for the humans who will use it,
while the broad training of liberal arts encourages "out-of-the-box thinking
in a digital age."[59] Parents are excited. And traditional faculty are nervous
that this tech turn signals the beginning of the end to their relevance.

Pundits have been announcing the death of the humanities for years. But
the Infosys collaboration at the downtown campus also raises questions

about the costs of positioning urban engagement as simply an investment strategy. This corporate partnership makes good business sense for Trinity. But if colleges and corporations are going to come together in the name of urban engagement, these partnerships have to directly invest in programs that meet the needs of their neighborhoods.

The bottom line is that the value of an urban liberal arts experience can't be determined by its capacity to train workers and produce wealth. And community investment must reach beyond a college's real estate deals.

=

In 2019 the Trump administration had finalized plans for its Opportunity Zones Program in all fifty states. This initiative encourages direct capital investment in low-income communities by letting investors defer their capital gains taxes (the rise in value of a property between its purchase and its increased value after investments). Colleges and university neighborhoods fall within the program's broad rubric of low income because even though campus areas may contain significant wealth, they include unemployed students. Because of Trinity's location in the Frog Hollow census tract, the college was eligible for the opportunity-zones program.[60]

Trinity administrators and alums with deep pockets were eager to take advantage of the opportunity. However, many across the country are concerned that opportunity-zone developments would become a gateway to gentrification. Investors see profits only when the value of a project increases. And there is already talk of "impact washing," with investments in self-storage centers, luxury condos, or other projects that will not benefit low-income communities. As property values rise, rents also increase, which can lead to displacement. Therefore, we have to look at this program as more than an advantageous tax tool and create inducements for projects that leave profits in the community, especially if campus neighborhoods are going to be a key fulcrum in the opportunity-zones program.

There is good reason to remain suspicious of making higher education areas eligible for opportunity-zone benefits, just because of students' unemployment status. But with public pressure, the tax-exempt status of schools could force investments in campus areas to include certain safeguards against residential displacement. City schools could mandate things

like zip-code–based hiring on all construction, affordable-housing requirements, and job training and apprenticeship earmarks. Development deals
could also include partnership requirements with small-business suppliers
and restaurants within a specific distance from the project. Some Trinity
administrators, including President Berger-Sweeney, said that the investments tied to the college must add to the current neighborhood and not
simply extract profits from a tax loophole. The possibilities were exciting.

But Melvyn Colon, the current director of SINA, brought more context to the conversation. Colon pointed out that Trinity's interest in opportunity zones is part of the school's broader financial investment portfolio.
CTNext, the state's strategic venture capital arm, has designated the space
between Trinity, Hartford Hospital, and the Connecticut Children's Medical Center as an "innovation place," which comes with a portion of a $30
million grant.[61] The major aim of this designation is to help generate excitement around a live/work/play space to draw entrepreneurs from the
health-care and tech industries and to provide local job opportunities for
Trinity graduates. But according to the proposal, there also aren't enough
food establishments and other cultural amenities in the area to draw staff
and visitors to what they hope will become a biotech hub.

Colon warned that these new development strategies are all based on
drawing in outside investment to revitalize what is seen as a "dead zone."
But that, he argues, is the wrong approach. Colon is in no way opposed
to attracting business investors from outside Hartford, but he also points
out that residents and small businesses are already working to build community in the targeted area. Why not invest in them also? He explained
there are about fifteen thousand people who live in the community and ten
thousand people who come to work every day. But institutions like Trinity
don't encourage their employees to live in the area or patronize the many
restaurants that already exist. Colon noted that, for example, Trinity employees still don't hear about the home-ownership incentive program: "I
don't believe that there are formal messages being sent down, but new employees are being informally told to look for housing outside of Hartford, in
areas that are perceived as 'safer.'"

His impression of the opportunity-zones push is that the college has
some very wealthy trustees who can invest in building an economic market

to draw interest from the outside, while almost none of Trinity's faculty or staff live in the city, let alone the neighborhood: "If you're gonna try to develop the neighborhood, you should truly start at home and getting your own people thinking about the neighborhood." But presently, Trinity's ambitions in the "opportunity zone" have largely stalled while real estate speculators from New York and New Jersey slowly make their presence felt in the area. We are left to wonder if future development projects will look at the existing neighborhood as a roadblock to real estate revenues or a community worthy of investment.

Still, Colon gave me a lot to think about, especially when considering the long dance between Trinity and the city it calls home. The traditional vision of a liberal arts college doesn't imagine a campus fully immersed within an urban experience. But for various reasons of enlightened self-interest, Dobelle tasked Trinity College with revitalizing a city in rapid decline. After he appeared to overreach, it seemed that invoking the liberal arts signaled a quick retreat to strategies of enclosure, isolation, and security. And the turn inward found the college pointing fingers at the city beyond while remaining silent about the systemic problems within.

The school is now peeking out again from behind the gates. And Hartford residents continue to take pride in the fact that such an esteemed educational institution sits in their city. Espinosa suggests that under Berger-Sweeney Trinity may be undergoing its best relations with the city because at least there are no glossy brochures so far out in front of what is actually possible. Now the college's urban ambitions fall more in line with its fiscal capacity. Espinosa points to Trinity's Center for Hartford Engagement and Research (CHER) as a positive example of the new urban possibilities. But an anonymous faculty member who worked heavily on urban outreach projects pointed to CHER as part of the problem.

This person said that the current urban engagement initiatives through CHER exhibit a "limited capacity for understanding local Hartford." The college hired two staff members with elite pedigrees but with no familiarity or knowledge of Hartford. There was an almost complete disconnect between the community initiatives targeting communities of color and the capacity to prepare students to serve on those projects. "What does it mean to send privileged college students into low-income Black and brown communities with little to no community-organizing–like training?" this faculty member wondered. It's been said that in the desire to establish a higher profile and attract funders, Trinity's urban engagement initiatives continue to ignore the wealth of local knowledge and expertise that could make their work truly innovative. But CHER underwent a leadership transition in 2019, and perhaps this change will bring a new outlook.

It's still not clear what Trinity means by urban engagement as it fights to keep a liberal arts college, stuck in a poor city, relevant to wealthy students and their families. Both Trinity and Hartford exist in the shadows of more-prominent cities and schools. Trinity is not Yale, and Hartford will never be New York. So the school and the city look across the street at each other with ambivalence, afraid to admit a bond because of their shared deficits. But the smaller scale of both Trinity and Hartford makes new models for urban development very possible. The city and school could turn to each other. No one else is coming to save them.

CHAPTER THREE

THE SCHOOLS THAT
ATE NEW YORK

In February 2005, New York City Mayor Michael Bloomberg invited New York University President John Sexton to a retreat on Staten Island. The mayor wanted Sexton to help his city hall staff envision an economic blueprint that reached beyond the city's historically dominant finance, insurance, and real estate industries—or what many urbanists shorthanded as FIRE. Sexton talked to commissioners about the possibilities of turning New York City into an "idea capital."[1]

Since his earliest presidential speeches, Sexton had traveled the world selling the promise of placing universities, NYU in particular, at the center of an international economy networked through global cities. Sexton was a powerful man. He had been on Law Review at Harvard and was the chairman of the board at the Federal Reserve Bank of New York. But Sexton loved to emphasize his high school days among Irish and Italian working-class kids at Brooklyn Prep. As NYU president, he used this city-kid hustle

NEW YORK CITY

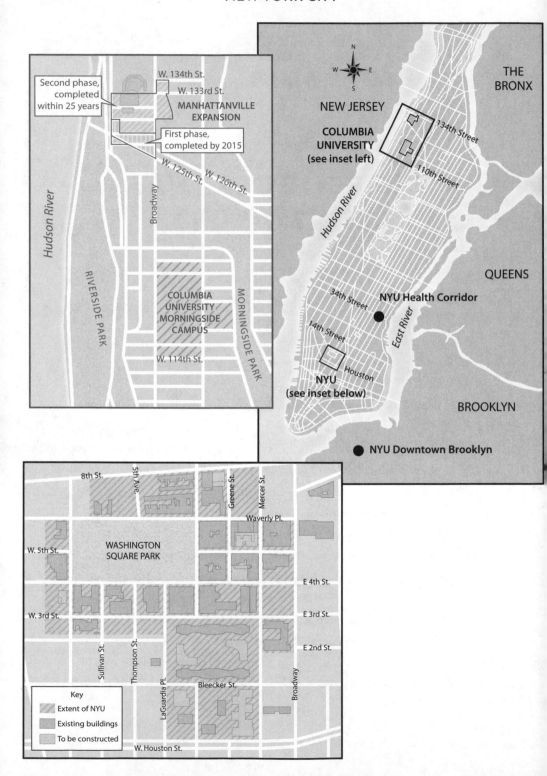

Second phase, completed within 25 years

First phase, completed by 2015

W. 134th St.

W. 133rd St.

MANHATTANVILLE EXPANSION

W. 125th St.

W. 126th St.

Hudson River

Broadway

RIVERSIDE PARK

COLUMBIA UNIVERSITY MORNINGSIDE CAMPUS

MORNINGSIDE PARK

W. 114th St.

N
W E
S

THE BRONX

NEW JERSEY

COLUMBIA UNIVERSITY (see inset left)

134th Street

110th Street

Hudson River

QUEENS

34th Street

NYU Health Corridor

East River

14th Street

Houston

NYU (see inset below)

BROOKLYN

● NYU Downtown Brooklyn

8th St.

5th Ave.

Greene St.

Mercer St.

Waverly Pl.

W. 5th St.

WASHINGTON SQUARE PARK

E 4th St.

E 3rd St.

W. 3rd St.

Sullivan St.

Thompson St.

E 2nd St.

Broadway

LaGuardia Pl.

Bleecker St.

W. Houston St.

Key

Extent of NYU

Existing buildings

To be constructed

narrative to sidestep many charges of crass materialism when the university purchased prestige by poaching top scholars from elsewhere and dumping millions into campus expansion.

Instead, NYU earned the compelling brand of city builder, an educational profile different from its more-reclusive rivals in the Ivy League. Sexton was known for discussing what he called urban universities' "locational endowment."[2] He described city schools as carrying a seemingly inherent drive to reach beyond campus walls and connect with their urban locales. It was an explicit rebuke to the pastoral ideal of retreat held by the older Ivies and to the more ambivalent relationship that smaller schools like Trinity had with cities.

After the Staten Island summit that winter day, Sexton started rolling out the slick slogan that would carry him forward as not just an engaging university president but also a titan of Gotham. In what became his landmark 2007 speech, Sexton announced the decline of the city's once-dominant FIRE economy and the parallel rise of the intellectual, cultural, and education industries, or what he called the ICE sector.

Through the catchy "FIRE + ICE" paradigm he explained how the computer technology of fiber-optic cables freed the finance industry from New York City. By contrast, the economic growth generated within the ICE sector required "geographical proximity" to a specific locale.[3] The lifestyle of undergraduate students and the intellectual property produced by medical researchers were enhanced by New York's specific cultural assets: from the resources in its museums, libraries, and hospitals to the stimulation of its nightlife and iconic skyline. In short, because urban universities depended on their cities, these schools made the ideal anchor institutions to help bolster cities within the new economy. Sexton offered the succinct quip: "ICE can keep FIRE from being extinguished."[4]

Sexton's "FIRE + ICE" catchphrase soon became the advertising copy to drive his NYU 2031 plan calling for a massive expansion of the campus. But students, faculty, and residents balked at the project's looming threat to take over Greenwich Village. Some derided NYU as "a real estate company which also issues degrees." Still, the NYU president wasn't moved. In a New York magazine article aptly titled "The School That Ate New York," Sexton insisted, "What's good for NYU is good for the city."[5]

By 2013, NYU stood as just one of the many colleges and universities at the center of a construction surge in the city. Residents watched as building cranes pierced what seemed like every inch of New York City's skyline. Schools soared past real estate moguls and Wall Street speculators to spark a building frenzy projected to add millions of square feet in classrooms, residence halls, and laboratory spaces over the next two decades. Richard T. Anderson, president of the New York Building Congress, made it plain that "education is a big business in New York."[6] The now retired Sexton appeared prophetic in his arrogant zeal for the promise of an ICE economy. But the intimate relationship between the university president and the mayor on that day back on Staten Island spoke to something far more pernicious.

The New York story highlights the death of public authority that has come with the rise of universities, in particular NYU and Columbia, as dominant power brokers in the city. When people questioned the public benefit of both the NYU 2031 plan and Columbia's Manhattanville campus, local residents and politicians said that the universities bought off government agencies, disbanded advisory councils, sidestepped community boards, and breached long-standing policy agreements to push through two of the most controversial building projects in Gotham. And even when the universities were not directly making decisions, other private entities scrambled to reshape the neighborhood to provide campus amenities. For example, developers chased the greater profits of upscale student units over the local needs for affordable housing. In these campus communities, university interests have become the public interest.

Ultimately, New York City schools are wielding their growing political influence to become quasi-autonomous republics in the middle of the biggest "college town" in the country.[7] But we can still hear the frustrations of longtime residents and their legitimate fears when higher education privatizes local power. If a university has become the governing force in West Harlem or Greenwich Village, where do New Yorkers level their complaints against the university? The meaning of urban citizenship is grossly diminished when people are struggling on the fringes of what is becoming a campus city.

=

Chants of "Hell, no, we won't go" filled the Harlem air during a rally on the morning of July 10, 2006. About a hundred protestors descended on Marcus Garvey Park, at 5th Avenue and 125th in the heart of Harlem's commercial district. This group of mostly tenants yelled, "They say rent hike, we say rent strike!" amid a sea of colorful placards in English and Spanish with slogans like "Stop Hurricane Columbia." The Harlem Tenants Council (HTC) had come together with another group, the Coalition to Preserve Community, and rallied under the umbrella title *Nos Quedamos* (We Are Staying). Residents, local politicians, and concerned students mobilized in the fight against what they saw as illegal evictions and landlord harassment tactics that many tied to the expansion of Columbia University into West Harlem. And they grew increasingly worried as Columbia seemed to steamroll the political checks and balances of the city's community board system and even push the legal limits on eminent domain. People believed they had to mobilize.[8]

As Nellie Bailey of the HTC told the crowd, "If we don't organize, Harlem will cease to exist. It will become just a bus stop on tour buses from downtown. Columbia now wants to expand its campus into Manhattanville. And they don't want to work with the community. They have ignored all the proposals that were made by the Community Board and others. What they can't buy they are going to take using eminent domain. And we have to stop them!"[9] The rally of one hundred grew into a mobilized mass of more than six hundred people who headed to the Riverside Park Community Houses on Broadway and 135th Street. Changes to this housing complex encapsulated broader attacks on affordable housing taking place throughout the neighborhood.

In 2005 property owner Jerome Belson had opted out of the state's Mitchell-Lama Housing Program, which provided low-interest mortgages and tax exemptions to developers who maintained rent-stabilized units.[10] Protestors along the march and residents in the building believed that when Columbia circulated plans to build a seventeen-acre campus in Manhattanville, Belson was just one of many property holders who would see dollar signs in the housing complex sitting on the northern edge of the expansion project.

Riverside Park tenants were already seeing vacant units converted to market rates while their maintenance needs went unmet. *Daily News* columnist Juan Gonzalez published a series of reports detailing a "growing spate of strong-arm tactics by landlords to evict low-income tenants," from filing eviction proceedings built on flimsy claims to ratcheting up rents based on fictitious improvements. Companies say all of their actions were legal. But once Columbia encroached, residents feared, it would only get worse. The apartments could be rented to wealthier student and faculty tenants. All Belson had to do was get current residents out of the units.[11]

Columbia first announced its almost $7 billion proposal for a new West Harlem campus in 2003. And President Lee Bollinger immediately acknowledged the university's fraught history with the impoverished neighborhood. "I have done everything I can to put the ghost of the gym behind us," he said. "Columbia is a different neighbor now."[12] The specter of 1968, when residents and students like Karla Spurlock-Evans (see chapter 1) stopped Columbia's efforts to place a gymnasium in Morningside Park, was still on Bollinger's mind. But after spending the last fifty years intentionally tucked behind the gates of its Morningside Heights main campus—an area that locals started calling "White Harlem"—now Columbia claimed to be cramped and needing to spread its wings.

In the early proposal stages, administrators trotted out a graph showing that Columbia was at a disadvantage with just more than three hundred "square feet of building space per student," while its Ivy League peers, such as Yale and Princeton, provided six hundred or more square feet.[13] The square-foot-per-student metric seemed arbitrary, especially for a school in the middle of a dense city. But the pithy graphic also helped signal to city officials and financial leaders a sense of urgency around campus expansion as an act of both community building and competitive necessity.

The area targeted for campus expansion, from 125th Street to 133rd Street and west of Broadway to the Hudson River, had certainly seen better days: it was a largely industrial patchwork of warehouses, tenements, and car-repair shops. Some city booster had the audacity to dub Columbia's proposed expansion the "West Harlem Renaissance," a cheeky pro-developer reference to the neighborhood's celebrated Black cultural flourishing of the 1920s.[14]

The initial phase of the campus project promised to bring science re-search labs and new facilities for Columbia's business and art schools to attract or keep top scholars. The celebrated architect Renzo Piano said the expansion would sharply contrast the gated, stone layout of the main cam-pus; it would be replaced with the transparency of glass and steel buildings surrounding a large open area. The campus design of retail and open space was described as a gift of civil society to Harlem. Ground-level retail and art spaces would invite pedestrians to move from an enlivened 125th Street to a renovated Hudson River waterfront. "It's a piazza," he explained with an Italian lilt. "The people will come, there will be discourse."[15]

Columbia matched the design plan of transparency with a forty-person community advisory council. University administrators knew their cam-pus plan had to win the approval of local governing bodies. The advisory council offered an image of political consensus between the university and local residents, hoping that this would undercut the resilient sting of old wounds.[16] Most residents seemed optimistic about what this redevelop-ment could bring but remained cautious. Even the university's revival of the area's more historic name, Manhattanville, to describe an area that most

Columbia University's West Harlem (Manhattanville) construction site, 125th and Broad-way, 2008. Photo by Daniella Zalcman.

called West Harlem put everyone on high alert about long-standing fears of displacement.

Residents were clear: they wanted any expansion to adequately benefit the community through construction jobs, skill training, and opportunities for small businesses and local suppliers. The bottom line is that Harlem wanted to work as a partner in a development project that would dramatically transform the neighborhood. Altagracia Hiraldo, an advisory council member and executive director of the Dominican Sunday Community Service, confirmed in 2004 that "we have to be included in the process."[17] Decision making about the future of Harlem had to include its residents.

As early as 1991, Community Board 9 (CB 9) started developing a comprehensive redevelopment plan (197-a) to capitalize on the area's assets as a transportation hub and potential food corridor.[18] CB 9's plan was most notable because it invited Columbia to the neighborhood but insisted that the university build within the existing mixed-use landscape of manufacturing, affordable housing in historic buildings, and current property owners. The plan promoted "a diversity of incomes and ethnicity without displacement of existing residents."[19] And the community board welcomed the university as a partner in developing what some envisioned as a new Harlem for everyone. But Columbia had other plans.

CB 9 unanimously approved the 197-a plan in October 2005. But soon after, Columbia revealed its own 197-c amendment, calling for a complete rezoning of the entire seventeen acres. The university also wanted to reserve the right to use eminent domain if necessary. President Bollinger was emphatic that Columbia needed ownership of the entire parcel because it wanted a fully connected campus. He added, "I have said we would never ask for eminent domain against private residents. But if needed to fulfill our public service responsibility and if the state were willing [to] use eminent domain . . . it would be irresponsible to take it off the table." In reality, Bollinger was already preparing. By 2005, the university had already acquired twenty-eight of the sixty-seven properties in the targeted campus zone.[20]

It's important to note that Bollinger raised the issue of "public service" so that Columbia could reserve the right to deploy eminent domain and displace private residents. When cities and universities used eminent domain in the 1960s, a government agency could force the paid seizure of privately owned land only for public use, such as roads and public utilities. But in 2004, lawmakers changed eminent domain so that it could even more easily advance the development goals of private institutions.

The legal case *Kelo v. City of New London* ruled that private property could now also be seized for a private entity if the project produces public benefits, including jobs; increases tax revenues; or revitalizes a depressed area.[21] Private developments that may or may not directly help or be accessible to local residents were now deemed a public service. The *Kelo* decision introduced the expansive idea of public benefits beyond the stricter requirement of public use, which gave a private entity like Columbia significant leverage in rejecting a shared vision of the seventeen-acre campus zone.

Eminent domain remained a hot-button topic in March 2006, when Bollinger appeared on *The Brian Lehrer Show*, a popular program on public radio station WNYC. By this time, the president was still working to refine his messaging around the "public-benefits" justification for eminent domain. Bollinger first described Columbia as a "nonprofit, public institution" and described private property owners who resisted selling to the university as "standing in the way of developing neuroscience work which may actually find a cure to Alzheimer's." Lehrer quickly jumped on the president's error to point out that Columbia is in fact a *private* institution.[22] After this fumble, Bollinger grew nimbler to explain that Columbia's work was not driven by profit seeking and that its research was funded by public entities such as the federal government. In later press statements, the university reiterated that eminent domain would be used only as a last resort while emphasizing how its research served the public good and would also generate seven thousand jobs.

Abigail Daniel had lived in West Harlem her whole life. She grew up on the fringes of the expansion area, where Bollinger's promised public-good benefits rang hollow in the face of what residents saw as their inevitable removal: "I was in high school when 197-c was at the center of many heated debates in my building. We didn't care about what the plan meant. We knew that sooner or later we'd be kicked out, and nobody wanted that."[23] With good reason, residents remained suspicious as the university circumvented their demands.

Columbia continued to officially push a narrative of political transparency and mutual benefit. But Bollinger also diminished the standards of local accountability by talking about the university's contributions on a global scale: "We are trying to do things that help the world more broadly. The community is not everything."[24] And Columbia's actions, both public and private, would offer greater clarity about how the university had seemed to manipulate the democratic process to serve its interests over those of the neighborhood. In 2004 Bollinger disbanded Columbia's advisory board after members backed CB 9's 197-a plan, which didn't give the university total control over the development area.[25]

In 2005 the *Spectator*, Columbia's student newspaper, broke news about a secret correspondence between the university and the state of New York. Columbia had offered to pay the Empire State Development Corporation (ESDC) $300,000 in legal fees to "consider the condemnation of portions of the property not under Columbia control" and use eminent domain to transfer the deeds to the university. When the news broke, Columbia officials downplayed the significance of the agreement and called the letter a necessary part of any development project the size of the Manhattanville campus. The school also explained that signing a reimbursement letter was required to preserve the possible use of eminent domain, an option Columbia said it was never prepared to take off the table. The ESDC added that these private discussions were merely preliminary and that any property considered for condemnation would have to undergo an independent "blight study." Jordi Reyes-Montblanc was chairman of CB 9 at the time and expressed immediate outrage: "I am disappointed at Columbia, and I'm highly pissed off at ESDC. . . . Now we cannot trust either one."[26]

Columbia University wasn't merely raising the threat of eminent domain; the school looked like it was buying off a government body to ensure dominion over the targeted development area. The university couldn't deploy the weapon of eminent domain unless its desired section of West Harlem was deemed "blighted" by a state agency.[27] The ESDC's "neighborhood conditions" study would make that determination. In September 2006 the planning and engineering consulting firm Allee King Rosen & Fleming (AKRF) received the contract from the ESDC to conduct a blight study. Private correspondence uncovered by student journalists a year earlier proved that the university offered to underwrite all of the ESDC's costs related to the project. Columbia essentially funded the blight study.

Not surprisingly, AKRF chronicled a Manhattanville landscape drenched in darkness and decay. The study found an area "mainly characterized by aging, poorly maintained, and functionally obsolete industrial buildings, with little indication of recent reinvestment to reverse their generally deteriorated conditions."[28] But perhaps unintentionally, AKRF also revealed that by the time of the study's 2007 publication, all but two of the properties surveyed were under the control of the university. As a CB 9 member pointed out, "Columbia has basically blighted the neighborhood by buying it up and by keeping most of what they bought vacant."[29] Still, residents went beyond highlighting Columbia's role in accelerating neighborhood decline to question the highly subjective word *blight* altogether.

Residents once called the targeted area "Murderville" and still point to the gangs as major enforcers in the nearby Grant and Manhattanville housing projects.[30] But many still did not see the largely industrial landscape as "functionally obsolete." Kenny Nuñez swelled up with pride when walking past auto shops in Manhattanville: "I was good friends with one of the auto-shop owners; he was a Dominican, and tires were all that he knew. I spent a lot of time in his shop when I first came to New York City. While the area wasn't the greatest, and his shop wasn't the cleanest, it was a representation of his hard work. It inspired me."

Nuñez got offended when the owner told him that the blight study described the area as unsafe and having no space for pedestrians. He scoffed. "Go to Manhattanville and walk down Broadway. . . . I couldn't believe they could lie like that."[31] The study's blanket dismissal of all residential and commercial activity failed to see any utility in the existing neighborhood but almost blindly endorsed the blank slate ambitions of a master planned project, such as a fully contained campus. AKRF offered no comment. But the Empire State Development Corporation defended the vague definition of blight as appropriate. It said that it was unnecessary to identify a precise measure of deterioration; one simply had to exercise "common sense."[32] Still, the degree to which AKRF's findings aligned with Columbia's desires seemed more than coincidental.

Thomas Lopez-Pierre is a local real estate broker; like many, he believed that Columbia's insistence on calling the area blighted showed that the university was concerned only with the land and never cared about West Harlem: "You see how they drafted those reports and said that Manhattanville needed to be fixed? That's not true. Manhattanville was a vibrant community. It wasn't until they came in that the community started to suffer."[33] Other local business owners agreed and got together as part of the West Harlem Business Group in 2007 to file a petition with the New York State Supreme Court, charging the ESDC with colluding with Columbia by hiring AKRF.

Released documents reveal that AKRF had worked for Columbia since 2004, helping to survey and shape the proposed campus site before conducting the neighborhood conditions study for Empire State. It seemed that Columbia University paid for the study and made sure that one of its own subcontractors conducted the study. Did the university work behind the scenes to guarantee a favorable government ruling? The majority decision of the court of appeals saw it that way. Justice James Catterson, writing for the majority, concluded that "AKRF has consistently acted as an advocate for Columbia in seeking ESDC's adoption of Columbia's proposal."[34] Unfazed by the court's ruling, the ESDC still approved the Columbia plan by pointing to a secondary study from Earthtech Inc. This was a firm with no Columbia connections, but it conducted a neighborhood conditions study that, according to critics, not only confirmed AKRF's findings but replicated the same vague methodology for measuring blight.[35] The university, a so-called agent of the public good, didn't even seem to flinch at the optics of political corruption. Residents were outraged.

In August 2007, CB 9 held a raucous public hearing of about three hundred residents to discuss Columbia's rezoning application for the targeted campus-expansion area. The crowd booed former mayor David Dinkins, Bollinger, and other advocates of the Columbia plan. Still, transcripts of the hearing reveal that in testimony after testimony, residents and business owners generally welcomed the campus project; they just flat-out rejected any use of eminent domain. One resident, a Ms. Doty, explained that "if Columbia had taken eminent domain off the table, we would have had a lot more cooperation and better feelings toward this project. We want to include more people in our community and grow as a whole. I think this is a disgrace, what this university is doing." According to the *Columbia Spectator*, approximately twenty-two people voted in favor of the plan and seventy-three against. However, community boards in New York City are simply advisory.[36]

Despite what seemed like clear findings of university collusion and unrelenting community anger, both the New York Department of Planning and the New York City Council approved Columbia's proposal in December 2007. Mayor Bloomberg and Governor David Paterson added their stamp of approval in a joint press release touting the project's ability to "solidify New York City as a world-renowned center for higher education and scientific research and enhance New York's ability to attract skilled talent."[37] Various political forces had decided that Columbia controlled West Harlem, and they worked with the university to obliterate any attempts at shared governance. But the two remaining property owners took their fight to the courts.

In 2009 Tuck-It-Away Self-Storage owner Nick Sprayregen and Shell Gas Station proprietors Gurnam Singh and Parminder Kaur were the last two private landowners in the expansion area. These business owners filed separate lawsuits in the appellate division of the New York State Supreme Court. Singh and Kaur looked at the gas stations as their small slice of the "American Dream."[38] They had run their stations when violence flooded the West Harlem streets, and now the university wanted to push them out just as the neighborhood took a modest upturn. Singh and Kaur hoped to benefit as well and found the university's offers insulting. Both lawsuits challenged the blight designation and subsequent approval of eminent domain.

Tuck-It-Away had been the largest piece of land owned by anyone in the expansion site besides Columbia. Sprayregen became a multimillionaire running his garish line of orange storage warehouses. But in the face of Columbia, he had become the "little guy" raging against the powerful while also upholding the libertarian values of sacred property rights. Most certainly, if Sprayregen could overturn eminent domain, the value of his properties standing in the path of campus expansion would skyrocket. But he said the real fight was against a private university taking private property for its own financial gain. Always the savvy businessman, Sprayregen suggested that Columbia could work with him to help develop parts of the campus: "There's no reason why they have to own this in order to do this research."[39] Even though his interests were not purely altruistic, West Harlem had found an ally with deep pockets.

In a surprise to many, the appellate court ruled in favor of the business owners. The court focused on what it considered the "tangled relationships" between Columbia, the ESDC, and their shared consultant AKRF. The court ultimately ruled that the state could not use eminent domain on behalf of Columbia's private interests. Justice James M. Catterson wrote a blistering opinion that excoriated the ESDC, dismissing its use of the blight designation as "mere sophistry."[40] However, six months later the New York State Court of Appeals upheld the ESDC's state authority to determine blight. This court deemed the use of eminent domain legal because, according to the *Kelo* case, a private university can serve a "civic purpose."[41] Sprayregen's lawyer pointed out the crass irony that Columbia in fact caused the blight but could use such neglect to its own benefit.

The US Supreme Court dealt property owners a final death blow in December 2010, when it refused to hear an appeal. Writing for the *Atlantic*, Megan McArdle couldn't believe the outcome: "One's gut and one's social conscience positively riot" at the thought of turning a "large swath of Manhattan into a quasi-compound for some of the wealthiest and most privileged people in the city."[42] The needs and interests of local residents had gotten lost in the priority of campus expansion.

The tangled web of Columbia's land deals gave the impression that a private university had basically bought the rights to control the political sovereignty of the neighborhood. But part of the school's leverage for eminent domain derived from claims of serving the public good, particularly economic development in an underserved community. President Bollinger began celebrating the thousands of jobs that came with the development. He also boasted that a new campus would help the city remain a global center of lifesaving academic research. But Bollinger also realized that such grandiose claims meant very little in West Harlem. Columbia had to pay up.

University officials began to highlight the community benefits agreement (CBA) they officially signed with the West Harlem Local Development

Corporation (WHLDC) in 2009. This legally binding agreement stipu-
lated that in exchange for the right to build the campus, Columbia would
provide more than $150 million in benefits for the community, which in-
cluded funding for a university-supported public school, access to university facilities, affordable-housing assistance, related legal services, and $76
million earmarked for future community programming. The Teacher's
College Community School opened in September 2011. An attendee at the
school opening celebrated it as "an excellent example of the rare moment
when two visions intersect to become a reality to benefit a community."[43]
But as the years moved ahead, the contracted benefits didn't seem to reach
much of the community outside of the school. The devil hid in the details.

When benefits stalled, local residents started wondering to what degree
the WHLDC actually represented the community. Despite claims of community control, ultimately seven of the fifteen WHLDC board members
were appointed by politicians and Columbia allies, including US Representative Charles Rangel and Manhattan Borough President Scott Stringer.
Then in December, Jeff Mays of *DNAInfo* reported that WHLDC spent
more than $300,000 on consultants with ties to ex-mayor David Dinkins
while failing to develop a website, hold a public meeting, or disclose its
spending details. Attorney General Eric Schneiderman conducted an investigation and found that WHLDC was not guilty of theft, fraud, or mis-
appropriation of funds. But he also said the organization was not living up
to its purpose, largely because the board of directors failed to "develop clear
policies and procedures for grant making activities." Under a new settlement agreement with the attorney general's office, WHLDC was required
to abide by a clear conflict-of-interest policy, increase its public disclosure
about grants awarded, and more carefully monitor grant recipients.[44]

Local residents Nuñez and Daniel are both originally from the Dominican Republic and confirm that not only was there little outreach about community benefits, but efforts certainly didn't address the large population of
nonnative English speakers in the community. Nuñez remembers his cousin
talking, in Spanish, about the agreement: "What the hell was a community
benefits agreement? I didn't understand and he knew less than me! He's an
American, born and raised in Harlem . . . that speaks English. How is it
that they expected me, someone who doesn't know a drop of English to

understand what this agreement meant? To this day, I don't know what it all means."[45] Community members had been cut out of the very networks that set the terms of community benefits.

Under heavy fire, Columbia quickly pivoted to focus on its success in minority, women, and local hiring for the new campus-expansion project. The CBA required that 25 percent of all contracts and 35 percent of non-construction contracts go to minorities, women, and locally owned firms. It also required that large contracts be broken into pieces so smaller companies could compete. In a 2013 report, Columbia proudly announced it not only met but far exceeded the required hiring goals. But when the Harlem group of Black architects, Arch527, reached out for work, a university official told the group that the CBA did not have requirements for professional services, only construction.[46] This omission suggests that Columbia cared much less about sustaining professional services in the community, a sector where the university might find direct competition for the same services that it peddles in the knowledge marketplace.

But even in terms of manual labor, *DNAInfo* reporter Mays investigated further and found that although one local firm, Absolute Plumbing and Heating, was listed in the Columbia report, an employee told him that it wasn't working on the project. Another firm on the list, Pearlgreen, had actually relocated to New Rochelle, outside the local boundaries. In fact, Pearlgreen had been pushed out of Manhattanville because of the campus expansion. The ESDC promised to review Columbia's documentation.[47] Considering the ESDC's role in the blight controversy, no one held their breath.

Feelings are still raw when talking to Harlemites about Columbia not only pushing its campus plan through the political process but also limiting the effectiveness of its own CBA. University press reports continue to outline the benefits of the hiring practices, medical aid, shuttle buses, and other services. But West Harlem resident Abigail Daniel felt pushed aside.

She was a City University of New York student, and one day her local branch library closed early. But she really needed to finish some research. Daniel assumed that Columbia's library was open to all residents. Why wouldn't it be? After all, it was a university that talked big about public service, and the library was in her neighborhood. Before heading over, she recalled, "Something told me to call them and confirm that I could use their facilities, only to find out that it was not open to local residents. . . . But I live here. How could they tell me I couldn't? At that moment I knew Columbia did not care about me, or my neighbors."[48] There seemed to be a huge disconnect between the promised benefit of Columbia's campus expansion and its actual contribution to the local community.

≡

On October 25, 2016, Columbia held a dedication ceremony with great fanfare for the groundbreaking of its new Manhattanville campus. In his remarks, President Bollinger went as far to proclaim the project "the best thing that could happen to upper Manhattan."[49] He specifically pointed out the number of public-facing services that now occupy the development, including a wellness center to raise health awareness and train community health workers, a science-based education lab, and the Wallach Art Gallery. The street-level feel of accessibility also includes publicly accessible Wi-Fi in the Steep Rock Bouldering Gym and the Harlem-based coffee shop and eatery Dear Mama. Ultimately, the campus buildings will sit along a pedestrian path running north from 125th Street to meet a one-acre public square.

But Columbia's new values of integration and transparency toward the community seem largely confined to the architecture. The ground-floor amenities are all open to the public and are wrapped in a glassy skin, what principal architect Piano dubbed the "urban layer," meant to blur the boundaries between public and university spaces.[50] The buildings keep exposed their functional skeletons of air ducts and steel struts to suggest an integration of the campus into the neighborhood's rapidly fading industrial landscape. Piano went as far as to call the buildings "new kinds of machines for doing scientific research" set within a "factory of ideas."[51]

Still, this sprawling tribute to innovation also blocks Harlem off from a revitalizing 12th Avenue and the riverfront in ways that resurrect the ghosts of 1968 and the failed attempt to partition Morningside Park for university desires. Since campus construction, restaurants along 12th Avenue, including the landmark Floridita, have suffered a 30 percent loss in revenue. And although Columbia has claimed that the project will enliven 125th Street

Jerome Greene Science Center, 125th and Broadway, 2018. Photo by author.

leading to the waterfront, this once-public corridor is now largely owned by the university, and the new buildings are ensconced in what one journalist called a "hostile architecture" of security cameras, narrow benches, skateboard deterrents, and security patrols. Each gesture toward public accessibility further cemented Columbia's control over the neighborhood. The irony simmered beneath almost every celebration of the new campus.[52]

Architectural critic James Russell noted that the Manhattanville project intentionally eliminated the gates surrounding the main campus but that architectural openness was not enough: "The aura of institutional ownership and control is unmistakable."[53] On one of his many visits to the new Forum building's public lounge, Russell pointed out the multiple security officers positioned to guard the main elevator. Accessibility was just as manicured as the green landscaping that will dress the public square, a space that won't be visible from the edge of campus.

Writer Justin Davidson added that the transparent wall wrapped around Dear Mama was surely meant to evoke an urban living room, but instead of grand and casual, it enforced the chilly and somber feel of a museum: "Everyone is allowed in at the management's discretion, as long as they follow the rules."[54] The physical stature of the campus helped muffle a decade of community resistance. For those not in the know, the new buildings seem like simply one act in Columbia's inevitable showcase of neighborhood revitalization. As the community became a campus, residents were told that the privatization of the neighborhood was to their benefit.

Flores Forbes is a child of Black Power activism and is a long-standing Harlem advocate. He fits the profile of someone who would be directly at odds with the way Columbia handled campus expansion. Yet he was not. "I didn't see a controversy," Forbes told me. He arrived at Columbia in 2007 to work as an associate vice president in the university's Office of Government and Community Affairs, right at the high point of the battles waged over the future of West Harlem. Flores had little patience for what he called the "myth of gentrification." He pointed out that Columbia built on vacant land and the university did in fact help relocate anyone who lived within the footprint of the campus. In Forbes's mind, people were relocated to probably a better location, not displaced. "That's some boogey-man stuff," he chided.

Some might conclude that he was just a company man, voicing the official Columbia press release. But this university administrator wasn't the typical office jockey. And Forbes's perspective on the campus expansion may have much more to do with his storied biography than any fear of workplace retribution. He had been a leader in the Black Panther Party and was incarcerated because of a failed plan to kill a witness scheduled to testify against Panther founder Huey P. Newton. Forbes said that after coming out of prison he gravitated to urban planning as a logical extension of the organizing he did with the Panthers.[55] The focus on economics, politics, and land use was another avenue toward helping Black people. Forbes eventually worked as a planner under former Manhattan Borough president C. Virginia Fields before serving as chief strategic officer at the Abyssinian Development Corporation.

When Columbia came calling, he looked at the position as an opportunity "to do something significant in Harlem." Forbes wanted to use Columbia's backing to give Black people access to the university's ample resources. For him, the campus expansion was the perfect project. Its motive was simple; as he put it, "We're an academic institution. We're not a real estate developer." Under Columbia's control, the new campus would not only create jobs but also provide what he called "intellectual capital." I asked Forbes what he meant. Would Columbia take royalties from the research produced in the university's tax-exempt buildings and put them back into West Harlem? He quickly shifted the discussion: "Oh no, no!"

To explain intellectual capital, Forbes described how the new campus buildings will house scientists that solve world problems. But he also discussed the university as largely an exclusive agent of workforce training. Parents paid $60,000 per year with the expectation that their children would be placed on a career path. And now that Columbia offered forty scholarships a year to Harlem residents (for each class of about 2,200 accepted students), the university's elite network opened up to a wider talent pool. But Forbes most enthusiastically touted the school's programs that helped train the formerly incarcerated to become coders, to become entrepreneurs, and to work on campus jobs beyond construction: "You know, teach somebody how to fish."

Forbes made an extremely compelling case. But he had a difficult time reconciling individual achievements on a new campus with the direct and indirect losses created by Columbia's increased control over West Harlem. To be fair, Forbes did admit that a nearly $200 million community benefits agreement isn't a lot on a $7 billion project. He suggested to me that West Harlem should have received a percentage of the overall cost versus a fixed payout. But Forbes still didn't believe the CBA was compensation for any community displacement. He called it "buying economic goodwill," comparing it to the work that any corporation undertakes after a shock to the community, like a hurricane. Forbes believed Columbia didn't cause any present-day disruption and that the CBA was more a way to ease tensions over past missteps because of 1968: "You know, with the gymnasium—you have to show good faith."

This Columbia administrator and ex-Panther saw no relationship between campus expansion and community displacement. I mentioned census data showing that between 2000 and 2010, Manhattanville's Black and Latinx populations witnessed significant drops, by 22 percent and 9 percent respectively, while its white numbers exploded by 231 percent. At the same time, housing prices in areas that surround the project were rapidly increasing to capitalize on rising land values. As soon as the city approved the campus expansion in 2007, the Department of City Planning issued an impact statement estimating that approximately 3,400 university-affiliated residents would be attracted to the area within a half-mile radius of the project, which will lead to as many as 1,300 housing units facing rent pressure and involuntary displacement by 2030.[56] The racial and economic demographics in the area more closely mirror the Columbia profile. Still, Forbes said those numbers were a product of the broader "development process," not campus expansion.

But even just the promise of Columbia expansion drew upmarket investors to a still largely poor and brown Harlem. Property values are rising, and residents will get priced out, despite Forbes's dismissal of displacement. Ariel Property Advisors puts out a regular real estate sales report for submarkets in the city, and it verifies that "smart money investors are actively acquiring in West Harlem on the periphery of Columbia University's Manhattanville campus following the expectation that the university would bring prosperity to the area."[57] But not all local tenants and small-business owners felt hopeful about the prosperity that was supposed to follow the new Columbia regime.

Ambar Paulino grew up in the largely African American and Dominican neighborhood of Hamilton Heights, directly north of the new campus site, spanning from West 133rd Street to 155th Street. She returned home from college in 2015 and witnessed her neighborhood suffering the pains of Columbia's growth. Paulino pointed to local businesses and neighborhood institutions being replaced with new bars, such as Harlem Public, that specifically catered to the college-aged and to young professionals, with drink specials for students. She lamented that her neighbors felt like outsiders in their own community.

Hamilton Heights makes up about half of city council member Mark D. Levine's district. He welcomed the diversity of new establishments but fears the new interest is pushing out longtime residents. Levine was clear about the fact that Columbia expansion has driven "a real epidemic of displacement."[58] Small businesses were denied long-term leases, and landlords refused to maintain buildings or collect trash, hoping to force out rent-stabilized tenants and jack up prices.

To its credit, Columbia replaced some of the affordable housing destroyed for the campus with a new mixed-use building in Hamilton Heights. But right before their eyes, citizens watched as elected officials, state agencies, and public policies were rendered toothless in the face of Columbia's might. A private university wielded the power of the "public good" to undermine the local control of a neighborhood.

And this is not just a Harlem story. Greater swaths of NYC were increasingly wrapped up in debates about the decline of community oversight in the face of campus expansions. Pro-growth mayor Bloomberg, who some derided as "Mogul Mike," fully endorsed the "meds and eds" as potent economic engines driving the city's future. Only four miles south of Harlem, New York University got embroiled in a similar struggle to stretch its legs. But NYU faced a drastically different political battle when trying to squeeze more square footage into the well-heeled and well-connected Greenwich Village community.

═══

In the fall of 2010, I opened my mailbox and saw the biannual NYU alumni magazine. A bold title on the cover read *Planning for 2031*. Here was NYU rallying its alumni around an audacious plan to add as much as six million square feet across the city by 2031, the school's two-hundred-year anniversary. The prospect of a 40 percent growth in the campus footprint was massive. But the stories that drove the sales pitch were fine grained. They compelled readers to imagine the tragedy of offices the size of closets, dance rehearsals in hallways, and classes in a basement backroom. NYU had reached a tipping point, and the success or failure of the school depended on space. The article was very careful to avoid the phrase *real estate*. This was not an economic development project but rather a push for academic excellence that required campus expansion.

The alumni magazine is the first place I had ever seen the wonky "square-foot-per-student" ratio. I later learned that Columbia had already deployed this metric to justify its own campus expansion uptown. NYU wanted the world to know that with an even more paltry ratio than Columbia, at 240 square feet per student, its campus could barely breathe. I was a grad student at NYU in the mid-nineties and remember holding office hours at coffee shops because the shared graduate cubicles were often full. But did the remedy to coffee-shop office hours really require this kind of massive expansion?

The NYU 2031 plan hoped to extend from the Washington Square "core campus" out to the midtown "health corridor," from a downtown Brooklyn tech campus to possibly even Governors Island.[59] This new educational empire also included international outposts as part of what President Sexton termed his "Global Network University."[60] At the center of NYU 2031 were plans to add more than two million square feet to the already densely populated Greenwich Village, or floor space roughly the size of the Empire State Building. This part of the project included four new high-rise buildings and a swath of below-ground development, all double-stuffed on the two university-owned "superblocks" just south of Washington Square Park.

The article directly acknowledged NYU's history of flagrant disregard for public oversight. It noted the new strategic plan's "mea culpa tone about past development errors." The university had a horrible record of building out of scale with little concern for the existing neighborhood landscape or input from its residents. Alicia Hurley, former vice president for Government Affairs and Community Engagement, admitted that the university never sought consultation from "community boards unless we absolutely had to." She said that it only undertook projects that did not require government approval.[61] Just one year earlier, NYU had opened its much-reviled 26-story, 700-bed "megadorm" on East 12th Street, installing the tallest building in the East Village and totally overwhelming the rest of the neighborhood. Hurley conceded that it was time to more carefully consider how the university expands. But the dorm remained a cautionary marker amid a patchwork of what some onlookers saw as NYU's roughshod land grabs and broken promises, all without a larger planning vision. Residents rightly wondered if 2031 would reap the same results.

NYU's plans for its core Washington Square campus in Greenwich Village meant facing residents who were a notoriously active bunch. The Village reveled in its historic reputation as America's bohemian capital. A cabal of artists, intellectuals, and assorted malcontents stood strong in an offbeat neighborhood of winding, grid-repellent streets dressed in cobblestones and low-rise buildings.

The 1960s witnessed titanic land battles between internationally known urbanist Jane Jacobs and the "master builder" Robert Moses on land now occupied by NYU. Moses cleared fourteen blocks just south of Washington Square Park, declaring the area "blighted," to make way for massive highway building schemes modeled on his infamous Bronx Queens Expressway. But Jacobs's grassroots activism kept most of his Village projects forever on the blueprint table. She became the immovable object to his unstoppable force. Still, Moses and NYU forged ahead on a grid of nine square blocks in the slum-clearance area that were converted into three superblocks for campus housing and recreational space framed in concrete.[62] And residents of the Village have a long memory (especially where NYU is concerned).

The two superblocks targeted for the new NYU 2031 project already house the university's Washington Square Village (WSV), a massive project of twin residential slabs painted in primary colors and separated by the Sasaki Garden. The site also includes a commercial strip on LaGuardia and a playground. The southernmost block contains three I. M. Pei–designed thirty-story structures. Two of these silver towers house faculty and graduate students, whereas 505 LaGuardia operates as a co-op of moderately priced housing run through the Mitchell-Lama Program. Pei's "towers in the park" are also home to *Bust of Sylvette*, one of only two Picasso sculptures in the US. The buildings on these superblocks remain heirlooms from urban renewal, anomalies in this low-rise part of the city, massive and Brutalist in their stark, geometric design bathed in concrete.[63] But President Sexton promised a different day.

From day one, Sexton identified the gated pastoral quads of the high-toned Ivies as the antithesis of what higher education could be. He sold NYU as the hipper, urbane alternative, a place without "a single gate": in other words, the future.[64] Of course, there are gates at NYU and other kinds of landscaping and construction that make the clear architectural statement of campus borders. But as Mark Levine observed in the *New York Times*, Sexton is "a man temperamentally incapable of understatement."[65]

Since taking on NYU's presidency in 2001, Sexton often repeated the Daniel Patrick Moynihan saying "If you want to build a world-class city, build a great university and wait two hundred years." He was impressed with Richard Florida's ideas and sold NYU to local stakeholders as the physical manifestation of the "creative city."[66] And Sexton is the one who crafted the catchy image of an ICE economy to impress upon municipal leaders the interlinked fates of NYU and New York City. He wanted everyone to embrace the idea that not only the university's academic excellence but also the economic vitality of New York City rested on NYU's physical growth.

But Village residents remained leery after witnessing the university's continued transformation of the neighborhood with little community consultation. When Sexton was dean, the law school demolished an original residence of Edgar Allan Poe to make way for an academic building.[67] Did the Poe house simply foreshadow the kind of disingenuous cooperation that would come with the NYU 2031 project?

Well, the university's building ambitions certainly poked the bear of Village activism. And although many residents held firm to the image of quirky bohemians or a village of Jacobs-style "anti-building zealots," the area's median income and housing values had rapidly shot up in recent decades.[68] Unlike Columbia, NYU now faced a largely white and monied constituency in one of the wealthiest neighborhoods in the country. The ensuing battles between a powerful university and its formidable residents could rip the Village apart. Things had to be different.

Manhattan Borough President Stringer had worked to neutralize Harlem dissent against Columbia's expansion battles, and he sought to get out in front of NYU's 2031 plan before things got out of hand. In 2006 he quickly put together a task force so that university administrators, residents, and local politicians could sit at the table and work out differences before they calcified into warring factions. The prospect of all sides coming together for neighborhood development signaled an important turn of events.

Andrew Berman came to the task force with an open mind. He served as the executive director of the Greenwich Village Society for Historic Preservation (Village Preservation) and believed that Stringer was an honest broker for the community. Besides, New York City's building schemes were embedded in his blood. His mother's apartment got demolished to make way for Robert Moses's infamous Cross Bronx Expressway. He grew up in Co-op City, the initial destination for the borough's remaining working-class and lower-middle-class white ethnic residents during urban renewal. After attending Wesleyan University, he came back to work as the Greenwich Village community liaison for politician Tom Duane. But his lifelong interests in the built environment never diminished, compelling him to take the lead at Village Preservation in 2002.

Berman jumped headfirst into his role on the task force, attending most of the more than fifty meetings that discussed NYU's building priorities. In January 2008, Stringer announced that NYU had officially signed on to the guiding principles for campus expansion put forth by the task force, with a focus on reusing existing buildings and, when possible, pursuing spaces outside of the Washington Square area. The political viability of Village residents seemed to encourage a different university building outcome than what happened in Harlem. But Berman grew cautious very early when the task force negotiated a university development dispute that preceded the full NYU 2031 expansion plan.

In 2008 NYU sought to demolish the historic Provincetown Playhouse to make way for a new law school building. Widely regarded as the birthplace of "Off-Broadway experimental theater," this playhouse served as the artistic home of many legends, including Eugene O'Neill, Bette Davis, and Paul Robeson.[69] After loud grumblings from community members and theater lovers, the project came under review by the task force. NYU agreed to preserve the facade and structural walls while incorporating the old seating into a new theater. But then one day Berman received an alarming call.

A member of Village Preservation snapped a photo of NYU building crews demolishing a wall that the university had promised to preserve. This person lived on the same block as the playhouse, and their back window faced the construction site. According to Berman, NYU had created "tall construction walls on the street so that nobody could see what was going on." University spokeswoman Alicia Hurley admitted that "it was a mistake" but still dismissed the outrage as a political ploy by development opponents.[70]

For many community stakeholders, though, Provincetown became one more example of NYU's two-faced approach to partnership. Berman now realizes that the school's failure to honor the task-force agreement foreshadowed something larger: "We knew something big was coming, but we didn't know exactly what it was going to be. In retrospect, it was clear that NYU was working to make the rollout of the full NYU 2031 plan successful and dampen or mute community opposition."

In 2009 NYU began slowly offering the task force more-specific details about its expansion plan. University officials placed emphasis on the satellite points in midtown, Brooklyn, and perhaps Governors Island, but they couldn't hide the fact that almost half of the proposed six million square feet would be sited in the Washington Square area and specifically on the two university-owned superblocks. "We were pretty stunned and horrified, and it didn't abide by any of the planning principles that we had put forward at all," says Berman. He pointed out that right after September 11, the financial district clamored for investors in the area, including NYU. In fact, the NYU 2031 plan brought programs that were already in the Wall Street area back to Washington Square.

Former borough president Marty Markowitz had also constantly called for the Tisch School of the Arts to come to Brooklyn: "We're only how many subway stops away, 2, 3, 4? It's around the corner practically from NYU!"[71] And why couldn't film programs partner with the famed Silver Cup Studios in Queens? But administrators pointed out that half the plan *did* push beyond Washington Square and the half that remained didn't sprawl out into the neighborhood. Almost all of the construction would take place on university-owned blocks. University leaders argued that they were damned no matter what.

On April 14, 2010, NYU welcomed everyone to the first public showcase of its 2031 expansion plan at the Kimmel Student Center. As the crowd filed into the building, they walked past critics handing out fliers and stickers emblazoned with a war cry against expansion: "Overbuild, Oversaturate, Overwhelm."[72] Once local residents and other interested observers reached the tenth floor, university officials and architects pointed to various details on an impressive 3-D model.

The plan displayed a new boomerang-shaped building at each end of existing apartment complexes on the Washington Square Village superblock. The nondescript LaGuardia and Mercer buildings would rise to 125 and 215 feet, respectively, and were slated to extend below ground, serving academic purposes with retail on the ground floor. The central garden and playground would be replaced with a new recreation space on the outside of the structure, and a new sunken light garden would be accessible only from the new buildings "to ensure security."[73]

On the University Village superblock, NYU sought to add a four-hundred-foot tower to the Pei "towers in the park" design. As the tallest building in the Village, it would split uses between faculty housing and a university-owned hotel. The plan would also demolish NYU's Coles sports building and replace it with a massive million-square foot "zipper loft." The new structure would sit flush up against the Mercer Street sidewalk and be filled with fourteen hundred dorm rooms, academic space, and a new underground gym.

Now that NYU 2031 had gone public, the expansion plan had to navigate a gauntlet of nonbinding votes and recommendations that were meant to influence the final and most important city council decision. Opponents

Rendering of NYU 2031 expansion in Washington Square Park campus, February 2013.

mulled around the showcase fuming about the implications of the plan. But Berman still rolls his eyes at the suggestion he simply opposed development. He wanted a balance between the university and its community. NYU couldn't oversaturate the Village.

Berman looked at the proposed buildings with grave concern: "It feels less and less like a neighborhood and more and more like a company town or an extension of the NYU campus." At a June CB 2 meeting, he was far less polite. The room exploded with applause when Berman denounced the university plan as "a little like BP [British Petroleum] saying they show respect for the environment."[74] Community boards ensured that residents had the chance to voice concerns, but NYU didn't need their approval.

By the end of the summer, the task force had grown even more contentious when discussing the zoning ordinances that had to be amended to move forward with NYU 2031. The fourth tower required historic landmark restrictions to be overturned. The project sought commercial development in areas zoned for residential use. It called for the removal of deed restrictions on open space and the transfer of public land to the university. Many of these zoning limits had been negotiated to offset the original out-of-scale Washington Square Village and University Village developments on the superblocks years earlier. Task-force members generally argued that the proposed expansion would destroy the "neighborhood character" with its mix of small-town charm and urban density.

Stringer unceremoniously dissolved the task force in July without any notice to its members. He said it was time to suspend the task force and make way for broader public reviews of the NYU plan under the authority of Community Board 2.[75] Some members were surprised and disappointed because they thought the work of the task force had just begun. Similar to what happened at Columbia, it seemed that when the neighborhood stakeholders didn't support university development, advisory boards were disbanded, and the veneer of joint authority quickly fell away.

But the task force found a powerful ally in architect Pei. On November 10, 2010, NYU quickly withdrew its proposal for a fourth building to complement the "towers in the park" when Pei's longtime business partner and public representative, Henry Cobb, issued a letter calling the additional tower "highly destructive."[76] Pei looked at the tower as closing off a design that was meant to be open. The proposed structure also blocked views of Picasso's sculpture. In response, the university shifted to propose a building half the size at the site of an old Morton Williams supermarket it owned on the same superblock. Halting the fourth tower signaled a major win for critics.

But residents fighting to preserve the neighborhood character started to face their own critics. Far too many New York residents struggled to simply find quality, affordable housing, and the battles here over zoning technicalities, architectural intentions, and NIMBYism ("Not in My Back Yard") in an already-affluent neighborhood sounded too much like rich "white folks problems." Some even nicknamed Berman the "Village Crier" for what seemed like his inflexible opposition to the NYU plan.[77] He said the NIMBY charge just didn't hold up under scrutiny. As Berman saw it, attacking him avoided the fact that NYU seemed to continually break agreements and now advanced a project that offered little to the community where it would sit: "I mean it would be one thing if we were saying here is some affordable-housing project or homeless shelter. But here was an elite institution that was looking to expand and become even more elite." Berman's critique of NYU's expansion became even more compelling when university faculty joined the fight.

=

In January 2012, more than forty residents testified during a marathon open forum. But something was different. For arguably the first time, many of the speakers identified as NYU faculty, and they all spoke out against the expansion plan. The next month, discontent officially announced itself as NYU Faculty Against the Sexton Plan (FASP).[78] For many on the faculty, NYU was both their employer and landlord. Without university housing, even a decent salary doesn't enable faculty to inhabit one of Manhattan's most expensive zip codes. Roughly 40 percent of the faculty live on the superblocks, so the 2031 plan would ensnare them in twenty years of demolition and construction.[79] And in the name of academic excellence, how could faculty then recruit the world's best and brightest to a land of jackhammer noise and particulate dust?

But it was the plan's financial risk that seemed to galvanize the broadest cross section of concerned faculty. Administrators remained tight-lipped, but the cost of NYU 2031 floated somewhere between $4 billion and $6 billion for a school with a relatively meager $2.5 billion endowment. (By comparison, Columbia sits at around $8 billion, and Harvard soars over $30 billion.) In a *New York Times* op-ed, faculty members Ernest Davis, Patrick Deer, and Mark Crispin Miller pointed out that the plan would cost more than double the school endowment, so how could the debt be covered? They pointed to the students and faculty.[80]

This costly campus expansion, they argued, would inflict a significant drain on a university budget where reportedly 57 percent of the university's annual revenue comes from tuition. With a small endowment, the school relied heavily on the $70,000 that it then charged students annually to further its development ambitions. NYU can rightly boast that it now offers free tuition to all of its medical students. But in 2013, *CBS News* reported that only 3 percent of the overall student body got their full financial needs met, whereas many other elite schools had started meeting the full demonstrated financial need of all their undergraduates. The result is that NYU students graduate with the largest debt load of any private university in the country. They are exemplars of a nationwide explosion of more than $1.5 trillion in student debt.

At the same time, roughly 60 percent of the teaching staff has shifted from secure tenured or tenure-track positions to contingent, temporary-contract status with limited benefits.[81] The Faculty Against the Sexton Plan suggested that the exploitation of students and faculty at an endowment-poor institution would only increase with the additional debt from an expansion plan. And growing dissent to the plan from the surrounding neighborhoods would only further undercut NYU's new public posture of openness and collaboration.

Thirty-nine of NYU's 175 departments and schools passed resolutions against the plan in 2012. The nearly unanimous votes of the Economics Department and the Stern School of Business were the most striking. Hardly bastions of Village activists, these departments feared the possibility of financial default. But faculty also spoke to a growing concern with what they

Opponent of NYU's 2031 plan dressed as a purple people eater, September 2012. Photo by Nick Pinto/*Village Voice*.

saw as Sexton's autocratic approach to university governance.[82] Sexton ruled among an elite few of well-paid executives and a board of trustees stacked with the 1 percent of financiers, real estate moguls, and even the owner of a company that issued high-interest student loans. Students might be expected to pay more and faculty to earn less, but the trustees led the companies that would construct, finance, litigate, and profit from the expansion plan.

That February, Community Board 2 unanimously rejected NYU's campus plan. They repeated many of the same concerns expressed by the task force and worried the Village would be transformed "into a private NYU campus." But they also pointed out some alarming testimonies from residents on the University Village superblock. Since 1967, the 505 LaGuardia tower had fallen under the affordable-housing Mitchell-Lama Cooperative. But now NYU held the lease, and tenants reported that when regulated apartments became vacant, there were efforts to deregulate the units by keeping them vacant or offering them to NYU faculty.[83]

NYU had wanted to avoid the public relations nightmare Columbia faced with its campus expansion, but it seemed that it was using the same questionable tactics to force residents' hands. The opposition to the NYU 2031 plan had grown broader than zoning laws or NIMBYist calls for Village preservation. It seemed NYU had breached housing protections for its own interests.

In order to push through the plan, university leaders had to find a way to downplay the loss of public authority. So administrators rallied their troops around a vision of NYU 2031 as good for students, faculty, and the city's economy. In March 2012, Greenwich Village Chamber of Commerce President Tony Juliano joined local unions at a press conference on the steps of city hall. He was backed by "25 burly hard hats" draped in American flags while holding purple-and-white signs exclaiming "BUILD IT!" They focused on NYU 2031 as an economic engine for working people.[84]

According to the *New York Post*, the expansion would add more than 18,000 unionized construction jobs, 9,500 permanent jobs, and $6 billion in hard and soft money. Former mayor Ed Koch exclaimed, "NYU spread your wings," boldly declaring Greenwich Village "the East Coast version of Silicon Valley."[85] NYU officials also responded to student and faculty dissent by arguing that the plan would help meet increased needs for faculty housing. Not surprisingly, Mayor Bloomberg endorsed the plan on April 9. Stringer followed suit with his nonbinding support two days later. Even Columbia's Bollinger came downtown to offer words of support, calling universities the "creative spirit of New York."[86]

The warring factions converged at the June 29 testimonies before the city council subcommittee on zoning. The mood in the room was tense. Panelists sat around the well-traveled 3-D model of NYU 2031, its impressive detail almost signaling the plan's approval as a foregone conclusion. Sexton and his army of suits made their case to the subcommittee. He professed to speak in the name of students who felt "compressed." NYU needed to give families more value for what they were paying. Members of the faculty coalition retorted by dismissing Sexton's claim as "nonsense." NYU's academic excellence, they insisted, was not tied to its physical growth. They conceded that some additional space was needed for classrooms and studios, but the scale of the current plan was unfounded. They also suggested that NYU already underused space by having few classes on Fridays and more than a hundred NYU-owned apartment vacancies.[87]

And then, "of course," as a *Village Voice* reporter scoffed, "there was the requisite grumbling of a privileged movie star" who lived in the Village. In this case the star was Matthew Broderick. One expansion opponent said onlookers "were basking in the shimmer of Matthew Broderick." But he was quickly upstaged by an eight-year-old girl who wondered aloud why college students were incapable of taking a subway for a class or two when she took the train to school every day.[88]

Broderick admitted later to me that he wasn't particularly sharp that day. But he came to offer testimony as someone who grew up in the Village during the 1970s. Broderick once lived in an apartment on Washington Square North, and he offered a unique view of NYU's growth.[89] He waxed nostalgic about a time before NYU had shrouded the park in shadows. The actor offered a compelling description of the old Village as a "nice mess" with community playing fields where the Coles student gym sits. And the park was a "little dangerous," with drugs, music, hippies, and old men playing handball. But it all became a campus, and the school had "eaten all the things that make the neighborhood attractive and distinct." He called NYU a city dropped in the middle of New York.

After a nine-hour meeting, the public testimonies were delivered, and negotiations began between NYU and local politicians. All roads led to the final July 25 city council decision. Before Speaker Christine Quinn could utter a complete sentence, she was drowned out by a chorus of boos and hisses. The protestors, numbering around a hundred, were told they could hold their signs—which read NYU2031: Wrong for NYC, Wrong for the Village, Wrong for NYU—only at chest level and not above their heads. Quinn offered a few warnings of silence amid repeated outbursts of "Shame on you!" and "This is democracy!" Rumors swirled that backdoor compromises had been between NYU, the speaker, and the Village council rep, Margaret Chin. Moments before the vote, people started to chant "Chin and Quinn did us in!" Then Speaker Quinn pulled the trigger and ordered the upper gallery cleared of the protestors.[90]

With a vote of 44-1, the city council approved a modified version of the proposal. Chin never directly addressed the claims that she followed the lead of real estate interests, but she pointed to her success in scaling back NYU's plan. The negotiated agreement created more open space for public use on the superblocks. Negotiations also included a 700,000-square-foot reduction of the zipper building, and the boomerang buildings were made smaller in order to avoid making the Washington Village green space an enclosed courtyard. And there would be no hotel at University Village. NYU celebrated the victory as a successful balance between its space needs while "addressing concerns of our neighbors."[91]

However, Berman wasn't pleased. He said the plan broke all existing zoning and urban renewal agreements: "Here's a neighborhood with some of the lowest ratios of open space per capita of any in the city. And this was particularly precious green space because the community fought for it and won it in their fights with Robert Moses." Residents, including a number of faculty and students, were left wondering how the neighborhoods that they, and Jacobs before them, had fought to preserve were now part of the new campus city.

═

After the city council win in 2012, Sexton and his NYU 2031 plan seemed unstoppable. But then the school's reputation got bloodied and bruised by Wall Street–style controversies that threw the victory lap off course. News reports found that the school spent lavishly on bonuses, multimillion-dollar apartments, and mortgage loans for a few academic stars and top-end administrators.

In June 2013 the *New York Times* followed up with a deep dive into Sexton's lavish compensation package. The board of trustees provided him an annual salary of $1.5 million, a $2.5 million "length-of-service" bonus in 2015, and guaranteed retirement benefits of $800,000 per year. A related foundation also gave Sexton a $1 million forgivable loan to finance his beach house on Fire Island. Even Sexton's son seemed to get in on the deal. During the 2002 faculty housing shortage, the *New York Post* learned that the son and his wife lived in an NYU-owned Mercer Street duplex while serving no official university function.[92]

All of this lavish spending pushed Senator Charles Grassley to question universities' tax-exempt status. His inquiry was part of a larger Republican attack on higher education in general, but the senator's observations still highlighted NYU's apparent hypocrisy of passing the costs of campus expansion on to faculty and students. Grassley chided, "It's hard to see how the student with a lifetime of debt benefits from his university leaders' weekend homes in the Hamptons."[93]

NYU quickly ended the vacation home loan program, but the school's armor had been dented. The middle of 2013 ushered in a frenzy of "no-confidence" votes against Sexton by five of the university's various colleges, including its largest, the College of Arts and Sciences. And that December, Sexton announced he would step down from the NYU presidency in 2016.[94]

As a final blow, a collection of community stakeholders took the city to the New York Supreme Court. In January 2014, Judge Donna Mills ruled in favor of the plaintiffs that the city illegally handed over public parkland to NYU. She pointed out the public had been using the various open spaces on the superblocks as parks for years, the areas received city funding, and one even had city park signage. Mills called the green spaces "implied parkland." And only the state legislature can designate a different use for public parkland. But ultimately the State Court of Appeals reversed the decision, and NYU maintained its right to build.[95]

Despite university scandal, community protest, and the alleged breach of previous agreements, NYU pushed ahead with its 2031 expansion plan. Construction moved forward on the massive Mercer Street zipper loft. I asked Berman what lessons he learned after grappling with an institution of higher education that is also a developer. He quickly pointed out that NYU is not just any university: "Their board is the 1 percent of the 1 percent of the 1 percent. It was like taking on this almost star chamber of the most powerful, well-connected people in the country with a vested interest in the construction and real estate industry."

Village Preservation, Berman noted, had worked with Cooper Union and the New School when there were concerns about zoning ordinances during campus expansions. Both schools immediately complied. But as he saw it, NYU is different. Berman said he went to great lengths to work with the university, to connect it with communities beyond the Village that were yearning for the kind of investment and population density a campus could bring. Village residents had the power to make a lot of noise. But

NYU still didn't have to play ball. It had become the governing authority in the Village.

Now that NYU continues to build, Berman pledged to join others in the city insisting that universities live up to their responsibilities to the community. The NYU conflict foreshadowed the city's current fight for an urban democracy. There are university-driven building projects happening across the boroughs, from Lehman College in the Bronx to the College of Staten Island. Alongside Union Theological, the New School, and Cooper Union, Rockefeller University will add two acres of biological and medical research space to the Upper East Side. Fordham plans to remake its entire Lincoln Center Campus over the next two decades.[96] And in 2017, Cornell Tech moved into its Roosevelt Island Campus. These developments simply crystallized national trends in a concentrated form.

As schools traipse across their cities, who will protect the interests of urban citizens? Harlem and Village residents saw firsthand how clashes over land use or housing costs are not resolved within a truly democratic process but according to the complete hegemony of corporate rule wrapped in an ivory tower. In cities like New York, residents are used to wondering what the point is of having deed restrictions to protect public space or laws against political collusion when such policies can be so easily overturned. But communities face new challenges when universities are the corporate and political power players operating ostensibly in the interest of the public good.

In Hamilton Heights, Councilman Levine believes that stronger laws protecting tenants' rights are the only way to slow down Columbia's influence on inflated property values. Urban planner Sylvia Morse says that the NYU case forces us to rethink the city planning process. She calls for "binding community-based neighborhood plans" to guide all future university developments.[97] The bottom line that many have accepted is that city schools are going to continue to grow. Community neighbors just want to have a say about decisions that shape their neighborhoods while sticking around to reap the benefits. As protestors were ushered out of the city council meeting to decide the fate of the NYU 2031 plan, one of them yelled "Democracy is dead!" Well, maybe not yet.

Given the political power of NYU and Columbia, it's hard to imagine a university with even more authority in its city. But the University of Chicago has, in fact, dominated that city's South Side for more than a century. Chicago isn't the home of the 1 percent of the 1 percent of real estate and finance titans, but it's one of the most segregated cities in the country. And UChicago is a wealthy white school that holds court over a Black community by wielding the twin forces of land acquisition and police control. Its dominion highlights the apparent specter of violence that a university can deploy when building an expansive campus citadel in the middle of a city.

CHAPTER FOUR

THE "800-POUND GARGOYLE"

Brandy Parker grew up in Woodlawn, just a few blocks south of UChicago's Hyde Park campus. But his neighborhood felt like a world away from the university's bucolic oasis in the city, filled with ivy-covered Gothic buildings and sleek, glassy research facilities powered by some of the wealthiest families in the world. By contrast, Woodlawn was and still is a neighborhood ravaged by urban violence and poverty. Parker moved to 61st as a preteen and remembers that his mother wouldn't even let him venture away from the block until he was fifteen or sixteen. In fact, he didn't even know a place like Hyde Park could exist so close to where he lived. So as soon as he could, Parker immediately joined his teenage friends and explored the campus. Hyde Park was so different from Woodlawn, he remembered, that "we would walk around just to get away from my environment, from the violence and stuff, you know."

Whereas Parker, now twenty-one, looked at UChicago as a refuge, others tagged him as a threat. Today, he reflects back on those days with a mixture

CHICAGO

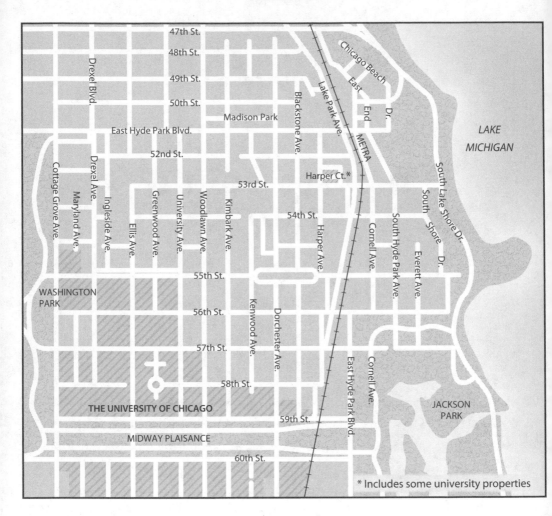

47th St.
48th St.
49th St.
50th St.

Drexel Blvd.

Madison Park

East Hyde Park Blvd.

52nd St.

Blackstone Ave.

Lake Park Ave.

Chicago Beach

East End Dr.

METRA

LAKE MICHIGAN

53rd St.

Harper Ct.*

54th St.

South Lake Shore Dr.

Cottage Grove Ave.

Maryland Ave.

Drexel Ave.

Ingleside Ave.

Ellis Ave.

Greenwood Ave.

University Ave.

Woodlawn Ave.

Kimbark Ave.

Harper Ave.

Cornell Ave.

South Shore Dr.

South Hyde Park Ave.

Everett Ave.

55th St.

WASHINGTON PARK

56th St.

Kenwood Ave.

Dorchester Ave.

57th St.

58th St.

THE UNIVERSITY OF CHICAGO

59th St.

MIDWAY PLAISANCE

Cornell Ave.

East Hyde Park Blvd.

JACKSON PARK

60th St.

* Includes some university properties

of irritation and fear: "Every time I used to step my foot on university campus, they always used to follow us." Parker would hear his physical description on a nearby walkie-talkie ("Black male with a mohawk"), or campus police would just flat out declare, "You don't belong over here; what are you doing over here?" Students didn't outright question his presence, but he noticed how they "crunched their backpacks." He would think, "You could be one of those college students that finna go shoot up a school. . . . I should be crunching *my* damn book bag!" Parker believed that he had every right to enjoy the tranquil green spaces and different environment just blocks away from home. But the feelings of harassment wore him down. He devised elaborate, if inconvenient, routes to walk around the main areas of the campus. But UChicago police were everywhere: "I can't escape from them."

It was hardly an exaggeration for Parker to say he could not "escape" the University of Chicago Police Department (UCPD). In 2011 the city's Commission on Public Safety passed a municipal ordinance that expanded UCPD's jurisdiction far beyond the campus boundaries, going north to 37th and as far south as 64th.[1] In short, UCPD, an armed private police force that answered to a private university, was given the public authority to make arrests on city blocks. And its jurisdiction spread all the way from the historic Black neighborhood of Bronzeville right down to the heart of Parker's Woodlawn. He explained to me, "It's just like if you hire your own police force, you make your own police force." And the consequences of this expanded jurisdiction were real.

Many residents were happy to have the additional police presence, given the city's violence. However, Parker was getting stopped by UCPD three or four times a week. He had committed no crimes and could not be found in any criminal database. He told me that cops sometimes jumped out before the car even stopped, screaming their almost standard mantra, "Where the guns at, where the drugs at?" Parker began to wonder "what they really protecting. . . . Is they really protecting the people, or is they protecting the soil, the land?"

Parker pointed out that he met some really good police officers who encouraged him to go to school and even welcomed him on campus. But with the UCPD expansion, the campus already spilled over into his neighborhood. He now felt just as unwelcome on his own block as he did in

Photographic "parody" of UChicago control over the community, June 2010. Photo by Quinn Dombrowski, Flickr.

Hyde Park. And it became clear to him that UCPD was "just protecting the university property." Parker's experiences speak to the ethical slippage of handing over a city's public policing power to a private institution like UChicago. And policing serves as simply the most visible—and violent—expression of the university's new desire to incorporate greater swaths of the city into its development ambitions.

As its history makes clear, no other private school used urban renewal dollars to shape its own campus surroundings better than UChicago did. This South Side university used public money to demolish whole blocks, which helped fortify the campus from a perceived threat of Black and working-class residents in the surrounding areas. But in the twenty-first century, city living had become a draw. UChicago needed to cultivate assets that would attract students, faculty, and their families looking for a secure urban lifestyle. University affiliates were no longer satisfied with turning their backs on the city; they wanted to be *in* the city.

Instead of filling emptied blocks with classrooms and laboratories, UChicago has pushed its retail, museums, and boutique hospital services out into the existing communities. But the persistent fears of poverty and violence on Chicago's South Side pose challenges to this curated design of an urbane university life. For the project to succeed, UChicago seems to have replaced the bulldozers with police patrols as the frontline weapon to make city blocks safe for university consumption. The 2011 municipal ordinance applied UCPD jurisdiction to any neighborhood area that contained university buildings.

Through UChicago, we see how city schools can deploy the blunt force of campus police, along with the soft power of university amenities, to enact what seems to some as a violent confiscation and control of local communities. And Parker's story illustrates what happens when policing helps turn neighborhood blocks into what he calls "university property." South Side residents haven't yet experienced wholesale displacement, like what happened to residents in West Harlem, but they still have to fight hard to resist becoming outsiders in their own city.

=

The reverberations from urban renewal's bulldozers could be felt well into the twenty-first century. UChicago acknowledges its past actions of institutional fortification and now celebrates its more humane approach to community outreach. But it is hard to see much difference between the brutal demolition of community blocks during the heyday of urban renewal and the aggressive policing and seizure of those same neighborhoods for today's campus expansion.

Don Randel was about to hand over UChicago's presidency to Robert Zimmer in 2006. Randel found himself haunted by the school's urban renewal past when stepping down. Perhaps, because he had one foot out the door, Randel could afford to be a bit reflective. He had come a long way from being a Cornell music professor to lead UChicago in a multibillion-dollar capital campaign, and he was now on his way to helm the prestigious Mellon Foundation.

But even with such notable success, Randel grew especially thoughtful about unfinished business on the South Side. He gazed down upon the inner campus from his fifth-floor office and reflected with candor on what the outgoing president called the university's "isolationist heritage." It's not surprising that UChicago's campus architecture brought this scholar of medieval music back to a time when the "cloisters and spires and filigreed arches"

General campus aerial view, 1911–1920. Special Collections Research Center, University of Chicago.

of medieval universities were intentionally designed to invoke a sense of "retreat, of keeping apart from the outside world."[2]

A little more than a year earlier, Randel had spoken in more detail about how the legacy of retreat was embedded in the "DNA" of the university. At a crowded Saturday-afternoon speech in the university's International House, he offered a plainspoken description of UChicago's role in fostering national urban renewal policies during the 1950s and 1960s that closed the campus off from the surrounding areas. He first lamented that the very architecture of the quad, with its Gothic-style "street side stone walls hiding well-manicured inner quadrangles," evoked exclusion from the world beyond. But the university did not stop there. Randel said the school went on to "lower the gates. Raise the drawbridges. Dig the moats deeper" in the face of "what was seen as a threat from the outside."[3]

However, those Black residents who lived in the shadows of the medieval spires were quick to remind anyone willing to listen that UChicago's urban ambitions had never stopped at the proverbial front gates. The university was called the "800-Pound Gargoyle" for a reason.[4] UChicago's interests significantly determined the quality of life not just in the immediate campus community of Hyde Park but also in the blocks beyond the campus, which were filled with empty lots, deteriorating graystones, and brick two-flats struggling to come back from decades of divestment.

In fact, during the Checkerboard Lounge controversy in 2003, Black residents argued that the university's decision to move the blues club from Bronzeville to Hyde Park "recalled urban renewal days" from the 1950s. A "Friends of the Checkerboard Lounge" letter to the *Hyde Park Herald* said it wasn't by chance that the amenities and economic infrastructure in Bronzeville lagged behind that of Hyde Park (and hence struggled to support businesses like the Checkerboard). The university has long determined where development would, and would not, take place on the city's South Side. Not only has UChicago directly influenced city decisions about development, but as the most powerful institution in the area, its endorsement or disinterest in projects can dictate where investment happens.

Local Checkerboard advocates marked UChicago as "a key reason for the stark differences between Hyde Park and Bronzeville." Those differences reflect what Bronzeville historic preservation administrator Paula Robinson termed a "Tale of Two Cities."[5] The university had never simply turned its back. And today, UChicago's selective outreach in local communities works as a distorted mirror image of its racially biased divestment from surrounding neighborhoods in the past.

Two figures at the forefront of the "Friends" campaign were longtime Chicago residents Paula Robinson and Harold Lucas. For them, the university acquisition of the Checkerboard marked just one example in a long list of what Lucas described as "cultural theft." Lucas and Robinson were part of a growing set of South Siders who, in the 1990s, witnessed a growing "back-to-the-city" movement. After decades of divestment from Black communities, white civic leaders and developers expressed a renewed interest in the Bronzeville area, which was wedged between the city's Loop commercial corridor and the UChicago campus.

In response, Robinson and Lucas had joined others, under the banner of "Restoring Bronzeville," to control what they called "cultural assets" as part of Black efforts to profit from a fledgling heritage tourism market. Chicago's South Side was the home of pioneering innovations in jazz, blues, gospel, art, publishing, and politics: it became a cultural and commercial "mecca" at mid-century. Local entrepreneurs, preservationists, and activists had to figure out how to capitalize on the emerging commercial value of this Black past. If they didn't, developers would swoop down and turn historic Bronzeville into a cookie-cutter bedroom community for new urbanites.

Robinson was born in Bronzeville and grew up in Hyde Park in a solidly middle-class family under the care of her mother, a high school assistant principal. After college, she worked as a public relations executive in the 1980s and 1990s, handling big accounts in the downtown Loop, and then turned to marketing community development on the South Side. Described as a "connector," Robinson became the perfect Bronzeville advocate, especially as local stakeholders sought to "dress" the neighborhood for tourists and investors.[6] She quickly realized that promoting Bronzeville also meant preserving its deteriorating buildings, the ones that had historical significance and that she described to me as "our cultural antiquities." Robinson was most proud of saving the historic arts and crafts Rosenwald Courts building, where luminaries such as musician Nat "King" Cole, writer Gwendolyn Brooks, and boxer Joe Louis lived in the 1930s and 1940s. Saving the Rosenwald Courts, she said, was "one of my biggest success stories."

But there were also many failures. Robinson fought to save the Pickford, where pioneering Black filmmaker Oscar Micheaux screened his films, and the Metropolitan, a key venue of Jazz Age Chicago and later the headquarters for Jesse Jackson's Operation PUSH organization. However, the city ultimately ordered the demolition of both theaters. And the home of blues legend Muddy Waters still sits crumbling and vacant. But Robinson's voice grew especially intense, during our conversation, when talking about Gerri's Palm Tavern. For decades the tavern served as a watering hole and refuge for musical luminaries that included Duke Ellington, Dizzy Gillespie, and Muddy Waters. The community fought valiantly to keep the doors open until the city used eminent domain to forcibly evict Mama Gerri Oliver from the premises in 2001.

The deterioration and demolition of historic Bronzeville wasn't simply a matter of poor business practices or unfortunate events for Robinson. She believed that invisible hands were at play. And if big changes took place on the South Side, UChicago was almost always in the mix. As with the Checkerboard Lounge controversy, Robinson remains emphatic that the historic and present-day deterioration of Bronzeville is intimately tied to the actions of the university. She tells me that after years of retreat, "the 'Ivory Tower set' let down the walls, and there are certain areas they want—Washington Park or the South Lakefront—and they call it empowerment, but what they are really doing is engulfing."

Lucas, a third-generation South Sider, agreed but used far less polite language: "It's murder!" Self-named "the Bronzeville Curmudgeon," Lucas described himself as an entrepreneur, impresario, and organizer "ensconced in the bottom up." He shared Robinson's desire to turn Black heritage into an economic market but took a different path. "At thirteen I hit Hyde Park with a Woodlawn gangster mentality," he says, identifying the riches of Chicago's Black culture as a clear site of struggle. He believed that taking ownership of Bronzeville—rather than letting it be stolen—would ultimately help "us get out of the rust-belt condition." From the north, developers target Bronzeville as a potential bedroom community for South Loop professionals while UChicago selects certain Black cultural assets, like the Checkerboard, to showcase in downtown Hyde Park. Lucas scoffed at these moves.

"I represent the authentic experience of Walter Lee Younger and Bigger Thomas," says Lucas, referring to classic characters from works by Chicago writers Lorraine Hansberry and Richard Wright. Lucas explained that major South Side players, like the university, recognize both the value of Black culture and the land it sits on. But now, the real estate is more valuable than the people who live on it.

Lucas's observations speak to an important twenty-first-century shift, where city blocks surrounding the campus have been reimagined from dangerous Black neighborhoods to potentially lucrative real estate. And the expansion of a "university lifestyle" across greater swaths of the South Side underscores the pervasive violence of urban renewal. UCPD surveillance and control are the most obvious examples. But we can't ignore what psychiatrist Wendy Fullilove has called the violent "root shock" that comes from the debilitating cycle of urban divestment, renewal, and displacement. When neighborhoods are targeted for campus expansion, the people who live there face the enduring traumas of losing their homes and the physical disruption of their cultural ties.[7]

≡

Beginning in the 1990s and intensifying during the 2000s, cities and urban life became desirable again. In order to remain competitive, UChicago was forced to change the way it went about the business of urban renewal. In the 1950s and 1960s, the university's urban renewal schemes of demolish and fortify left the area with little of the "urban lifestyle" that commercial developers now like to promote. Walking through Hyde Park today, you might still see T-shirts describing the university as "The Place Where Fun Comes to Die."[8]

UChicago had taken its "nerd culture" notoriety as far as it could go. The campus neighborhood certainly contained the research laboratories, conference rooms, and computer stations to draw the highly sought-after creative class. But the school failed to possess the campus culture of wide sidewalks teeming with cafés, galleries, retail, and nightlife to keep the creatives and their families. UChicago had fallen far behind the national trend of turning urban neighborhoods into an expanded campus district in ways that could be profitable for both the university and the city.[9]

Even locally, schools across the city had outpaced UChicago with new urban renewal projects to develop their surrounding areas into campus communities. The Illinois Institute of Technology (IIT) opened its Rem Koolhaas–designed McCormick Tribune Campus Center and "State Street Village" dormitories in 2003. IIT carved out a secure zone of student housing, retail, and recreation right in the heart of the struggling Bronzeville neighborhood. On the near west side, the University of Illinois at Chicago leveraged public funds to clear sixty acres of land and create a fully planned campus town of residential and commercial properties to service the "ready-made population" of students. Many are concerned that this "South Campus" has raised property values beyond the means of the Latinx Pilsen neighborhood nearby.[10]

UChicago realized that it had to design an urban environment that could help stave off the steady stream of student and faculty dollars flowing away from campus, what retail specialists describe as "leakage." And the upgrading of Harper Court was its first significant development project.[11]

The original Harper Court commercial district had been created in 1965 as a limited refuge for artists and small shops displaced by the university's first urban renewal initiative in Hyde Park. Maybe it's poetic irony that once commerce became a centerpiece of UChicago's growth strategy, Harper Court took on new meaning. The summer it first opened, Harper Court celebrated with literal fireworks. It served as one of the four designated shopping centers after the university had demolished commercial areas under the Hyde Park–Kenwood Urban Renewal Plan.[12]

After several decades and little investment, the bungalow-style shops and public square grew dated and worn down. But Harper Court remained an important, racially diverse social space in Hyde Park. Residents continually recall the army of Black chess masters plying their craft in front of anyone who walked by while low-rent pizza shops, chicken shacks, and other affordable fare dotted the storefronts of the 53rd Street corridor.

Dominique James was a high school student and artist in Hyde Park during the years just before Harper Court's grand reopening in 2013. She described the old 53rd Street as "definitely beat down," but it was a place where Black kids could just "post up" without having to buy anything.

The "old" Harper Court, Chicago, Illinois, 2008. Photo by Eric Allix Rogers, Flickr.

There was even a graffiti permission wall for young artists. Harper Court was familiar but limited in its offerings, and all agreed that it could use improvements. So most were excited when UChicago announced its renovation of Harper Court in 2010. This development would bolster larger efforts to "reimagine" 53rd Street as a commercial corridor for the campus. The university's community news officer, Kadesha Thomas, described the project as an effort to "make sure we will be able to shop, eat out and have fun, without leaving our neighborhoods."[13]

Public figures loosely described the Harper Court redevelopment project as a "public-private" partnership, simply because the city owned an adjacent parking lot that would be incorporated into the larger plan.[14] The city injected the Harper Court project with an infusion of public capital of approximately $27 million through the sometimes-controversial Tax Increment Financing Program. Tax increment financing (TIF) is a contemporary version of urban renewal funding, where property-tax dollars are transferred to a centralized fund and then distributed to specially designated TIF districts. This program focuses on private projects that claim to eradicate blight and bolster development in communities that would not otherwise see investment. Once the TIF district receives attention for investment, property values usually rise. But under a TIF agreement, any future tax revenue increases within the district are diverted into a separate city fund to pay back the initial bond used to finance a project.

Ben Joravsky, staff writer at the *Chicago Reader*, was an unrelenting critic of TIFs in Chicago. He focused on the lack of public supervision over what he described as a "shadow budget" under the mayor's control that, in reality, also underwrites big developers in affluent neighborhoods. A big concern, raised by Joravsky and others, is that when property values rise and the additional value goes to the city fund, there are no additional monies to support public services.[15]

In August of 2012, teachers and activists protested the use of millions from a TIF fund to build the Hyatt Hotel for Harper Court, arguing that financial resources should support schools, not hotels. The decision was especially controversial because Penny Pritzker sat on both the Hyatt board and the Chicago Board of Education (BOE). She was a major player both locally and nationally; a good friend of Barack Obama, she even served as the secretary of commerce during his second term. In March 2013, Pritzker ultimately resigned from the BOE, some argued, to avoid the optics of a conflict of interest. Pritzker explained that she wasn't receiving the TIF funds directly. Hyatt added that the Hyde Park Hyatt would operate under a franchise agreement; hence, it would not be directly owned by Hyatt Hotels Corporation or Pritzker. These technical distinctions did little to assuage those concerned about the distribution of public funds for private companies.[16] The hotel debate raised the broader question of how to build and support community development. Many agreed that Hyde Park benefited from a new hotel, for example, but did the area really need TIF funds to make it happen, especially as public schools crumbled?

Amid the controversy, UChicago and the city pushed forward with their selection of the Danville, Illinois–based Vermillion Group to redesign Harper Court as a $200 million mixed-use complex. The company's "portfolio of projects in university towns" made it an immediate draw. As Vermillion confirmed, "We obviously want to create a *destination* for Hyde Park." The plans required demolition of all but one of the four main bungalow-style buildings in the court, making way for two new perpendicular, block-long private streets and a performance space where the streets could be closed off into festival grounds.[17]

The proposal also created a separate retail corridor and retail on the lower levels of office buildings, a two-hundred-room boutique hotel, two mid-rise apartment buildings, and a condominium tower on top of parking. Susan Campbell, former associate vice president of Civic Engagement, explained that the university's primary interest was to create a venue where the office space and hotel ensure a captive consumer base "during both daytime and evening hours."[18]

Faculty and students were understandably excited by the Vermillion catchphrase "Live/Play/Learn/Work" and the possible death of the "retail desert" that Hyde Park had become. But others feared that boutique hotels and high-priced condominiums would reproduce what one resident described as an economic and lifestyle "moat around the university area."[19]

The final layout and primary tenants of the new Harper Court seemed to confirm some concerns that this development was crafted to exclusively serve the still largely suburban interests of students and potential tourists

The "new" Harper Court, Chicago, Illinois, 2013. Photo by Leslie Schwartz Photography.

through the design of a simulated city experience. The two perpendicular private streets (almost alleys) frame an architectural layout where all actions within the space are regulated by the dictates of buying and selling. There are benches and sidewalk commerce but no public restrooms or public streets. Missing are the walls and ceilings of the suburban mall. They have been supplanted by the "open-air enclosure," a privatized public experience of socializing under the shadows of office and retail towers made of glass and steel.

Most shops became what *Chicago Tribune* writer Joel Hood described as "casualt[ies] of the growing pains of a neighborhood on the move." Gone was the Dixie Kitchen & Bait Shop restaurant, a onetime favorite of Barack Obama, and the Hyde Park Hair Salon, which once trimmed the locks of Muhammad Ali, Obama, and Harold Washington, also did not make the "cut" of revitalization and was relocated.[20] These community institutions were replaced with more-recognizable retail chains, including Starbucks, Chipotle, LA Fitness, and the Hyatt Place Hotel.

But at the same time, elements of Chicago's Black culture are alive and well. The Jamaican eatery Ja' Grill, the clothier Sir and Madame, and the eclectic clothing and home-goods store Silver Room now occupy the court. Owner Eric Williams closes down the L-shaped commercial corridor every summer for the showcase event: the Silver Room Sound System Block Party. And the highly popular restaurant and music space, the Promontory, sits across the street in a former Borders bookstore.

Now back from college, Dominique James told me that the graffiti wall is missed, but she certainly enjoys the new offerings surrounding Harper Court, especially the existence of Black businesses. "But which Black?" she asked. With eighteen-dollar burgers at the Promontory, James explained that racial diversity is alive and well in the court, but the class dynamic is *very* different. She tied the feeling of class difference not just to elevated price points but also to the loss of a public life.

James said that the new restaurants have outdoor seating but nowhere to stand. The increased UChicago police presence overwhelms Harper Court's perpendicular streets; people move through the court with a strictly commercial purpose. Former university employee Chester Blair was more direct in his assessment: the university wants "an environment of stores and restaurants its rich students are used to going to."[21] In short, this carefully curated university playground became what architectural critic Michael Sorkin called one of the country's "Variations on a Theme Park."[22]

In 2017 I wrote about Harper Court as part of a larger story about university-based urban development for the *Chronicle of Higher Education*. Soon after my piece appeared, I received an email from Matthew, a former administrator in UChicago's Office of Civic Engagement, who asked that I not use his real name. He had read my article with great interest and wanted to confirm that my observations were just the tip of the iceberg. It was through him that I began to fully understand the real dangers of letting a university's profit motives drive urban renewal. Matthew worked at UChicago right at the time Harper Court underwent redevelopment. He said that yes, Harper Court was billed as an amenity for the greater South Side community, as a more humane project of urban renewal. But it was actually designed with the exclusive interests of the university in mind. If there were residual community benefits, that was fine too.

In subsequent conversations, Matthew explained that to maintain its world-class reputation, UChicago needed to cultivate a certain urbane university lifestyle for its students, its researchers, and their families. These experiences have nothing to do with academics. Amenities such as Harper Court were meant to attract potential university affiliates, with big grants or drawing power, that were considering a move to Hyde Park.[23] So then how does the university lure those that remain apprehensive about the South Side's reputation as a haven of poverty and gun violence? Urban renewal efforts, administered by the Office of Civic Engagement, became the vehicle for a wide-ranging "image campaign," but it seemed with little concern for community interests.

As a young administrator, Matthew quickly learned that projects in the community, including Harper Court, were meant to serve what he called a "PR machine." And the audience for these development projects wasn't even the community where they sat. Matthew said he was directly told by his boss to develop initiatives that UChicago's "peer institutions will read about: Columbia, UPenn, Harvard." But he pressed on, believing that it was his primary job to go out and speak with residents first, to try and heal old wounds from the university's past actions of demolition and apparent duplicity. He held meetings with residents before decisions were made; he pushed forward a "buy local" initiative for university purchase orders; he even helped restore a mural in the community. But he said his bosses weren't interested.

Matthew said everything seemed to really go downhill when the commercial real estate division was placed in the Office of Civic Engagement. He understood that using community outreach to ease the pain of university land control started to make sense "because our job was to put out fires on outward-facing projects." Matthew was told that some people would be angry about UChicago's development projects in communities. He said it was his job to tell administrators how they could still do whatever they wanted but without making the residents angry. The civic engagement staff members were stuck working to support a real estate development process they didn't control. And Matthew's beliefs about the university's deceptions around community engagement became most clear in his work with the Office of Communications.

Matthew was not allowed to make any public statements before every word was vetted. Administrators grew nervous about how the community would respond to UChicago's presence in the broader neighborhood. If the media called, Matthew referred them to the Communications Office, and then Communications would tell him what to say: "I came from a full meeting with a complete rendering and details about a development, and then it was our job to say that there is no development at this point." Matthew found the lack of transparency enforced on him extremely frustrating. He believed that his goals for actually engaging with the community were completely misaligned with the goals of the university.

The more Matthew worked in the Office of Civic Engagement, the more it became clear that his idea of an "urban campus"—which included the interests and input of what he called "the larger family"—ran directly up against the university's goal to build a "campus lifestyle." UChicago's leadership, under president Robert Zimmer, was primarily concerned with the goal of "un-nerding" the school, which meant moving from the quad and foisting amenities for the university onto neighborhoods surrounding the campus. For many university administrators the key function of the racially diverse Hyde Park was to reflect the needs of a profit-generating research hub. Upscale clothing stores, theater and art, and high-end residential options would bolster UChicago's reimagining of the South Side. However, it was unclear to what degree nonuniversity residents would actually benefit from the new terms of community engagement. And Harper Court was just the beginning.

=

As UChicago announced its bid to renovate Harper Court, residents also noticed the declining array of community services provided by the university's medical center (UCMC). Both changes raised a critical issue. To what degree should residents benefit from the university amenities placed in their neighborhood? A hospital would seem to have a moral obligation to serve its community. The UCMC's tax-exempt status also legally required indigent care. UChicago was not responsible for the area's violence and economic disparities. But what many perceived as the university's heavy-handed policing practices and self-centered urban renewal projects failed to address those problems and largely worked to let them fester. For the hospital, urban renewal meant upscaling its offerings in luxury private suites and cancer research to draw both publicity and profits. Meanwhile, the hospital had closed its Women's Health Center on 47th and Woodlawn. Whether or not the UCMC would agree that the hospital was abandoning its public-good mandate, local residents were paying the costs for the new directions in care.[24]

In August 2010, eighteen-year-old Damian Turner got caught in the crossfire of a drive-by shooting. Turner was in his Woodlawn neighborhood when it happened and hence just four blocks from the UCMC. But first responders had to drive him nine miles away to Northwestern Memorial. Despite the unrelenting epidemic of gun violence on Chicago's South Side, it hadn't had a level one adult trauma center, prepared to treat gunshot victims, for more than twenty years. Turner died at 1:23 a.m. His death brought to life a grassroots movement for an adult trauma center, and UChicago's Medical Center became the target.

For years, activists held protests, sit-ins, and other forms of organizing. They even signed up for and infiltrated a 2013 tour of the new $700 million "Center for Care and Discovery," where a focus on high-cost specialty care certainly did not service the needs of gunshot victims. Alex Goldenberg is a local activist and director of South Side Together Organizing for Power (STOP). He remembered that on the tour, "the optics were kind of absurd."[25]

UChicago continued to object to a trauma center, based on the exorbitant costs, while pushing ahead with an expensive new medical complex. Many people mentioned that the UCMC continued pulling back on services for the poor and indigent. According to *Chicago Tribune* writer Bruce Japsen, this move freed "up space for specialized patients who can generate more revenue." But perhaps UChicago finally saw the handwriting on the wall when activists leveraged their protest power to unsettle the university bid for the Barack Obama Presidential Library. With chants of "No trauma, no 'bama" making national headlines, the university knew it had to play ball.[26]

UChicago also had ambitions to build a new cancer institute. This would help showcase UChicago's medical brand in the lucrative cancer-treatment market. But the university soon realized that any plans for a new build-out, especially one asking for state dollars, would now have to include trauma care. So after years of various fits and starts, in 2016 UChicago unveiled its bold $270 million plans for an adult trauma center, offset by an additional 188 beds to offer more-profitable services in specialized surgery and cancer care. The center finally began seeing patients in 2018.[27]

Not one UChicago official has been willing to publicly admit that grassroots activism shaped the decision to build a trauma unit. At the 2016 groundbreaking, then-mayor Rahm Emmanuel praised just UChicago for the trauma outcome. But Cook County Board President Toni Preckwinkle subtly signaled the power of grassroots organizing in the campaign: "Great institutions like the University of Chicago benefit on occasion from encouragement from the community to do the right thing."[28]

Quite a few residents looked at the trauma center as a moment when they successfully pushed back against the university PR machine to help build a hospital that would serve a broader vision of urban renewal. But even this cautious optimism was quickly tempered. Local media exposed a campus policing strategy to suppress trauma-center activism that reinforced the university and the medical center's already woeful neglect of community needs.

In February 2013 a UCPD detective went undercover to get intel on the activists demanding the hospital trauma center. An anonymous source provided photos to the *Maroon* student newspaper of Detective Janelle Marcellis, of the department's Investigative Services Bureau, posing as a demonstrator. She could be seen trying to blend in, holding a protest sign with a sticker over her mouth that read "Trauma center now." With this one photo, the university got caught in an embarrassing rebuke of civil liberties. President Zimmer quickly denounced the campus police actions as "totally antithetical to our values."[29] In March the school fired Milton Owens because he was Marcellis's commanding officer. But Owens responded by filing a lawsuit claiming that he was made a "scapegoat" to downplay a pattern of policing campus activism by UCPD leadership.[30]

His suit detailed the horrendous police actions at an earlier protest where video showed officers forcefully restraining protestors and throwing them to the ground. Though off duty, Owens came to the scene and was shocked by what he saw as clear violations of protocol. People under arrest were not read their rights, witnesses had not been interviewed, juveniles were not properly processed, and the arresting officers had left the scene.

No investigation followed because the university said it saw no misconduct and there were no complaints. The jury did ultimately side with Owens on the wrongful termination and awarded him $150,000 in damages.[31] The university disagreed with the verdict but also lost on appeal. Beyond Owens's individual plight, the case also exposed layers of what looked like systemic police misconduct. Most importantly, the testimonies and evidence raised much broader questions about the disturbing lack of clarity around the UCPD's procedures, especially as it was also tasked with policing nonstudent residents beyond the immediate campus.

=

UCPD's actions during the trauma center protests and its treatment of South Side residents like Parker demonstrate how far campus police have come. Campus police departments have existed for more than a century, with the first officer at Yale in 1894. These security units initially performed a "custodial function" as student caretakers. But they now hold policing authority in significant parts of our cities. As colleges and universities experienced student unrest in the 1960s and 1970s, campus police began to look a lot like their city counterparts. Majority-white schools in declining, multiracial cities faced the additional burden of signaling a safe campus environment to potential families. Police became the answer.[32]

By the new millennium, most states had passed laws authorizing campus police in some form. Federal Bureau of Justice statistics show that as of 2011-2012, 92 percent of public colleges and universities and 38 percent of private campuses have police officers. Nearly all carry guns, and about nine in ten have arrest and patrol jurisdiction off campus. According to the *New York Times*, as of 2014, more than a hundred colleges were also armed to the teeth from the infamous Department of Defense 1033 Program, which transferred excess military equipment to civilian law enforcement agencies.[33]

More than half of Chicago-area universities have armed police forces. But UChicago stands above them all. According to the department website, the school's police unit deploys "approximately 100 sworn personnel" alongside a legion of unarmed private security guards provided through a contract with Allied Universal. This makes UCPD one of the largest private security forces in the world, outside of the Vatican.[34] But the implications of this police power drastically increased after the 2011 city ordinance expanding police jurisdiction far beyond campus.

In many ways, UChicago's security workers have become the unfettered front line for extending an urbane campus lifestyle out into surrounding neighborhoods. Wherever there was a new university development project in the city, the extended jurisdiction of campus security applied. Students and residents, in Chicago and across the country, began to raise questions about whose interests are served when a university's security force does the work of the city police. And no answer rang louder than the name Sam DuBose.

On the evening of July 9, 2015, a Cincinnati police officer named Ray Tensing pulled over Samuel DuBose for a missing front license plate. Minutes later, a shot rang out, and DuBose was dead. Tensing was an officer of the University of Cincinnati Police Department, and he had pulled DuBose over on a public street blocks away from campus. DuBose was not affiliated with the university or suspected of committing a crime on university property or against a university affiliate.[35] This death raised additional

UChicago security officer at Harper Court, 2017. Photo by author.

outrage because it occurred in the wake of recent police killings of unarmed Black victims like Michael Brown, Eric Garner, and Ohio's young Tamir Rice. And Cincinnati still hadn't fully recovered from four days of rebellion that followed the police killing of an unarmed Timothy Thomas almost fifteen years earlier.[36]

Not quite two weeks after DuBose was killed, Hamilton County Prosecutor Joseph Deters announced Officer Tensing's indictment for murder and involuntary manslaughter. Deters had previously been labeled "pro cop at any costs" by his critics.[37] But even the prosecutor could not conceal his outrage over Tensing's actions: "He wasn't dealing with someone who was wanted for murder, OK? He was dealing with someone who didn't have a front license plate." Video footage showed that after a bit of verbal back-and-forth, Tensing tried to open the car door and almost immediately pulled out his gun and shot DuBose in the head. He was killed over a traffic violation. Deters called it "the most asinine act I've ever seen a police officer make" and added, "I just don't think a university should be in the policing business."[38]

On the day of Tensing's indictment, the city braced for the possibilities of another "Timothy Thomas situation."[39] University of Cincinnati alum Brianna Bibb described the scene on campus that day as a military occupation, with armored cars patrolling the streets and what looked like snipers on the tops of buildings. Even after this community tragedy, it seemed the university and police priority was to protect the campus and its gentrified blocks. As Bibb remembers, "We were like, yo this is f-ed up. Oh, this is how UC feels? They don't even really care about Black people. The message was, don't you dare come out here and protest or riot or do anything. Get away from the campus and the community! Get away from UC!"

For Bibb, this militarized protection of the campus was just a sensationalized version of the normal approach to university policing. She helped funnel student outrage into the Irate8 movement, named after the meager 8 percent Black student body in a city that is more than 40 percent African American.[40] Many white students lived on blocks just off the main campus near largely Black neighborhoods, and parents, deeming these neighborhoods unsafe, wanted then-president Santa Ono to do something. The city and university quietly signed an agreement in 2009 giving the seventy-two-member campus police force authority to patrol nearby residential streets.[41] Bibb saw a clear link between this agreement and DuBose's death: "You sent your kid to a place in the middle of all Black people, so they feel unsafe. And that's kind of why they started hyping up the amount of stops." DuBose became the third unarmed Black person killed by University of Cincinnati police since 2011. Bibb grew incensed just thinking about it.[42]

A report prepared by an independent security firm found that in the two months prior to the DuBose shooting, stops and citations hit an all-time high, averaging 412 stops and 392.5 citations. By August of 2015, 69.3 percent of citations written by University of Cincinnati police were issued to African Americans, whereas 23 percent were issued to whites. Tensing, in particular, had pulled over a higher percentage of African Americans than any other cop on the force at the time.[43] For him, pulling over Black people was largely what it meant to protect and serve. And for the broader campus police force, traffic stops had become a crime-reduction strategy with deadly results.

The killing of DuBose loomed over all discussions of campus policing, especially on Chicago's South Side. There was no question that violence had ramped up in the neighborhoods surrounding Hyde Park, and many residents applauded the extra security offered by UChicago's campus police. "The UCPD is still welcomed," said Shirley Newsome, the current president of the South East Chicago Commission. She credited former UChicago president Randel with being the first to understand that "the university is only as secure as the communities around it." But as UCPD expanded its jurisdiction, students and community stakeholders worried about racial profiling or at least the undue surveillance of nonwhite citizens by a police force tasked with serving the interests of a largely white institution. Members of community organizations such as the Invisible Institute and STOP could rattle off countless stories of Black residents being directly harassed, thrown up against a squadron car, or followed by the UCPD.

Students of color also had their own accounts. When Matthew worked for the Office of Community Engagement, students told him about the many times they were asked for their ID and it was run through the police system. He grew incredulous recalling these incidents: "Who forges a student ID?!" University alum Aerik Francis outlined a strategy that I have heard from Black and Latinx students attending urban campuses all over the country. He made sure to present himself "as a student, wear[ing] UChicago gear," and regretted how the Hyde Park campus neighborhood "kind of has the vibe of a police state."[44]

Campus activists sought to investigate what appeared to be a concerning racial disparity in the way that UCPD treated students of color and residents within the larger campus community. But they continually hit a brick wall. Illinois's 1992 Private College Campus Police Act does not require a private security force to release information about the stops made or adhere to the Freedom of Information Act (FOIA). This protection for private campus police is common in most states. Ultimately, UCPD was a private police force serving a public function but without public oversight. Outraged, students organized the now-inactive Campaign for Equitable Policing (CEP) in 2012. They collaborated with local representatives in 2014 to draft House Bill (HB) 3932, through which campus police would be required to disclose similar—but not exactly the same—information mandated by the FOIA.

UChicago alum and bill cosponsor State Representative Barbara Flynn Currie said students came to her asking for more transparency in light of UCPD's expanded jurisdiction. "There were questions about the UCPD stopping more African American kids than white kids," Currie told the *Chicago Maroon*.[45] The private police force needed more public oversight. But legislative critics worried about subjecting private entities to public authority, whereas activists were concerned that proposed amendments to the bill didn't really increase UCPD accountability. Unlike the FOIA, there would be no chance to bring a case to court, and there would still be a number of items not subject to disclosure, such as recorded materials from campus security cameras. Why not subject campus police to freedom of information policies when they serve a public function? The bill ultimately died on the senate floor. But revealing insights still came from this political mobilization.

Just as the bill reached the senate, UChicago wanted to dull the potential consequences of public embarrassment by slowly releasing more information. As one of the leaders of Campaign for Equitable Policing, Ava Benezra, said of the move in 2015, "We're encouraged, but it's definitely not enough" and went on to point out that "it's a voluntary process that they can end at will." But arrest data the campus police made available did support long-standing charges of racial profiling. In 2016 African Americans made up 59 percent of the population under UCPD jurisdiction, but according to a report from the Illinois Department of Transportation, they accounted for 100 percent of UCPD's investigation stops conducted on foot.[46]

In 2018 Black drivers made up nearly three-quarters of all the drivers stopped by university police. And lest one argue that these numbers simply verify how Black people commit more crimes, the data did not include interactions with the majority-white student body. Former UCPD chief Fountain Walker confirmed that incidents with students are typically referred to the university. Campus activists charged that the glaring difference in treatment has created an unjust "two-tiered system of policing."[47] A student and a community member can be accused of the same infraction, but the former meets with the dean, and the latter is shuttled through the criminal justice system.

Despite the clear racial disparities of a two-tiered system, schools all across the country looked to UChicago as a model for policing urban campuses. After a 2017 spike in robberies and assaults in the Baltimore neighborhoods near campus, senior administrators at Johns Hopkins even made a trip to the South Side.[48] And in March 2018, Hopkins President Ronald Daniels and Hopkins Hospital CEO Paul Rothman sent a surprise email to the campus community announcing their intent to establish a private police department in Baltimore.

Hopkins officials insisted that a new hope rested in ramping up campus security, frequently citing a 2015 study lauding UCPD's ability to reduce crime by 45-60 percent.[49] Students and Baltimore residents also looked at UChicago as a model for campus policing, but what they saw horrified them. Apprehensive critics highlighted the 2018 UCPD shooting of a mixed-race student in the midst of a mental health crisis.[50] Although no one could deny the need for solutions to Baltimore's violence, strong local voices denounced the idea of a private campus police force as the remedy.

"It's akin to establishing a Vatican City within Baltimore" is how State Senator Mary Washington described the policing plan.[51] Her district includes the main campus, and she grew livid just thinking about the idea of this private, elite, majority-white school seeking to establish a security force in one of the country's most impoverished cities. She pointed out the racial and class disparity but also decried the idea of a private police force with the public authority of law enforcement powers in local neighborhoods.

Cincinnati and Chicago signaled a growing trend of private campus police authority in the cities, but such an approach was unprecedented in Maryland. Yet under the proposed terms, Johns Hopkins would sit as a quasi-municipality "with its own army, its own laws," Washington explained. Normally, public officials held what she called the "power of the purse," which allowed them to change police budgets or incentivize desired behavior. But here, the officers would answer to no one but the school's board of trustees and its donors. Hopkins already carried considerable weight in Baltimore. Still, not even its long-standing influence would compare to the authority of a private police force with no public oversight, except maybe the way that powerful political forces lined up behind the school's police proposal.

Former NYC mayor and Hopkins alum Michael Bloomberg endorsed the bill in January 2019, calling it "ridiculous" that the school didn't have an armed police force. This champion of New York City's racist "stop-and-frisk" policy had already donated $5 million to the Baltimore Police Department in 2017 followed by a $1.8 billion gift to Hopkins. It's considered the largest donation ever made to the university.[52] Then, on a single day in January, nine senior administrators and one retired Hopkins Hospital CEO contributed a total of $16,000 to the campaign coffers of then-mayor Catherine Pugh. Soon after, she endorsed the police bill only to resign from office months later, precisely because of her involvement in "pay-for-play" deals in exchange for contracts with the city. Hopkins was never implicated.[53] Baltimore Sun investigations later discovered that the university had also spent $581,000 on eight lobbyists working in Annapolis to push forward the police plan.[54]

Students, faculty, and local residents never wavered in the face of Hopkins's clear political power and mounted a strong case of opposition from the very start. Protesters demonstrated at the Garland Hall Administration building for the month of April 2019. They warned that Hopkins would use police expansion to gentrify neighborhoods while remaining silent about the largely white campus crimes of liquor violations and sexual assault.[55]

A Black faculty member, who would speak only anonymously for fear of university retribution, said that Black staff had been unlawfully bullied and harassed by their white peers on campus for years: "The introduction of police would heighten, not reduce, such instances. This would [also] empower ... white Hopkins affiliates to deploy lethal force on their nonwhite colleagues in the name of campus safety." Senator Washington backed the protest. She also pointed out that many of the community "sweeteners" included in the police bill to appease skeptics would actually come from the taxpayers, not the university. Critics made a strong case for rejecting the plan. But Maryland followed the national trend and allowed Johns Hopkins to establish its own private police force in the middle of Baltimore.[56]

With Hopkins on my mind, I asked South East Chicago Commission President Newsome about the pros and cons of giving a wealthy white university policing dominion over poor, brown neighborhoods. She conceded that there had been some unfortunate incidents. But Newsome believed that overblown outrage was largely coming from activists with what she called "ulterior motives" and from those who don't have to endure the neighborhood violence. But she also remained quite sober about why the university had extended UCPD's jurisdiction. As students move out into the neighborhoods and faculty and staff take advantage of the mortgage programs to buy locally, "it's in their best interest to have UCPD patrol the neighborhood."

But what does it mean when students and faculty are considered the top priority for a private police force charged with protecting the broader public?

In the summer of 2020, broad social protest against police violence also galvanized a campaign against the unjust practices of campus police and their growing public authority in cities. But policing merely served as the flash point for rethinking the disparate relationships between universities and their surrounding communities more broadly. Students and residents across the country joined forces to reignite long-standing calls for an antiracist university.

More than a hundred UPenn students and Philadelphia residents gathered on July 24 to protest Penn Police Department's alleged role in the teargassing of protestors on May 31 while also calling for the university to make payments in lieu of taxes (PILOTs) to support the community and local schools. Faculty and students at UCLA are demanding that campus police be replaced with preventative and anticarceral forms of community-based public safety. They also want the university to cut all ties with external law enforcement agencies after the Los Angeles Police Department used the UCLA-leased Jackie Robinson Stadium to detain and process protestors on June 1.[57]

Activists and residents are also identifying how expanding campus police jurisdictions increases the university control over the daily life of urban citizens. In Chicago, organizations such as Reparations at the University of Chicago (RAUC) have brought together students, faculty, and residents around a broad analysis of what they say is the university's long-standing role in fostering racial exploitation. They point to funds for the old campus that came from the Mississippi slave plantation of Stephen Douglas, as well as to UChicago's more recent hand in alleged residential segregation and displacement.[58]

Reparations demands include ethnic studies programs, more faculty of color, a community board with veto power over any campus project expanding into the South Side, and the transformation of UCPD into an unarmed emergency response service.[59] As people pushed back against campus police violence and neighborhood displacement, they began to realize that the future of US cities is up for grabs. And to overturn the powerful forces that shape our cities, we must pay attention to universities.

For many, it became clear that policing has endeavored to safeguard university citadels well beyond the main campus and that this fact is now central to the experience of everyday life in US cities. Alongside student and faculty housing outposts on the South Side, plans for the Obama Center in Woodlawn and the Theaster Gates Arts Corridor in Washington Park became UChicago's latest beachheads in the urban frontier. Here, university visions of urban renewal faced off against local understandings of real community benefits.

≡

In 2014 Obama announced plans to build his presidential library. Following recent trends, he wanted the library to be affiliated with a university. The Obama Foundation ultimately whittled down the pool to four finalists, two of which were in Chicago. The following May, the foundation announced it would partner with UChicago and ultimately selected Jackson Park as the location.[60] The Obamas had ties to the area that were both formative and sentimental. President Obama had taught constitutional law at the university. The First Lady grew up on the South Side and once served as vice president for Community and External Affairs at UChicago's Medical School. Moreover, it was the South Side where young Barack earned his community-organizer bona fides.

Never before had a presidential library been placed in an impoverished, predominantly Black neighborhood. It was hard to say anything critical about the South Side's prodigal son, especially when he was coming home. But the partnership between Obama and UChicago also reopened old wounds.[61] And residents began to grumble under their breath about whether the library served as simply a more polite version of campus police in the university's bid to impose its will on the surrounding community.

Shortly after the announcement, Obama began to hear demands for details. Some residents even called for a community benefits agreement (CBA) that would guarantee local hiring commitments and put a freeze on property taxes within a two-mile radius of the project to help stave off potential displacement. The former president met with stakeholders in person and by video conference to try and quickly dismiss concerns. Obama highlighted the job-training programs to be included along with what the foundation estimated would be a $3.1 billion economic impact, from construction up through its first decade of operation.[62]

Despite community concerns, Obama had little patience for talk about gentrification. "It's not my experience . . . that the big problem on the South

Side has been too much development, too much economic activity, too many people being displaced," he argued. "We have such a long way to go before you will start seeing the prospect of gentrification."[63] But real estate numbers suggested that Obama and other supporters may have underestimated the threat of rising land values.

The real estate analytics company Redfin named Woodlawn the third-"hottest" neighborhood in the US for the first half of 2017. The Nathalie P. Voorhees Center for Neighborhood and Community Improvement at the University of Illinois at Chicago released a July 2019 study examining housing conditions within a two-mile radius of the proposed Obama center. It found rising rents in both new and rehabilitated units while eviction rates were among the city's highest.[64] Residents watch as construction crews arrive and the neighborhood slowly scales up, but there is little they can do about any of it.

However, muted grumblings about the Obama Center grew to a groundswell in a place where any critiques of Obama had previously been deemed treasonous. One group sued to halt the project because it places a private Tiger Woods golf course on public park lands. More than a hundred UChicago faculty members signed an open letter in support of a CBA.[65] But the Obama Foundation held firm.

In 2017 Obama directly addressed a Chicago audience, via video, to explain that because the foundation is a nonprofit, no agreement was needed. That answer, given the community's history with UChicago, hardly assuaged frustrations. He went on to underscore his resistance to a CBA by highlighting his community-organizing roots and hence knowledge of how things worked in "the neighborhood." Obama said, "I know that the minute you start saying, 'Well we're thinking about signing something that will determine who's getting jobs and contracts and this and that' . . . next thing I know, I've got 20 organizations coming out of the woodwork."[66] Every time an agreement gets signed, Obama reasoned, there might be another group with their hands out saying they weren't included in the deal.

Matthew, the former UChicago administrator, heard these remarks and agreed . . . up to a point: "I believe there is no question that the Obama Library will have a positive impact. But if you are already promising to do all of these great things already, then why not put it in writing?" Another community leader who didn't want his name on the record was a bit more biting: "When Obama first came to Chicago, he ran to the Hyde Park liberals and the Black middle class. Obama played us like a $2 ho, and he's pimping us right now."

But after years of sustained activism, politicians are finally listening to local concerns and even trying to build in protections against the adverse effects that come from the profit-hungry developers that follow behind nonprofit renewal projects. At the end of 2019, city officials met with alderpersons and community advocates about an ordinance that would keep 30 percent of housing development affordable when city assistance is involved. It would also establish a community trust fund to supply property tax relief as land values rise. As well, the city is trying to buy up properties in Woodlawn, a short distance from the proposed Obama Center, with the expressed interest of allowing current residents the chance to stay in the neighborhood.[67]

Alex Goldenberg has been a stalwart young activist from his student days on the front lines of the trauma-center conflict to his current battle for affordable housing and equitable policing. Goldenberg is now the head of STOP. When I spoke with him in 2019, he said STOP supports the possibilities that come with the Obama Library and takes as good faith its pledge of community commitments. The Obama Foundation has already followed through on efforts to hire people of color and get them into the building trades.[68]

Goldenberg reminded me that the real culprit on the South Side remains his alma mater, UChicago. And he described an earlier struggle with the university that still guides his thinking. While he was a student activist, someone tipped him off to the fact that the university wanted to redevelop Woodlawn's Grove Parc Apartments on Cottage Grove. Through STOP, Goldenberg fought the university to ensure that those apartments would become a site of affordable housing. But now, he told me, "UChicago is taking the credit." The university doesn't simply want to be a good neighbor when it pursues "community engagement." Rather, as Goldenberg put it, "I think what primarily moves the university is a desire for prestige on a global scale." At best, it seems to Goldenberg that UChicago looked at community benefits as a cover for its development interests.

Community advocates attempted to offset rising land values, but UChicago capitalized on the real estate boom. The university partnership with Obama ignited a small building rush of hotels and other amenities, followed by the school's own 1,200-bed student housing complex as part of campus growth south of the Midway Plaisance and west of Washington Park.[69] In the 1960s, urban renewal tensions between UChicago and activists from the Woodlawn Organization led to a brokered compromise for the university to halt building south of 61st Street. It has long breached that line. According to university officials, trust has been built over time, and the expansion ban no longer holds. Susana Vasquez, from the Office of Civic Engagement, said the university hopes that "the line between the campus and the community becomes more seamless." And when UChicago continued to expand, the university used the arts as the cultured face of its aggressive development objectives in South Side neighborhoods.[70]

The Logan Center for the Arts opened on 60th Street in 2012. Its refined galleries and community events served as the avant-garde—the advance guard—softening the blow for waves of academic buildings and residence halls that followed. Soon, Woodlawn will house more students than Hyde Park, with university employees also receiving financial incentives to live in this neighborhood.[71]

During the build-out of what's now called the "South Campus," reporters discovered that UChicago had also quietly bought up twenty-six properties in the Washington Park neighborhood to the west. Some old-timers and university insiders told me the school had long wanted to clean up the dilapidated Garfield Boulevard corridor and hoped to curate a more appealing west-side gateway to campus for visitors coming off the I-90 freeway. The university bought properties from speculators who lost big when Chicago failed to host the 2016 Olympics, with Washington Park targeted for the main stadium.[72]

UChicago ultimately became the only private-property owner on a four-block stretch of Garfield just as Washington Park stood as a finalist for the Obama Center. Alderperson Pat Dowell and community groups rang the alarm of campus encroachment. The university quickly hosted a series of public meetings. And in September 2011, UChicago announced the opening of an art gallery with Black art impresario Theaster Gates.[73]

It's perhaps telling that Gates describes himself as a "real estate artist" who turned abandoned buildings on Chicago's South Side into spaces of Black art and life.[74] His rehabilitation of cast-aside properties became an art practice in itself. He quickly rose to stardom on the power of his 2009 Dorchester Project and its elegant archiving of Black history and culture. For example, Gates turned one of the properties, a former candy store, into the Listening House, which was filled with the inventory from Dr. Wax Records after the shop got kicked out of Harper Court.[75]

In 2013 Gates bought the dilapidated Stony Island Trust & Savings Bank building from the city for $1. He reopened it two years later as the Island Arts Bank, with a majestic exhibition hall and library housing the archives of the Johnson Publishing Company, creators of the iconic *Ebony* and *Jet* magazines, alongside the record collection of house-music legend Frankie Knuckles. After the subprime housing crisis, Gates also grabbed up properties for artists and local tenants that he kept at below-market rates. *Art Review* dubbed Gates the "Mick Jagger of social practice" and the "poster boy for socially engaged art."[76]

UChicago found Gates's "art-as-development" style appealing for its own strategies of urban renewal, especially after mounting concerns about university expansion to the west. In 2011 the school appointed Gates director of its Arts and Public Life Initiative. Gates reimagined university properties on Garfield Boulevard as an "arts block" for Washington Park. A discarded landscape of vacant lots and boarded-up buildings became an arts incubator of galleries and studio spaces. He created Peach's at Currency Exchange Café and Bing Arts Books. Gates also helped launch the massive Green Line Performing Arts Center, which opened in 2018, just south of the transit stop. The properties are beautiful.[77]

All of these projects advance Gates's vision of "ethical redevelopment" and seek to turn his South Side properties into a "destination." But he also understood the potential costs of playing with power brokers from the art world and from the university. Gates is explicit in the desire to "leverage the fuck out of them as they were leveraging me." He walks the trickster tightrope of using the institutional power of a university—which has powered

Black displacement—in order to create what he understands as an art network of "Black space."[78] And opinions about Gates are just as complicated as his development strategy.

Lucas (aka the "Bronzeville Curmudgeon") calls Gates "brilliant," but with a wry smile. Local preservationist Robinson explained that "you know I am jealous of Theaster in a developer-envious way." She admired his ability to move around and get money to complete his projects but concluded that "the reality is Theaster is an operative of the university."

Lucas and Robinson see complexity in Gates's practice, but others have flat-out dismissed his brand of ethical development. On April 20, 2017, Black staff members at his nonprofit Rebuild Foundation set Twitter ablaze with charges that Gates fostered a "racialized hierarchy" between Black frontline workers and a "white managerial class." Critics also accused him of "artwashing": using culture-driven development as what they termed a "feel-good money laundering facility" for UChicago real estate deals.[79] Perhaps this critique was a bit harsh. There is no question that Gates was inventive in his approach to Black historic preservation and the curation of culture. But couldn't his desire for a Black destination coexist with the university's development of an arts corridor on Garfield?

It seems that the balancing act weighed heavily on Gates. After the controversy, he took a three-year residency at Colby College in Maine and no longer directs the Arts and Public Life Initiative. And some wondered aloud: when Black artifacts help dress up campus properties in the neighborhood, what about the residents, the children of those who made the culture?[80]

=

Naomi Davis watched UChicago's various roles in urban renewal, from Woodlawn to Washington Park, and she had her own ideas about what it all meant. Davis had been a lawyer and community organizer who moved to Woodlawn in 2010, looking for cheap housing after the foreclosure crash. But once there, her organization Blacks in Green (BIG) stood at the forefront of advocating for sustainable communities to weather the storm of gentrification.[81] We spoke over breakfast at Daley's on 63rd and Cottage Grove, the city's oldest restaurant, just before it moved across the street under the new Woodlawn Station affordable-housing complex.

Shaking her head, Davis looked out the window at some boys standing on the corner under the train, worried about how they would fare on the city's mean streets. She then began to wax a bit nostalgic about the historically Black middle-class community of St. Albans, Queens, where she grew up, and her desire for places like Woodlawn: "It's what we now call the walk to work, walk to shop, walk to learn, walk to play village." And memories of home merged with the principles of what Davis has dubbed "green village building" to animate her vision of Black urban development.[82] For Davis, "going green" means addressing things such as malnutrition, underemployment, hyper-incarceration, and cultural self-hatred, all toward building a healthy community ecosystem. To create environmental sustainability in Woodlawn, her vision had to move far beyond the typical markers of recycling, bike lanes, and Leadership in Energy and Environmental Design (LEED)–certified buildings.

Like Gates, Davis believed that culture was central to sustainable urban development. And she also gained the attention of UChicago because it wanted to embrace the new green economy. Davis loved teaching in the Center for the Study of Race, Politics, and Culture. But she got frustrated with how university administrators, up the food chain, seemed to promote her class through "showpiece marketing" to their peer institutions in places like New York: "Look what UChicago is doing!" Instead, she reimagined the way she taught the class to resist getting pinned down by university marketing. Davis took students out into the streets and prioritized building relations with the Woodlawn community.

Students helped coordinate with three local businesses to use their storefronts and put on a free program called "The Old Mississippi Fish Fry and Hip-Hop Storytelling Revival." At this four-hour event, they placed sustainability teaching tables in the grocery store—for example, signing people up for energy-saving programs. The middle store featured a vegan soul food plate (and added catfish). The final room showcased a performance of hip hop, jazz, and tap mixed in with stories about Woodlawn. Like Gates's Garfield corridor, Davis imagines 61st Street as its own cultural tourism destination, but one controlled by residents. With this work, she has received some support from UChicago but remains leery about what the university really wants.

Davis looks across the Midway as UChicago's police and building projects continue to head south in her direction. She appreciates the university's interest in her work. But when a school says it has to grow to stay in business, Davis knows what that means for places like Woodlawn: "That's telling me I'm coming for you. I need what you've got in order to live." The university talks about "campus community partnerships," but Davis does not think such a thing exists with UChicago: "This is like Santa Claus, and I'm gonna write the list, buy the gifts. And then I'll be damned if you're not gonna like them. That's not a partnership; that's self-interest at a hyperbolic rate."

She believes that someone like Gates has successfully leveraged the university for his own needs. "But who owns his shit?" Davis asks with a huff. Given the university's long history of exploitation, in her mind there is only one way that UChicago can invest in sustainable urban renewal: "They must devote their considerable assets in creating vehicles for the community to own itself." She believes the university should create something like an endowment that could support technical assistance and help finance local developers. All the money that will be made revitalizing Woodlawn must benefit the local economy. In short, she said it should be Black money: "You want to be Santa Claus, right: that's what I want for Christmas." Anything else is what she called "rape and rescue."

Davis and her vision of a self-sustainable village in the majority-Black neighborhood of Woodlawn are compelling. It is difficult watching UChicago continue to insert its development islands in the middle of depressed neighborhoods while speculators seize on the spotlight of the Obama Center to raise housing costs above the means of local residents. But at the same time, Davis's focus on Black development, ownership, and management is noticeably top-down in some of the same areas for which she denounces the university. She prefers a Black face on standard capitalist strategies of investing in developers with a belief that prosperity will trickle down. Such a vision does not explicitly engage other local demands for workforce housing and fair living wages no matter where residents work, especially while the university remains the largest employer. The village concept is enticing, but what if the Black-controlled financing doesn't trickle down?

Still, organizations such as BIG, STOP, and other members of the Community Benefits Coalition all agree that benefits must be negotiated and not simply handed out. And while the university-backed Obama Center is the current target of community concern, the eight-hundred-pound gargoyle in the room has always been UChicago itself. The university continues to hold leverage in Chicago and exercise significant control over the city's South Side. Its campus police are just the most obvious example. This power has been wielded to bolster the economic value and prestige of the campus at the expense of the poor Black neighborhoods that surround Hyde Park. Now UChicago moves into Bronzeville, Washington Park, and Woodlawn not simply guided by a past history of racist divestment but driven by what seems like a new desire for neighborhood control.

Higher education's urban renewal no longer means bunkering down behind the walls of campus buildings. UChicago now embraces a velvet-hammer approach to expansion, where retail and museums follow behind a militarized version of the campus police who secure various sections of the South Side for university development. What remains, no matter the expansion strategy, is how little concern UChicago and other universities have for the needs and interests of the longtime residents fighting for a right to remain. The Chicago model has been duplicated across the country, from the University of Pennsylvania to Washington University in St. Louis. With this template, city blocks are valuable only when they can be retrofitted to reflect the exclusive image of a university's global brand.

But what if a school can't bank on the brand of aged elitism and selectivity? For public schools without a big-city pedigree or a big endowment, the development plan shifts from exclusiveness to access. The Southwest is filled with states that offer little funding to their public universities while underwriting high speculation in real estate. So schools such as Arizona State University need to find a different approach, and often that looks like eschewing snobbery by packing the campus with as many students as possible and by converting their public land into a for-profit gold mine. We now turn to the Wild, Wild West, where a public university has become one of the biggest guns in the region's already outsized real estate economy—and all without any public oversight.

CHAPTER FIVE

A "PHOENIX RISING"?

They say the idea for an Arizona State University (ASU) downtown campus all began "on the back of a napkin." Phil Gordon told me that, when he was running for mayor of Phoenix in 2003, he couldn't keep the central city off his mind. Gordon first glibly described his interest in downtown as the lure of any city's density, its vitality, "stuff to do . . . getting everything at once." But upon greater reflection, he remembered being impressed by Michael Crow, who had become ASU president a year before Gordon's mayoral victory. Crow boldly promised to build a "new American university." His vision stressed broad access to education and a commitment to "social embeddedness": his cryptic support for a socially engaged campus community.

The new school president set Gordon to thinking: "Who better than ASU"—the largest university in the country—"to invest in central Phoenix" and anchor a "twenty-first-century knowledge economy"? A new downtown campus could help activate the newly opened light-rail system and support the city-funded biomedical campus built on nearby vacant lots.

PHOENIX

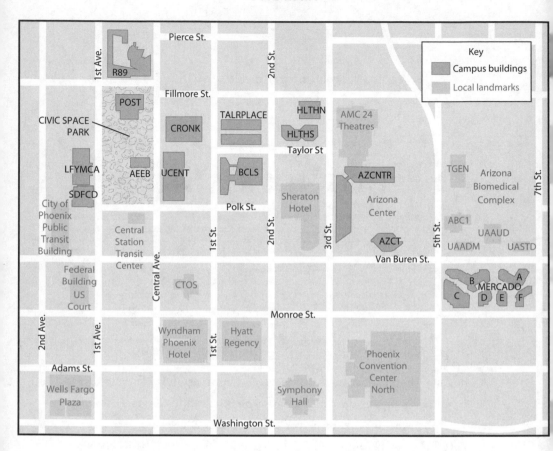

Key
- Campus buildings
- Local landmarks

Pierce St.

1st Ave.

R89

Fillmore St.

2nd St.

POST

CRONK

TALRPLACE

HLTHN

AMC 24 Theatres

CIVIC SPACE PARK

LFYMCA

AEEB

UCENT

BCLS

HLTHS

Taylor St

AZCNTR

TGEN

Arizona Biomedical Complex

7th St.

SDFCD

City of Phoenix Public Transit Building

Central Station Transit Center

Central Ave.

Polk St.

1st St.

2nd St.

Sheraton Hotel

Arizona Center

3rd St.

AZCT

5th St.

ABC1

UAAUD

UAADM

UASTD

Van Buren St.

Federal Building US Court

CTOS

Monroe St.

B

MERCADO

A

C

D

E

F

2nd Ave.

1st Ave.

Wyndham Phoenix Hotel

1st St.

Hyatt Regency

Adams St.

Phoenix Convention Center North

Wells Fargo Plaza

Symphony Hall

Washington St.

So in 2003 Crow and future mayor Gordon met for breakfast in one of the many suburban-style strip malls on Camelback near Central Avenue. There they sketched out the basic plans for the ASU-Downtown campus on a "plain white restaurant napkin."[1]

Crow says he arrived in Arizona as an "academic entrepreneur" at a time when ASU wanted a "builder," meaning someone to restructure the university and maximize its impact on both a local and national scale. Before his arrival in the Southwest, Crow served as vice provost of the Earth Institute at Columbia University, where he garnered attention while creating revenue for the school by making academic research available to private industry. Crow brought his sometimes gruff, always direct, and frequently fast-paced and broad-ranging vision of a "user-inspired" education to what he very explicitly understood as the "academic enterprise." Unlike New York City, Phoenix seemed to Crow like a relatively new and open town with fewer rigid traditions, a place where this wheeler and dealer "could get more done."[2]

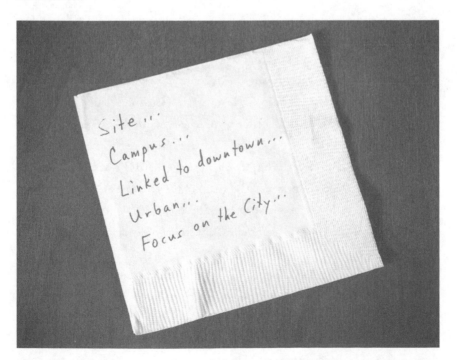

Reconstructed image of "the napkin." Image from Marshall Terrill, *Downtown Phoenix Campus—Arizona State University: The First 5 Years* (Tempe: Arizona State University Press, 2011), 12. Copyright © 2020 Arizona Board of Regents.

Over breakfast, Gordon explained to Crow how important downtown was to the future of Phoenix. The university president agreed and said he would love to have ASU in the urban core. In fact, Crow wanted to move entire colleges the ten miles from the Tempe main campus to downtown. But there was a catch: ASU would supply nothing else but a campus. In the words of Crow, "You give me the land, you let us design or renovate the buildings, you let us pick the spot, and we'll be down there." The university wanted total control . . . for free.

Crow believed the campus signaled an achievement for Phoenix because he could complete a major building project at a faster pace and greater scale than could any other institution. His oversized ego supplied the public service. Crow bragged that within eighteen months of that first meeting on Camelback and Central, "We stood for public election, in a [\$233 million] bond election . . . and won. And within two years from that day we had the whole campus built." Crow and his leadership team believed the mere presence of an ASU campus in the central city could confirm the university's ability to help revitalize downtown Phoenix. The mere presence of the campus would be the public benefit.

Crow then uttered a phrase that I heard over and over from many in the Phoenix elite: "There was nothing down there." In the same way Columbia University called West Harlem a "dead zone," Crow described the downtown Garfield area as "basically a failed neighborhood." The press materials for a five-year retrospective on the downtown campus reinforced this claim: like the proverbial Phoenix rising from the ashes, ASU revitalized a "desolate urban landscape."[3] But was the neighborhood where ASU ended up actually empty, as blank as the white napkin on which Mayor Gordon and President Crow planned the campus? Or were whole blocks *made* available for ASU downtown?

The power of "Big Real Estate" in Arizona looms large here. It seemed like almost everyone I met—whether politicians, activists, or academics— at least dabbled in real estate, and neighborhoods were largely discussed as land deals of financial profit or loss. The downtown Phoenix campus was no different. ASU's description of downtown as an empty frontier—just sitting there, waiting for revitalization—is a compelling but largely misleading narrative. Communities existed in the central city, even when suburban

sprawl started gutting the urban core in the 1950s. But downtown neighborhoods did not generate the kinds of massive dollars per square foot that
drove the city's dominant suburban home-building market. Within a real
estate logic, downtown neighborhoods might have residents, but the land
was seen as vacant until it could generate big profits.

Developers slowly figured out ways to make money from a more urban
lifestyle after overspeculation in suburban Phoenix atrophied the regional
economy. At the same time, ASU was looking for other revenue streams in
the face of a shrinking state budget. These interests in profit converged, and
a public university turned its downtown campus into a lucrative land deal.
The university initially sold the campus as an educational project in order
to win votes for the municipal bond. But ASU-Downtown was always a
real estate transaction. The school packaged its public land to investors as a
closed market of student consumers and as a shelter from the property-tax
burden for private industry.

Downtown small businesses not affiliated with the university struggled to compete in what has become a commercial monopoly, which fun-
nels students into select food franchises and retailers contracted with the
university. Bioscience industrialists and property-development firms also
hide under the cover of "higher education" to profit off of the school's tax-
exempt land. What should be tax investments for the city become direct
payments to ASU, all while property taxes on small businesses rise, funding for the public-school district drops, and public oversight disappears.
And in the process, a public university has become one of the most powerful real estate developers in the city.

═══

We can't understand the importance of ASU-Downtown as a land deal
without situating this project within the history of Phoenix real estate.
Phoenix is the fifth-largest city in the country, but it doesn't house the typical markers often associated with an urban experience. It's often described
as a "doughnut city," with a hollowed-out urban core that has repelled far
more residents and tourists than it has attracted.[4]

When I first visited the city in 2012, the ASU-Downtown campus
was only six years old. It was surrounded by a checkerboard of empty and

overbuilt lots that chronicle the "boom-bust" cycles of the downtown Phoenix real estate game, from dirt patches and cracked concrete to massive but (partially built) block-sized complexes almost falling on top of the few remaining modest bungalow-style houses from earlier times. I looked around at the hollowed-out neighborhoods and wondered: Why did downtown Phoenix look like Detroit, only with a lot more sunshine?

If suburbia could once be described as the physical manifestation of the American Dream, then Phoenix embodied the dream on steroids. But suburban sprawl was not inevitable. Journalist Jon Talton is a fourth-generation Arizonan who knows this history well. After a news career that took him all over the country, in 2000 he got the dream opportunity to come home and write a column for the *Arizona Republic*. But Talton was immediately horrified by what he saw upon his return. He said there had once been a fairly diversified economy of cattle ranching, mining, and early forays into aerospace. These industries were soon overwhelmed by a dependence on real estate development.

Talton used his columns to critique this shift, writing detailed warnings about the state's almost singular "pro-growth" strategy of land speculation and its insatiable appetite for all resources, including vital desert ecosystems and water reserves. Talton recalls that his columns were a threat to what he called "the real estate industrial complex." The pushback was enormous. He received death threats, and then said the paper finally told him, "You can stay, but you can no longer be a columnist." But Talton wasn't in town to be silent.[5] His departure confirmed what many had told me: in Phoenix, real estate is king.

In the mid-twentieth century, white Phoenicians followed the pull of federally subsidized highways, housing mortgages, and even cheaper gas out to the urban periphery. "White flight" marked a demographic shift that happened all over the country, but hardly anywhere else could match the scale and speed of movement found in Phoenix. Yet the word *flight* also obscured the fact that residents were not running away from downtown. Like white urbanites across the country, Phoenicians were actually sprinting toward the publicly funded and racially exclusive economic opportunities found in suburban parts of the city.[6]

Talton detailed a history that I had heard from so many about the city's overreliance on the real estate profits generated by a suburban life. Vacation resorts and home building became *the* economy: "We attracted people with the sun and put them to work building hotels and homes to attract people here to build more hotels and homes. A Ponzi scheme!" All around town you heard "Grow, grow, grow." And after paving over more and more desert, real estate developers hired anyone who could pick up a hammer to build the cheapest homes while pocketing the money. At the peak of the home-building boom, in the 1990s, the urban core was surrounded by planned communities of 200,000 and 300,000 acres. Banks offered bags of credit, based on the belief that everyone desired a single-family home in the middle of the desert. The Homebuilders Association of Central Phoenix became a political force, sustained by the idea that growth, in itself, was an economic strategy.[7] The city became the poster child for suburban sprawl.

The Great Recession of 2007 rocked the nation; most Americans, politicians included, had ignored the economic warnings that had begun as early as 2001. Cities like Las Vegas and Phoenix were hit the hardest because of their commitment to real estate as the primary economic driver. By the end of 2009, Arizona's unemployment rate sat at 10 percent, and the massive home-building "factories" were crippled. One major real estate developer, Fulton Homes, went from serving as one of ASU's largest donors to filing for Chapter 11 bankruptcy.[8]

You could travel across the sprawling Phoenix landscape and see construction signs amid tumbleweeds, massive planned-community graveyards, and housing developments halted in mid-construction. Phoenix was forced to rethink "fast growth" and the almost singular fixation on building the best suburban city. So Phoenicians increasingly turned back downtown. But developers brought with them the same grow, grow, grow land-speculation ethos that had eviscerated the urban periphery and now set its sights on downtown.

=

Brian Kearney saw it all. He came to Phoenix in 1987 and witnessed the city come late to almost every national fad in downtown revitalization, from sports stadiums and convention centers to commercial megaprojects and finally the "meds and eds" campus.[9] He first served as an economic development administrator for the city of Phoenix before moving to the private sector. Kearney worked as the project manager for America West Arena, a sports entertainment venue that he identified as one of the first public/private partnerships of its kind: "The city agreed to pay for the acquisition of the land and pay for 50 percent of the design and construction of the facility, and the city would retain ownership while the Suns [NBA team] would operate the facility." Because the city still technically owned America West, it required a small lease payment instead of what would have been a much more substantial property tax. In many ways the suburban strategy of relying heavily on government funding to underwrite private development got transferred to downtown.

When I asked Kearney why an "entitlements culture" ran so roughshod over the downtown, he sighed and eased into his chair. Kearney made it clear: developers couldn't think outside of the broader suburban economy of land speculation, which relied heavily on public aid. He proceeded to rattle off the massive tax cuts given to various "big-box" development projects downtown, like the America West Arena, that profited from significant public aid. In the booming times of the market, landowners bought land, demolished buildings, and overbuilt massive structures to squeeze the maximum profit from every square foot. And during periods of bust, they just "land banked": sitting on the land and waiting for values to rise again. The downtown became filled with vacant lots, and the city of Phoenix felt forced to step in and purchase the properties.[10]

In places like Chicago, tax increment financing (TIF) has been a very popular tool used by municipal governments to encourage urban development. But Kearney said Arizona preferred the even more developer-friendly government property lease excise tax (GPLET). Under the GPLET, the city takes ownership of the land and then leases it back to the developer at a significantly reduced rate that replaces the normal property tax. Complete tax abatement can last for eight years, and in many cases the city and developer have negotiated a reduced rate that lasts for an additional nine to ninety-nine years. There were very few projects built downtown without some type of tax entitlement.[11]

But in 2002, when the city wanted to plow through the Evans Chur-chill neighborhood to make way for another sports stadium, some resi-dents fought back. Much of the working-class Latinx community had been pushed out of the Evans Churchill and Garfield neighborhoods to make way for sports stadiums and convention centers in the 1980s and 1990s. Of those who remained, many fled under the cover of night in the face of displacement by police raids and racial profiling after Arizona passed its notorious anti-immigration bill, SB 1070, in 2010.[12]

However, a group of primarily Anglo artists and small-business own-ers had also set up shop along the crumbling Roosevelt Row commercial corridor in the area. The difference is they owned their art spaces and had more power as property owners and landlords. They came together as part of the Downtown Voices Coalition (DVC) to halt the stadium push. Their manifesto, "Downtown Voices: Creating a Sustainable Downtown," situ-ated calls for increased density, mixed land use, and walkability within a much broader discussion of affordable housing, historic preservation, and socioeconomic diversity in the city.[13] Their vision of community building posed a direct challenge to business as usual in the downtown. Residents had begun to reimagine downtown development as a site of democratic de-bate, and they demanded a voice in the conversation.

By the turn of the twenty-first century, powerful Phoenicians were forced to expand their understanding of urban development beyond the simple land grab. As Kearney conceded, "I had been intimately involved in stadiums and arenas and convention centers. But we also need the little things to happen in between. . . . To a large degree, they're still struggling with that." When the economic promise of stadiums and convention cen-ters failed, Phoenix wanted to reimagine itself as a hub for the lucrative information-technology and bioscience industries. And politicians and de-velopers slowly began to see the need for neighborhoods filled with "the little things," from local music venues and art galleries to shops that could draw people to work and live downtown.

The "meds and eds" campus seemed capable of offering what both resi-dents and real estate developers wanted. It could turn city blocks into labo-ratories for knowledge-based commerce while also cultivating a local culture to attract its workers and their families. But as much as local stakeholders celebrated campus building as a new day, this development scheme still reinforced the city's unrelenting faith in real estate as the only saving grace.

=

In the 2000s Dave Kreitor served as chief of staff for Mayor Gordon. He saw downtown Phoenix get overburdened by an extremely suburban focus where convention centers and arenas hardly created the promised results. The seasonal home games and other periodical events were not enough to activate downtown or stimulate the economy on a regular basis. Arizona Governor Janet Napolitano agreed. She proclaimed, "We need to turn this city into a destination," and she assembled the Commission on Sustainable Tourism in 2000. The Phoenix City Council followed with its 2004 Downtown Strategic Plan, hoping to reorganize the city in a way that was attractive to those seeking an urban life.[14]

A large segment of millennials had grown frustrated with their lives of isolation, especially in the hyper-suburban sprawl of Phoenix. At the same time, a youthful start-up culture emerged that was organized around data science and digital media. And young people wanted to cultivate a dense urban lifestyle where they could feel connected to their neighbors and their neighborhoods. The info-tech and bioscience industries tended to follow their potential workforce—as in cities like San Francisco, Denver, and New York—and Phoenix fought to compete with other cities for the revenue streams that might come from this synergy.[15] The "meds and eds" campus became a viable land management model for capturing investors, workers, and the urban lifestyle to bring it all together.

The first big infrastructure shift came when the Valley Metro light rail began running in 2008, serving as the connective tissue between academic research in the ASU college town of Tempe and potential new industry downtown.[16] The light rail helped activate the multimillion-dollar investment the city had also spent repackaging a section of downtown into the Phoenix Biomedical Campus (PBC). It opened in 2002 on the lots that were assembled and cleared for the failed stadium bid. This city-owned campus was described as "six million square feet of biomedical research, academic, and clinical facilities."[17]

Phoenix boosters got Jeff Trent, famous as head of the team that mapped the human genome, to come home and build his Translational Genomics Research Institute on the biomed campus. The University of Arizona (U of A) opened a branch of its medical school in the renovated former Phoenix Union High School. ASU and U of A, usually staunch rivals, joined forces in the Arizona Biomedical Collaborative Building (ABC 1). And the new Phoenix Union Bioscience High School was touted as a training ground for tomorrow's scientists and medical professionals.[18] These various facilities became the incubators for cutting-edge work, especially in cancer, neurological, and infectious-disease research. But groundbreaking scholarship wasn't enough; the campus also had to produce tangible economic returns.

By 2009, less than ten years after it opened, the campus claimed an annual economic impact of $77 million in jobs, taxes, spin-off businesses, and the commercialization of research.[19] Phoenicians celebrated the knowledge economy as a shift in how they imagined urban development. But the biomedical campus also confirmed the degree to which people still prized land as a vehicle for quick and cheap economic returns. In a very telling promotional brochure titled *BioIndustry in Phoenix*, city hall revealed how it designed the campus to package and steer a range of tax abatements and "angel investments" toward the biotech industry.[20] Before, the suburban home or the sports stadium had been the best design model to extract public money for private profits. Now land developers looked to the meds and eds campus. And no project demonstrated the resilience of old real estate values in the new knowledge economy better than the ASU-Downtown campus.

Wellington "Duke" Reiter was a Midwestern boy from Akron, Ohio. But by the time Reiter got to Arizona, he had dressed himself up in a "back east" pedigree with a Harvard degree and an MIT professorship. As an architect, his portfolio wasn't of much note. Yet as dean of ASU's College of Design, he cultivated the reputation of a pragmatic, corporate-style administrator who, like President Crow, could get things done. He specifically billed himself as a key player in building the ASU-Downtown campus.[21] When we spoke, he started by recalling his earliest Phoenix days in a way that reinforced the popular, if dubious, southwestern motif of tabula rasa. Reiter looked at the city as a "lunar landscape, so different, otherworldly." He said that arriving in the city in 2003 presented him with the "opportunity to participate in what this city would become, because everything was being conceived for the first time."

By describing the city as a blank slate, Reiter carved out the space for his own importance as an urban expert. In fact, he had just returned from a keynote address in Denver before a group of urban leaders from across the Rocky Mountain West, hungry to replicate the Phoenix model. Reiter converted his experience setting up the downtown campus into a consulting niche for postindustrial urban-design projects, the architectural version of Richard Florida's creative-city model.[22]

Reiter was still in salesman mode after Denver. He wanted me to understand that even amid suburban sprawl, the whole region depended on a vital and active urban Phoenix. So he promoted the campus as an act of what he called "civic ambition" by helping to get people downtown. When Reiter arrived, he joined the city manager and others on a tour of city campuses in New York and Boston, among many places, to help them see how "the city benefits by having a great university." In the run-up to the $233 million bond election, Reiter wanted to convince city hall that a downtown Phoenix campus could work like NYU in Washington Square Park by creating density to improve commercial activity.[23] But Phoenix offered a very different context: "We're talking about filling empty parking lots. Those universities are weaving themselves into an urban fabric that's already dense." He said the campus would serve as an economic "game changer" by helping to insert a density to connect the dots between the growing biomedical clusters and urban living.

The campus plan targeted Central Avenue, which also serves as the commercial spine of the city. Reiter said they first demolished structures to "provide" a civic space (avoiding the word *park*) to the west of Central that signaled a bridge between campus and community. On the east side of Central sat an old big-box building that had once been headquarters to a bank and then to Arizona Public Service (the local electricity utility). This structure was reimagined as the University Center (UCent), the physical anchor for the campus and home to the College of Public Programs. East of UCent, the development team closed down Taylor Street and retrofitted an old Ramada Inn for temporary student housing until building the Taylor Place dormitories. It also converted office buildings into a College of Nursing (Health Innovations 1 and 2). And north of UCent, ASU built the entirely new Cronkite School of Journalism.

Within the new Civic Space, the development team renovated the old AE English building into a mixture of university offices, retail, and public-use venues. ASU also preserved the post office, which sat on the northeastern edge of Civic Space. And the downtown YMCA, just west of Civic Space, was initially shared between local residents and students for their recreation center. In very real ways, the design of ASU downtown became a physical manifestation of partnership.

But Reiter's chronicling of partnerships seemed to always go one way: ASU saving the city. He bragged that ASU "saved" the downtown post office, which was going to be decommissioned, by keeping it open for general business in the front and turning the rest of the building into a student union. Reiter described Taylor Street as "nothing" and contended that by closing it off and placing student dorms and other school buildings around

Aerial view of ASU-Downtown campus looking up Central Avenue, 2012. Photo by author.

its perimeter, ASU had revived the area as an "axis" between various parts of the campus and community. But he spoke less about the ways that a downtown campus also benefited the university.

Underneath all the wonderful declarations of civic ambition, more than one person told me in confidence that the real drive for a downtown campus was to move bodies and make way for profitable research in Tempe. State contributions to the school had plummeted during the Great Recession. It seemed that President Crow pushed hard to make up the losses by turning the school's public land into a for-profit factory, churning out academic research that could generate commercial patents and licenses. But ASU needed more space. It is the largest university in the country, with more than fifty thousand students at its main campus. And it's still growing. However, the main campus in Tempe is landlocked. The school needed room to grow. But no matter the true motivation, the new downtown campus had the capacity to get more people excited about the city center in a still largely suburban town.

Reiter believed that his planning and design of the downtown campus taught suburban Phoenix how to *be* urban. When it came to the light rail, he said, "Our students have quite frankly shown people how to do it." But there were already people in the central city, of course. ASU administrators all said there was "nothing" downtown, yet artists, preservationists, and everyday residents lived in the city and believed that their community could shape the new campus and not just the other way around.

=

For those already in the central city, the land where ASU-Downtown would sit was more than a real estate venture. The Phoenix campus had to attract new investments while engaging the community that already existed. Nan Ellin was an ASU professor of architecture and tireless advocate of arts-driven development during the planning of the campus. She told me that in 2000, two years before Crow arrived, she had organized public downtown events with community members and appealed to resistant administrators about the benefits of an increased ASU urban presence.[24]

Ellin said that when Crow came, he immediately embraced her efforts to physically integrate the university with the city. But then, she laments, things drastically changed after Reiter became dean of the School of Design in 2003. Crow was a very iconoclastic figure; he preferred attention-grabbing pronouncements over the nuts and bolts of a project. The president left the details to Reiter. Ellin says Reiter abandoned the vision of a campus dispersed throughout downtown. He seemed driven by ambitions to be celebrated as chief architect of the new campus, what she called "architectural megalomania." Reiter needed a "clean slate," Ellin believed, because the adaptive reuse of older buildings would not "get you in the architectural magazines."

Other faculty and administrators agreed that the grand ideas of an urban campus like NYU quickly turned into a suburban-style fortress of buildings sitting adjacent to one another. Despite all the public money and promises of civic engagement, the physical design seemed to close the university off from the city. By choosing pragmatism over idealism, ASU acquired buildings that were available and was able to get the campus finished.

Local architect Will Bruder was initially considered for the project. Called the "dean" of Phoenix architecture, he had a proven track record of building truly inclusive civic spaces that aligned with the vision of a campus integrated with the community.[25] But he lost the bid.

Bruder shared his version of events with me on a tour of the main Phoenix Library he designed in 1995. There I saw people from all walks of life flowing in and out of a visibly open and welcoming space by foot, bus, and car to convene around a reading room modeled on the Bibliotheque Nationale de France. Bruder seemed like the perfect designer for an urban campus. When I asked him why he hadn't been chosen, he lamented that "it was Duke's game, Duke's party." Still, Bruder assessed the final results from a practical point of view: "If ASU had not come downtown, what would we be left with? There was a vacuum."

When I spoke to Brooklyn expat and local developer Michael Levine, he didn't have time for diplomacy: "Duke is an eloquent, slick, glib guy but fucking delusional."[26] Levine remembers Reiter and his team coming down to the warehouse district to scout buildings for a dispersed campus plan, but immediately rejected the idea with a backhanded dismissal: "What if a girl gets raped down here?" When I told Levine that both Crow and Reiter had said there was "nothing down there," he gave me an incredulous laugh before exclaiming "Go fuck yourself."

Levine went on to explain that the area where the current campus and Civic Space now exist was a bit seedy—there were strip clubs, bars, and a welding business—but the structures never had to be demolished. "It's not about the strip club; it's about the buildings," he reminded me. Levine supported the idea of a downtown campus, but he charged that ASU could have easily built up and over existing structures, helping to integrate the new school within the architectural history and culture of the community.

Not only did ASU gut the existing streetscape, but according to Levine, the university also replaced it with "crap." For him the final project looked more like a "moated campus" with all the backs of the buildings facing the streets while the Taylor Place dorm included a water-retention area "like in the suburbs." ASU and city officials argued that they ultimately created a more traditional campus because it was pragmatic to establish a clear anchor to build around. But Levine said the city assembled the buildings from its extensive list of properties all over downtown. ASU could have built however it wanted. For Levine, the final campus design was not simply practical but also consistent with the Arizona building model; it was intentionally suburban. He scoffed with finality: "What they built sucks."

Opinions on the architectural design of ASU-Downtown were clearly varied and hotly debated. These different views speak to the competing ideas about how a campus could enrich the urban landscape. The "clean-slate" approach to campus building suggested that ASU looked at the new school as primarily a real estate transaction for its exclusive benefit. A dispersed physical footprint, as opposed to what ASU had ended up building, might have included local businesses in the profits that followed ASU to the city. But whatever ASU had in mind, residents, workers, and students had their own vision for the downtown campus and the value it might add to Phoenix, in ways that exceeded profit.

Before Crow and Reiter had even thought of moving to Arizona, fringe artists like Beatrice Moore pioneered the First Friday art walk in the early 1990s. With a peak of thirty-five thousand attendees, the event was the largest of its kind in the country.[27] Art walks like First Friday blend entrepreneurialism with sustainability and point to a development ethos I continually heard from residents. They wanted to ensure that all of the excitement about the new campus wouldn't lead to the displacement of those who made downtown attractive in the first place.

When I relayed ASU's suggestion that there was "nothing" downtown, Cindy Gentry chuckled, followed by a knowing nod. Gentry worked as the executive director of the nonprofit Community Food Connections. She promoted food security through a network of small, local grocers and producers serving neighborhoods that needed fresh, healthy food.[28] We sat together talking in the shaded parking lot adjacent to the Phoenix Public Market Urban Grocery and Wine Bar, located just north of ASU's Cronkite School of Journalism. Our meeting coincided with the weekly open-air farmers' market that Gentry started in 2005. It has turned into a community institution.

Gentry told me advocates of the farmers' market heard Reiter's call for partnerships and wanted to work with him, but he passed. "He felt we weren't refined enough; he wanted Boston's Faneuil Hall, more sophisticated galleries," she said. But Gentry was proud of what they had accomplished, pointing out to me the people buzzing around from produce stands to food trucks with music playing in the background. This indigenous spectacle of urban revitalization exposed a blind spot in real estate claims that the downtown was "empty." And the metric of dollars per square foot couldn't capture the abundance of value already there.

Phoenix Public Market and shaded parking lot that houses the weekly farmers' market, 2012. Photo by author.

Gentry loved how Crow turned his attention downtown, acknowledging that "he's formidable; he doesn't mess around." She even talked about offering the market space up to ASU's School of Sustainability as an urban laboratory: "They could put in some solar panels, use us to measure heat island effects, create internships. They can bring 150,000 people down here." But Gentry also believed she had something else to offer ASU. For her the farmers' market was the impetus for making community happen.

Reiter talked about the campus as connective tissue, but Gentry described the farmers' market as "the excuse" for relationships, for "setting the table." She too thought about "the market" as an incubator, but not as an incubator for million-dollar engineering and science discoveries. It thrived as a place where ex-felons, immigrants, street people, and refugees grew and sold food locally for a living wage. Gentry told me that she had lived in Phoenix for more than thirty years but that the connections she helped sustain finally made her think about staying. The only question for her and others was how an integrated ASU campus could add to a more inclusive vision of urban development already taking shape.

Members of the DVC were excited about integrating ASU into the existing neighborhood. However, the "moated campus" seemed to send a clear signal of "stay away."[29] They still remained hopeful that aggressive outreach could break down walls and draw out students and faculty as engaged downtown neighbors. But the university established policies that suggested the community was a space to avoid, even fear. When DVC members took students to an arts festival only one mile from campus, they were required to have security and private vans, which reinforced a fear of the neighborhood. And residents pointed out that even though students shared the downtown YMCA, in the name of safety they were provided separate locker rooms.

Kimber Lanning of Local First said that a culture of fear also allowed ASU to make students a captive market. Because of fears about the neighborhood, faculty and student dollars didn't support the city's restaurants; they were funneled through franchises that benefited the school only. She pointed to the contract between the university and the food service giant Aramark. Despite all of the interesting local food options downtown, first-year students were required to purchase a meal plan that restricted them to the cafeteria. Even their more flexible Maroon and Gold (M&G) dollars were limited to chain outlets at the base of campus buildings, such as Subway, Chick-fil-A, and Starbucks. If local restaurants wanted to pay for an M&G card reader to serve students, they were charged exorbitant fees.

Lanning understood that the Aramark food service contract was for all of the ASU branches but believed that it should have taken into account the distinct nature of the downtown campus. She saw the management of the campus as a clear obstacle to stimulating an integrated urban life. All financial, and by extension, social transactions were kept inside the campus. And historic preservationist Jim McPherson pointed out that if it hadn't been for ASU administrators Debra Friedman and Jill Johnson, the university would have remained a suburban campus in the middle of the city.

Friedman became the chancellor at the University of Washington Tacoma in 2012. But before that role, she had really made her name in urban higher education as the first vice president of the ASU downtown campus.[30] Many grumbled to me, off the record, that Crow's vision of a socially embedded campus was all talk, good PR for the bond election. But Friedman persisted as a true believer. Crow told her the downtown campus was "the most exciting project in the nation," and she jumped in before the bond even passed.

As soon as she got to Phoenix, however, Friedman found that much of the talk was more strategy than substance. She told me the "napkin story was apocryphal," a compelling myth that came after the fact to celebrate the campus as an inevitable success. Friedman also said ASU sold the campus as an economic anchor to downtown residents. However, in the bond election they buried the campus line item under a larger push for "education" because polling data said there was little public support for university funding but big support for K–12 schools and parks.

Before she died of lung cancer in 2014, Friedman told me the political gamesmanship forced her to realize that the messaging of social embeddedness was mostly a marketing tool to help generate additional public money. Nonprofit higher education had become a great face for lucrative land deals. Yet Friedman saw the greater value, for students and Phoenix, of having a campus in the community. She got involved with local faith-based organizations, spoke at rallies against SB 1070, and even fought to make sure that all campus buildings remained open to the public. But not everyone at ASU wanted to continue the work she'd begun. A week after she moved to Washington for her new job, Friedman told me, "They closed off the buildings. . . . Claims to a people's university are not credible." Her departure left a significant void among university administrators. Jill Johnson was one of the few left continuing to push students out beyond the moated campus.

Johnson worked as a program manager at the downtown branch of the school's Honors College. Because honors students are required to live in a residential community for at least their first two years, Johnson had to organize a large amount of social activities for them. And she believed a positive urban outlook was key for retaining students on the downtown campus.[31] She knew it was an uphill battle.

Her students had largely grown up in the suburbs, so they equated the city with danger, even though the main campus in Tempe had higher crime rates. But Johnson also said the university didn't help. As she told me, "ASU sells the idea of an urban laboratory experience, but we operate as a fortress of buildings within the city." For Johnson, the height of embarrassment came in 2008 when administrators gave rape whistles to female students even though no assaults had been reported downtown. For her the message was clear: "People who don't look like you are not safe. Stay on campus. But crime statistics show, you need to be more afraid of the frat boy than the homeless person." She agreed with others that administrators used security as a cover to manage control over public land in ways that could maximize ASU profits. By depicting the world beyond campus as dangerous, ASU turned students away from the city and made them a captive market for the retailers and restaurants affiliated with the university.

Johnson described ASU's decision to build downtown as "monumental," but she also believed that the local community had good reason to criticize the double-talk of social embeddedness. Security became a dog whistle for placing university interests over the collective use of public land. She saw historic buildings that didn't need to be torn down to make way for the campus. Although the facilities that remained were "public" in name, they prioritized ASU needs: "If I wanted an event at the A.E. building, my name went to the top of the list. Events in the public park were closed off unless you have an ASU card, but there is free food that will be thrown away" after the event.

Still, Johnson fought hard against the fortress mentality. Her "cultural encounters" course took students to neighborhood events and out to speak with community experts about urban life in downtown Phoenix. She also patronized local businesses that brought in local food for campus events. For Johnson, "These young people are not just students but citizens of the downtown area."

Despite legitimate critiques, Johnson said there were clear examples where ASU's abstract notion of social embeddedness helped transform students from consumers to citizens. Students in social work, nursing, and other related fields offer health services and counseling to senior residents in the historic Westward Ho building, which was renovated for subsidized housing.[32] And with the *Arizona Republic* facing severe cutbacks, the student-run *Downtown Devil* has become the paper of record for the central city.

One former student, Vaughn Hillyard, told me that Johnson changed his life. While an undergraduate at Taylor Place, he participated in her course and went on the bus tour. But Hillyard felt bad that her programming serviced only the honors students because the impact on the students was so profound. He said, "The Barrett students are so much more connected, and it's not because they are honors students. It's because of what they are introduced to, and it's amazing. Just look at the amount of activities they partake in, the number of places they know. Their feeling of community is so much stronger."

Like others, Hillyard saw a huge disconnect between ASU's stated principle of social embeddedness and its application in the actual city. He told me that the "little L" design of the campus created an enclosed portal reinforced by what he called a "food monopoly." He said such policies also trained students to stay among their peers and to fear difference. One student disgusted him when she ran for student office on the platform of protecting students. According to Hillyard, she said students needed protection from prostitutes on Van Buren and called for a separate Rec Center because sharing the Y was dangerous, which for her meant the building was old and included "government housing." He laughed because although there were sex workers on Fortieth and Van Buren, that was miles away: "She didn't even know her own city!" The disconnect between the university and its urban community is what pushed Hillyard to act.

Hillyard became a full-fledged citizen of downtown, writing a column for the *Downtown Devil* student paper and advocating for local businesses.[33] He had mixed results trying to secure rental space on campus for a local bike co-op and working to find additional parking in empty campus lots for local businesses when construction blocked public spaces. Hillyard then shifted focus and cofounded the student organization Downtown Alive, which served as what he called a "good corridor," a way to connect students with the community where they live. When he saw students slowly venture over to Food Truck Fridays at Phoenix Public Market or grab coffee from Jobot on Roosevelt Row, it was more than commerce; it signaled urban citizenship. He had little patience for students' fear of the neighborhood: "This is a city; it's an urban environment; it's where you live."

But policies continued to amplify the university's nagging insistence on dictating the public use of campus space. One day in 2012, I noticed something new. There was now a metal placard on the glass of the University Center door: "The ASU Downtown Phoenix Campus buildings and facilities, including the common areas, are for the use of ASU students, faculty and staff, individuals or groups associated or affiliated with or invited by the University, and building tenants and their invitees. Any other use without the permission of Arizona State University is prohibited." It seemed to me that a publicly owned and funded campus had created an ASU-only trespassing policy. The university explained that although the city owns the land, it is leased to ASU, so it can dictate how the land can be used.[34] But with a public university campus now claiming basically private use, residents wondered whose interests was ASU actually serving.

That same year, Greg Stanton became the new mayor of Phoenix. He pointed to students and residents sharing the downtown YMCA as representing the best integration of a public university and its community. But I thought of the new Sun Devil recreation center, where both facilities would still remain shared, yet students had their own locker rooms and Y members were excluded from the rooftop pool.[35] These distinctions between student and resident gym use may seem minor, but they took on different meaning within the context of the new university "trespassing" policy.

I wanted to know if the mayor saw the ASU-Downtown campus as a truly public space. Did the value of the campus extend beyond its function to serve those who paid tuition or generated other kinds of revenue for the university? Does the wider public have a say about the terms of campus integration and land use? Stanton looked a bit pressed by my questions but maintained that the common areas in campus buildings "must remain open to the community; they must feel welcomed, or it won't be successful. . . . Tax dollars are used here." Then Stanton paused, took a deep breath, and looked back at me with a firm gaze: "The campus cannot become the University of Chicago."

≡

I went back to Phoenix in 2018. Six years had passed. Things were certainly different. Stanton had ascended to the US House of Representatives. Hillyard had become a political journalist at *NBC News*. Gentry had parted ways with the Phoenix Public Market Urban Grocery and Wine Bar, and in 2012 it closed. It reopened one year later as a "chic/bar eatery," the Phoenix Public Market Café, which buzzed during my visit with a very different clientele of tourists, businessmen, and soccer moms. After protest from Downtown Voices, ASU had taken the trespassing signs down. The university even started to disperse its downtown campus in 2016 after relocating graduate art programs to the Grant Street Studios, a building in the Warehouse District that it had purchased from Levine.[36]

ASU also "phased out" Johnson and her Community Encounters course in 2014. Everyone told me that students were all over downtown. Some said the course was no longer needed. According to a 2018 press release, the ASU campus sat "in the thick of the whirlwind resurgence that has made downtown Phoenix an enviable hot spot."[37] This bold claim was part of a self-promotion package, but it's hard to deny the impact of a reported 13,000 students, 7,000 residential units, 400 tech and creative companies, and hundreds of thousands of tourists that followed behind ASU-Downtown.

The new vibrancy of downtown Phoenix was certainly alluring. I mingled at a well-attended Phoenix Art Museum event where I met D'Lisa Shayn. She had recently moved her hair salon downtown from the well-heeled suburban enclave of Scottsdale, which had long been the hub for the affluent resorts and golf courses driving the snowbird tourist economy in the state. We stood at a wall-sized window looking at the light rail amble down Central Avenue. When it passed, Shayn pointed to a new apartment complex across the street, where her salon sat in a storefront at its base. She giddily explained to me that she never would have been able to come downtown had it not been for all of the development that followed the ASU campus.

Shayn grew particularly animated when she matter-of-factly proclaimed, "As far as I am concerned, ASU can gentrify the whole thing." She went on to tell me that the bulk of her clients are university graduate students, many of them living in the apartments directly above her shop. Shayn then whispered, "They are the only people living downtown who can afford my Scottsdale prices." She understood that all of this new development would make it harder for longtime residents to afford the rising real estate prices. And I could hear guilt in the way she began speaking to me in low tones. But as an upscale-salon owner, Shayn welcomed the benefits that came when ASU drew developers back to the central city. Not everyone felt the same way.

"They steamrolled us," Stacey Champion replied when I asked her about the impact of urban revitalization on the downtown community. In January 2015 she helped lead a protest in the drizzling rain, marching up and down Roosevelt Row with signs and a coffin marking the death of the arts community.[38] The properties that were demolished on 3rd and Roosevelt made way for iLuminate, one of the many upscale student or luxury apartment complexes now casting a long shadow over the few bungalows that remained. She agreed with other locals who screamed from the headlines, "Stop Calling Roosevelt Row an Arts District."[39] For many, the name Roosevelt Row had become simply a real estate designation to draw in tourists, developers, and students as blocks of tall, cookie-cutter apartment buildings now overshadow the murals, grit, and quirkiness of the neighborhood.

Champion reminded me that their fight against the current downtown land rush wasn't simply nostalgia for the good old days. Residents had struggled for a right to inhabit and not just serve those in the new city: "Five years ago, folks could pay 5 to 600 bucks to live in Garfield with gallery space in the front and housing out back. But a tiny studio in these new apartments are $1,200 to $1,400 a month." She worried there was no housing for artists in the arts district or for the low-wage workers who cooked in the restaurants, cleaned the offices, and took care of students at the downtown campus.[40] And another group that rarely got included in discussions was the small-business owners, who also struggled to remain.

"No one pays taxes," Kurt Schneider blurted out with a huff. Schneider described himself as a "culturally interested developer." He owned the property that housed the Public Café and the farmers' market. Schneider grew up in Seattle going to Pike's Place and remained committed to supporting a balanced combination of local retailers and national franchises that could make a real urban neighborhood. A few years ago, however, Schneider saw his property taxes skyrocket. He did some digging and discovered that because his downtown properties were surrounded by buildings with the GPLET tax abatement, small-business owners were left picking up a larger share of the tax burden.

In reality, the GPLET did not raise Schneider's taxes directly, but a 2009 state policy included the value of these tax-free properties when calculating the amount of state aid that a school district received.[41] Because of this new calculation, Phoenix Public Schools received less funding, and the difference was covered by non-GPLET property owners like Schneider. Far too many big developers didn't pay taxes, small businesses were left to pick up the slack, and residents lost vital resources that got paid for by taxes. "You're enriching someone else's private property at my expense," Schneider said. "I am being slowly condemned. It's like a reverse condemnation."

Schneider found out that some of the massive new apartment complexes, including Roosevelt Point, paid no taxes. Roosevelt Point also got financial support from a fixed contract with ASU to supply upper-division student housing. The downtown market may not have been able to fully support all of the new luxury apartments, but the financial aid given to projects like Roosevelt Point helped support what Schneider called a "false economy." The GPLET didn't cover ASU, but as a nonprofit public institution on city land, it also added to the list of properties that passed the tax burden on to non-GPLET property owners. Schneider still said he liked having ASU downtown, "but I didn't know that by having them there I was going to be paying for it." Public outcry forced slight reforms of the GPLET, but the changes had little concrete effect.

Still, the spotlight placed tax-exempt ASU under greater scrutiny.[42] Phoenix had certainly entered new times. Now higher education had joined the list of developers profiting from the same old deals. And everyone wondered how the urban development focus on "meds and eds" would catapult ASU to an even greater position of power.

In January 2018 I attended the monthly DVC meeting. The group continues to serve as a sort of civic association reporting on various activities affecting the downtown community while also hearing reports from developers and small-business owners attempting to garner support for their projects. On this day, Bob Woodruff from Wexford Science + Technology came with Rick Naimark, who had been recruited from city hall to serve as ASU's associate vice president for Program Development Planning. They shared plans for a 200,000-square-foot building as part of a larger "innovation center" on city-owned vacant lots at the north end of the Phoenix Biomedical Campus.[43] It was just blocks south of the transformed Roosevelt Row. ASU proposed to lease half the building, with the rest occupied by private companies in the bioscience sector.

In his presentation, Woodruff immediately started by dangling the carrot of "Cambridge and Palo Alto," places where MIT and Stanford used city land to convert academic research into profits, making them vital economic engines. "Everyone else is playing catch-up," he stated frankly, with a long pause for dramatic effect. Woodruff also went to great lengths to discuss how this project was *not* an enclosed campus. It would be what he called a "district," a space that is welcoming, walkable, and available for community events alongside food trucks, pop-up retail, and temporary parks. "We don't build where you have to have a badge to get in," he assured the crowd.

There was no question that at a DVC meeting, Woodruff knew his audience. But the emphasis here on a permeable district and community use was not without context. In the same moment, ASU was battling growing outrage over what many described as the public university using its tax-exempt land to provide a tax shelter for private companies on the main Tempe campus. Would ASU produce an additional tax burden on downtown residents with its new Wexford project?

That same month, with a six to one vote, the Tempe City Council approved an Omni hotel and conference center project that would pay almost no sales tax for up to thirty years. It would also pay no property taxes because it would sit on university land owned by the Arizona Board of Regents (ABOR). The state had continued to pull back on its contributions to public higher education, and ASU began to look for new revenue streams.

University administrators realized that they could lease their tax-exempt land to private companies, and instead of shelling out property taxes, these companies could make a lower direct payment to ASU. Elected officials would have no authority over how the money could be spent. The Omni hotel deal showed how ASU found a way to profit from its nonprofit land within a heavily deregulated real estate economy. Tempe is such a college-dependent town that business leaders and council members fell in line, simply parroting the ASU media message that the project promised to create jobs and spark tourism in the area.[44]

Kolby Granville was the lone dissenting council member and said he had good reason to vote the way he did. First, Granville explained there was little public oversight or residential input before the vote, with only closed executive meetings for two years. Second, he pointed out that two of the seven council members worked for ASU and that no one raised concern about the conflict of interest. Finally, Granville criticized the impact that tax-exempt projects had on the surrounding communities. "We are landlocked, and gentrification is a real thing," he said. The tax-free status of these ASU "innovation zones," along with the regular campus, raised property values to the point where ASU graduates couldn't afford to buy in town. With tax exemption, the university also didn't contribute to public services: police, road maintenance, K–12 schools, etc.

But he didn't fault ASU. "I applaud the universities!" Granville told me. President Crow explains that it is crucial that universities find other revenue streams in the face of shrinking state contributions to higher education: "We have found a new revenue source . . . for the things that we need to balance the operating budget and to advance the interests of the university."[45]

Granville called it a creative tactic to offer private companies shelter from taxes in exchange for a reduced payment that can be used for university expenses. But he did lament, "No one contemplated tax-exempt status was to pay an extra $300,000 for a football coach." Granville was referring to ASU's successful recruitment of former NFL coach Herm Edwards.

Sean McCarthy, unlike Granville, had little sympathy for ASU's stated plight. He is a research analyst with the Arizona Tax Research Association. And after reading an *Arizona Republic* article about the Omni deal, McCarthy put together a scathing policy review detailing the long history of "tax free zones" at ASU.[46] He specifically identified the State Farm Insurance complex on campus as the height of university corruption. The Arizona Board of Regents holds the deed to the land and leases it back to State Farm, which allows the largest commercial development in Arizona to pay ASU a fraction of what it would disburse if the company's property was on the tax rolls.

Arizona Attorney General Mark Brnovich shared McCarthy's outrage, and in January 2019 he sued the Arizona Board of Regents for essentially renting out its tax-exempt status to private businesses. Few were surprised when Brnovich lost the case in developer-friendly Arizona.[47] But residents in Phoenix watched all of this political theater with great interest. How would ASU's franchising of tax-free zones shape its partnership with the Wexford innovation district just off Roosevelt Row?

I asked Naimark about the financial structure of the Wexford project. He told me that with city land, the taxing structure was determined by the county assessor, but the lots were designated for educational purposes. Therefore, Naimark anticipated that Wexford would not have to pay property taxes. When I pushed him on the loss of tax revenues to service city needs, especially in light of the Tempe controversies, Naimark got a bit defensive. He first said those empty lots were city owned and had never produced tax revenue, so there is no conflict. But he quickly added, "Look, the anticipation is there will be no property tax, but if there is a property tax, there is a property tax."

I could hear the anger rise in McCarthy's voice when I told him what Naimark had said. He described ASU's approach to these educational land deals as "cavalier." For McCarthy, the university had a duty to ensure that its tenants or developers paid the correct taxes: "It's a dodge to say it's all on the assessor." He went on to explain that the classic "but for" argument was unacceptable. One can suggest "but for" the Wexford–ASU arrangement, those empty lots wouldn't have generated tax revenue anyway. But especially given the growing interest in development around Roosevelt Row, the city could have sold the land to a taxpaying private entity. In the end, McCarthy said it was fine if Wexford wanted to build ASU a space. But if any private, for-profit work takes place on that land, it should be taxed for the benefit of the public. He was emphatic on this question: "A private concern should not be exempt, period!"

Real estate developers and university leaders promised a new prosperity. And the largely white urban residents downtown fought for walkability, density, and urban excitement. But we still hear so little from those invisible voices in Phoenix. The experiences of Latinx, African American, and Native American residents who struggled to hold on in the central city or were pushed to the fringes told a different story. These were the Phoenicians who, in the words of Gentry, "have their nose on the glass looking at downtown." ASU had successfully shielded its raw real estate ambitions under the cloak of higher education. But it wasn't just artists who looked beyond profits to imagine how land could be developed differently in the changing city.

Diana "DeDe" Devine reminds us that downtown Phoenix is also a historic Native American neighborhood. Devine is the president and CEO of Native American Connections (NAC), an organization that has served the Phoenix area Native community since 1972. Devine told me that, initially, American Indian men were pushed to central cities, such as Phoenix, after the federal government wanted to take land from reservations: "They would get off at the bus depot and find themselves homeless on the streets of Phoenix. You know, in the bars, and it was a skid row downtown at the time." NAC began with the name Indian Rehabilitation, working to create a grassroots support network. It originally provided supports for Native men struggling with homelessness and alcoholism after being displaced from reservations and thrown into the racism and rootlessness of Phoenix.

She said that advocates quickly saw that Native American residents were not doing well in traditional problem-focused treatment practices. Devine explained that addiction had to be understood as part of the larger trauma of dislocation, the cultural annihilation of Indian boarding schools, and the consequences of American colonialism. NAC began integrating Native cultural and traditional healing practices—sweat lodges, drumming, spiritual counseling—within a more comprehensive behavioral health program of wellness. NAC insisted on creating pathways for people to transition from addiction to a supportive, drug-free environment.[48]

Devine showed me a little house on 3rd Avenue between Roosevelt and Van Buren. It was the first place where NAC integrated drug treatment, housing, and job placement with a sweat lodge in the backyard. And Devine's ears pricked up when the city made announcements about the light rail and ASU coming downtown in the early 2000s. NAC's clientele lived in the city, and land values were rising, so NAC had to formulate a strategy to stave off Native American displacement. She explained that they took the sizable winnings from a bet and started buying properties in 2005 right along the projected light rail to stabilize their mission within a changing urban core. Just as ASU arrived, NAC popped up in the very same spaces with "services-enriched" affordable-housing complexes as the base of its own vision of urban revitalization.

Just two blocks northwest of the post office that ASU partially converted into the student center sits Urban Living 2 (UL 2). This complex is one of NAC's more than ten developments. Devine relayed to me the importance of these properties in the historic Native American neighborhood.[49] "It's not an apartment. It's a community to them." The services and structure of the buildings vary, but there was a general approach to community building in the heart of downtown. Unlike the real estate culture that dominated Phoenix, the NAC valued land for the stability it provided people more than for the profits it could generate.

Residents live in new units with stainless-steel appliances and pay rents between $300 and $700 per month, depending on the number of people, unit size, and family income. The apartments are built to face a community space surrounded by a range of family services from laundry rooms to child care and tutoring services. All of these buildings include a cultural matrix of sweat lodges, spiritual leaders, and ceremonies. I sat, awestruck, as Devine showed me a vibrant layer of downtown Phoenix that I had never

Urban Living 2 apartments, 2018. Copyright © Babe's Photos, photography by Babe Sarver.

seen before. This world of affordable, services-enriched community building seemed almost impossible, especially given the real estate assumptions
and political outlook governing Phoenix.

Devine confirmed that affordable housing was still a "dirty word" and
that most people used "attainable" or "workforce" as code-word covers to
service a wider swath of the population. But she said that NAC couldn't
afford to worry about the stigma of equitable housing. For the last twenty
years, it had used low-income-housing tax credits to underwrite its multi-
family projects.[50] The federal government issues tax benefits to state housing authorities, which then put out a request for proposals from low-income
housing developers like NAC. Once NAC wins a tax benefit, it finds an
investor—usually banks or insurance companies—that buy the tax benefit
with cash that's used to finance the housing.

Critics argue that the tax credit here benefits wealthy investors more
than the tenants. Instead, subsidies should go directly to community-based
groups that build resident-controlled housing. But it seemed NAC had
found a sort of middle ground by using the market to help fund its community building. I asked Devine why NAC didn't sell these properties along
the light rail in such a hot market. She smiled: "People don't get us because

our mission is not real estate development. Our mission is stable housing for people on transportation corridors, regardless of income, so that they can have a clean, quality place to live with access to the services and the amenities they need." NAC saw the depth, and not the emptiness, of life on Phoenix city blocks long before the university came downtown.

Without much irony, the story that ASU told about downtown mirrored tales of Columbus discovering the "New World" or the manifest destiny of homesteaders taming the western territory. Only this time it was a public university using the old motif of a blank slate to profit from the new metrics of real estate speculation. There was nothing there, the logic goes, so our mere presence is a public good in itself. But, of course, people were already there.

When Anglos were allowed to follow government-sponsored prosperity to suburban Phoenix, a whole world remained downtown. We know that Latinx residents created vibrant communities in Garfield and Evans Churchill right on the land that became the biomedical campus. A smaller African American population settled in the East Lake neighborhood on the southeast fringes of the central business district. Asian Americans lived up and down the Central Avenue corridor long before the light rail was built. And Native Americans turned skid row into a community of refuge when the doughnut city took shape. It is the living legacy of these urban stakeholders that could and should guide the design and management of an ASU campus and its claims of social embeddedness. The children of this legacy continue to live downtown, and their stories point toward a different urban future.

Devine said she wishes that market-rate developers would have reached out to NAC with a desire to include some affordability in their projects. She points to the lack of a political will among city leaders but also blames ASU for failing to cultivate a language around community-based development. Devine gives Crow credit for building the downtown campus and bringing ASU out of the ivory tower. But she also believes that university lobbying efforts focus only on the university's interests. "They fail as a community partner," Devine lamented.

ASU is often presented as the "savior" of downtown Phoenix because it used its campus as an incubator to raise land values and spur economic development. This public university points to the broad ways in which higher education is now being envisioned as an anchor in our cities. And we have to wonder about the cost of salvation when a public campus is restricted, residents are displaced, and private profits are sheltered—all land-use practices that serve the university's wealth-building interests to the detriment of the public good.

Whether ASU-Downtown will serve as a profit university or a people's university remains to be seen. Art Walk, the farmers' market, and NAC's Urban Living 2 housing complex all point to ways the university can learn from equitable urban development that already exists downtown. The promise of the campus is still being written into the concrete and steel of the city blocks. If anything, Devine's Urban Legacy housing developments remind us that ASU and the developers that followed must see themselves more as a guest rather than as a host in Phoenix. The city is not theirs alone to build out and govern.

And like Devine, there are people all across North America speaking back with their own visions about the way higher education can best serve their cities. The raised voices of students, the declarations of community groups, and the proposals of local leaders can become the blueprints for better universities sitting at the heart of our shared urban future. Let's listen.

THE IVORY TOWER
IS DEAD!

In the fall of 2017, I was in Canada, at the University of Winnipeg, giving one of many lectures about the increased role that colleges and universities are playing in our cities. The audience sat in stadium-style seating. And as I started to outline my case, a man in a suit, right at my eye level, kept staring at me with a very focused level of intensity. At different points in my lecture, he would smirk or vigorously whisper to the man sitting next to him. It was almost disruptive. I assumed that he was a university administrator who felt a certain way about my arguments. And when the lecture ended, he was the first one in line to talk to me. He introduced himself to me as Sherman Kreiner. And I was right; he served as a university administrator, and he did feel a certain way about my lecture. But I was wrong about why. "Have you ever been to our campus before?" Kreiner asked. And when I said no, he asked me to give him a few hours the next day for a tour. "I want to show you some things," he declared.

That next day Kreiner pointed out various buildings, and from the out-side it looked like one of the many urban campuses I had traversed over the years. But in fact, the University of Winnipeg was a city school I had never seen before. He revealed to me a place that might be the model for re-thinking the campus city. As we walked to the McFeetors residential hall, Kreiner gave me some history of the school.

In the early 2000s the university stood at a crossroads. The school was broke, the buildings were crumbling, and somehow student enrollment had exploded from six thousand to ten thousand students. UWinnipeg worked largely as a commuter school where students came to campus, took classes, and quickly left for neighborhoods on the city's periphery. But the school experienced a demographic shift toward First Nation and New Canadian (immigrant) communities who were adult learners with their own families and hence had nontraditional housing and support needs. The university could either continue to tuck away from the impoverished indigenous areas surrounding UWinnipeg or build a new relationship with its city.[1] When Lloyd Axworthy came to campus, he changed everything.

Axworthy was a political powerhouse. The onetime Canadian minis-ter of foreign affairs, he became the president of UWinnipeg in 2004.[2] Always interested in urban and environmental issues, Axworthy came to the university with a clear mandate for a broad sense of sustainable devel-opment that included not just the environment but also social, economic, and cultural matters. Under Axworthy, the school decided to bypass the costly consulting fees of outside developers and create its own nonprofit community-renewal corporation (UWCRC) guided by the four pillars of sustainable development.[3]

After giving me this brief history, Kreiner then pointed to McFeetors Hall and explained how its 2009 opening stood as one of the first mani-festations of the new sustainable philosophy. Not only is this residential hall certified according to Leadership in Energy and Environmental De-sign (LEED) standards, but it also combines dorm-style beds overlooking twenty-five townhouse apartments. These townhouses meet the needs of nontraditional students and their families by offering affordable rents at 60 percent of the city's median market rates for those who are eligible. Ten of the units are available to community members taking classes anywhere in the city. And the UWCRC worked with the student government to add forty spots to the day care behind McFeetors for the community. If that wasn't enough, Kreiner's associate, Jeremy Read, walked me farther through campus to tour the other major development: Downtown Commons.

The Commons opened in 2016 and was intentionally designed to serve as a crossroads for "new urbanites" excited to live in a diverse residential community. And the entire complex is sold out with a waiting list. Read explained that eighteen premium units help underwrite this fourteen-story, 102-unit mixed-income development. The premiums have balconies, slightly different finishes, and a suite laundry. "But all the rest of the units are interchangeable," he smiled. Thirty-one affordable units are reserved for UWinnipeg students and families. The remaining apartments are open to the broader community, including fifteen apartments for immigrant student families moving from transitional housing and, at one point, five units for Syrian refugees.

All of the units are available at both market and affordable rates, and eligible tenants can receive an additional rent-geared-to-income (RGI)

Downtown Commons, Winnipeg, 2020. Photo by Foxtower Photography.

subsidy.[4] Read said they wanted to avoid any stigma based on income. The community-renewal corporation got Manitoba Housing to exempt it from the modesty restrictions so that all units could have the same building materials and amenities, such as air conditioners. The common area is publicly accessible and properly ventilated to allow for indigenous smudging ceremonies. It also includes free Wi-Fi for those who can't afford individual subscriptions. And Read said that because the Commons invested in an electric car-charging station, it was able to get Peg-City Co-op to provide one free membership for the whole building. Tenants just have to pay a charging license and the per-use fee. I was overwhelmed by what I saw, but these two buildings were just the beginning.

As Read walked me back to talk more with Kreiner, he pointed out the Axworthy Health and RecPlex that opened in 2014. He reminded me that Winnipeg gets insanely cold in the winter, so it is vital to have indoor convening spaces. The UWCRC entered into a community charter modeled on the one crafted during the 2010 Vancouver Olympics. According to the charter, at least a third of RecPlex operating hours "during critical time" are reserved for community organizations. Requests are managed by a community representative who schedules everything from sports leagues to pow wow clubs and drumming circles. On the way out we also took a quick detour to the cafeteria.

Once in the dining area, I looked for signage from one of North America's university food service behemoths, such as Aramark, Sodexo, or Chartwells. But no. In the corner was a modest little insignia for Diversity Foods. That's where I met Diversity's chief operating officer, Ian Vickers. He was happy to show me around. As workers buzzed through the industrial kitchen, Vickers explained that at one point, UWinnipeg did have a contract with Chartwells. But according to lore, one day Axworthy was preparing to host an international delegation, and he sampled the food. It was horrible. Axworthy reportedly said, "I can't ask people to eat this food!" In 2009 Diversity Foods was born. Driven by the same broad pillars of sustainability, Vickers showed me how everything is made from scratch and 65 percent of the supplies come from small family operations within a radius of 100 kilometers. Every workstation has a compost bin, and cooking oil is shipped off and turned into biodiesel.

On the employment side, at least 65 percent of the workers must be "marginalized employees," whether that be new Canadians, indigenous, nongendered, or the formerly incarcerated. And many items on the menu, from jollof rice to butter chicken, are scaled-up versions of recipes that workers bring from home. Vickers said Diversity ultimately wants to create a workers' cooperative model for profit sharing. He admits that this vision of sustainability is hard to maintain in the food industry, but the catering work helps underwrite additional costs. Diversity also has off-campus kitchens at an environmental recreation center and a golf course to give workers summer hours that keep their benefits going.

Vickers was emphatic when talking to me: "This is not something you can franchise. We are focused on creating a sustainable ecosystem for our community. If your goal is simply to make money, the Diversity model is not for you!" He may have been right about the challenge to franchise Diversity. But UWinnipeg's sustainable-development model got so popular that the UWCRC started working off campus.[5] Among many new developments, Kreiner was happy to highlight a venture that his team consulted on in the predominantly indigenous north end. "They couldn't have done the Merchants Corner project without us," he said.

The day after talking to Kreiner and Read, I went to Selkirk Avenue, in the north end of the city, and spoke to Jim Silver, professor and chair of Urban and Inner-City Studies at UWinnipeg. I wanted to get another perspective on the university's innovative work. The university's renewal corporation consulted on the new Merchants Corner community complex in the north end where Silver worked. "I think Sherman [Kreiner] overestimates the importance of the UWinnipeg CRC," Silver bristled. "It's true; we needed technical support in the areas of development. But they earned a hefty fee, and if not them, we would have purchased the support elsewhere."

The UWinnipeg Renewal Corporation engaged with the community in ways that I rarely saw from a city school in the United States. Still, Silver reminded me that Merchants Corner was a project that included UWinnipeg but was not driven by university interests. Its mission was completely governed by the needs of the indigenous community where it sat. He said I needed some important context to understand the magnitude of what Merchants Corner was doing.

As we walked around the active construction site, Silver explained that in the early 2000s he was conducting community-based research in the north end. He knew the horrible history. Eastern European immigrants first occupied this community, literally on the other side of the tracks, working in the rail yards, factories, and packinghouses. After World War II, white families fled to the suburbs, leaving behind ramshackle workers' shanties. By the 1960s, indigenous people left the reserves in search of jobs and educational opportunities for their children. As they moved to the city, the only thing available was the broken-down, abandoned housing in the north end. And jobs had also left just as they arrived.

Indigenous people had escaped the dehumanizing residential schools but entered an urban environment of no jobs, poor housing and health conditions, and racism. When Silver arrived to do research, he confronted an area ravaged by substance abuse, gang violence, and municipal divestment.[6] But he saw something else amid the disarray, young people looking for new ways to explore their aspirations in a neighborhood that had been discarded by the city: "These guys are really smart; they just don't have access. Maybe we can do something different right here in the community."

In 2009 Silver asked his dean if he could move Urban and Inner-City Studies to the north end. The dean said no. After many efforts, Silver finally caught Axworthy's ear. The president liked the idea but said Silver had to find his own money. Eventually, he secured a grant from the Council on Post-Secondary Education to pay rent for a space in the north end and replace his position on the main campus.

Since 2010, Silver has been teaching what he calls "urban studies from the margins," with a focus on urban poverty, indigenous culture, and community advocacy. "We do things different here on Selkirk Avenue than the main campus," he told me. His reference to doing things differently offered a subtle confirmation of some grumblings at the main campus about Axworthy and his urban engagement focus on large-scale brick-and-mortar projects when some wanted greater resources for faculty and student services. Silver showed me that on Selkirk, the classes are smaller, they offer free tutorial and social supports, and they promote lived experience in the classroom. He said that the main campus is happy to celebrate what he has been able to accomplish, but for Silver it has always been an initiative driven by the community: "What we are doing here was not initiated by the university, not initiated by the senior administration. I have been very much left to sink or swim." And the Merchants Corner project signaled that they were doing far more than just treading water.

I came back only a year later, in May 2018, and was amazed to see the transformation of the Merchants Corner hotel. The community had turned this active drug-shooting den and illicit single-room-occupancy dwelling into an educational and residential hub in the middle of the north end. As we toured the building, Silver showed me how the entire structure is circular in design to coordinate with indigenous cultural principles. There are classrooms and offices on the first and second floors and a kitchen.

The Merchants Corner project has partnered with a Pathways to Education high school program that prepares meals and offers tutoring and mentoring after classes. And the urban and inner-city studies collegiate program draws students from the local community and the main campus. The UWinnipeg Students Association also pays for a satellite office in the complex. And there is an elders' office that provides culturally competent advising and chances to smudge, among other supports.

Merchants Corner Lobby, 2018. Photo by author.

On the third floor of the renovated hotel and behind the building are thirty units of housing, all priced at rent geared to income levels. The complex also includes an elder unit in the rear building. Lisa Strong and her two children moved into a unit in December 2017. Gang activity and opioid drug use had ramped up in her previous neighborhood. Strong almost quit school just to look after her kids: "It was just getting so violent, and I was getting depressed."[7] But the Merchants Corner community makes the difference. She stayed in school, she planned to join community organizations, and she put her kids in the Pathways after-school program.

Silver said that he worked hard to help turn this dream into a reality, but he makes sure to credit private donors, local groups such as the North End Community Redevelopment Corporation, and the fact that the province was governed by the NDP, a Social Democrat party. I asked him if he saw this complex as an extension of what was happening at the main campus. Silver was clear about the distinctions: "We are located in a low-income, largely indigenous neighborhood. We work to attract indigenous and newcomer students who wouldn't otherwise step foot on a college campus. Our whole operation runs against the neoliberal tide of universities today."

There were clear points of contention between the main campus and the Selkirk Avenue visions of the city school. As Silver suggests, UWinnipeg wasn't perfect. Jamil Mahmood graduated from the school and went on to work as the executive director of the Spence Neighbourhood Association, which serves multiethnic communities surrounding the main campus. He said we can't forget that UWinnipeg had a history of buying properties in the area, kicking out tenants, and converting the buildings into university accommodations.

Residents still talk about how the university built its Richardson Science Complex on land where a local skating rink had been demolished, a place Mahmood describes as "an amazing community asset." He concedes that the university's new mixed-income housing developments are wonderful additions to campus but argues that they sit on a history of displacement and that not enough local residents live in those buildings.[8] This conversation reminded me that although UWinnipeg's efforts far surpass what I had seen elsewhere, there is a difference between the campus-oriented developments downtown and the community-driven Merchants Corner project in the north end.

But I still left Canada just dizzy with the overall belief that another university is possible. Even with its limits, the school's efforts pointed to the possibilities of the university as an anchor that helps meet the local desires for affordable housing, sustainable food systems, cooperatively owned workplaces, and a shared right to the city. I wondered, though, whether, like far too many freedom dreams (especially for African Americans), if such a powerful reimagining of UniverCities is possible only in a nation like Canada. Fortunately, if you look hard enough, there are signs of change on this side of the border, too.

———

India Walton had had enough. The registered nurse and resident of Buffalo's Fruit Belt neighborhood woke up one night in May 2016, went to Walmart, and bought a roll of caution tape. She sat down with her four children early the next morning and had a very frank conversation with them: "If I'm not back here by 8:30, you all go ahead and go to school, and we'll follow up later. 'Cause I don't know whether I'm gonna go to jail or what."

Walton knew she had to do something. The Buffalo Niagara Medical Campus had loomed over the historically Black Fruit Belt neighborhood since 2001.[9] But the complex continued to expand with new tenants, including the University of Buffalo medical school and its Center of Excellence in Bioinformatics. Additional low-wage health workers couldn't afford the costly parking on campus, so they took over street parking in the neighborhood. Black residents, especially community elders, had to carry groceries sometimes two or three blocks just to reach their homes. Some workers had the audacity to block driveways. Incredulous, that morning in 2016 Walton staged a "one-woman protest" by barricading open parking spots with the caution tape, waving medical workers on to find parking somewhere else.[10] News crews arrived just before the police came, when she packed up and left. Message received.

A parking-permit ordinance got passed by the New York State Senate shortly after her protest.[11] But Walton made certain I understood that her one-woman stance was just one piece of a much broader community campaign. The Fruit Belt neighborhood had waged battles against the explicit and unspoken consequences of the medical campus's growth for years. In fact, she admitted to me that she was initially part of the problem, as a gentrifier. Walton had graduated as a registered nurse and was living her best life. She explained, "Like many people in my position, you feel like you're the one who made it out. So you celebrate, and you forget that there are people who are still very much vulnerable and suffering."

But things changed when Walton's employer, Oishei Children's Hospital, relocated to the medical campus. She wanted to be near her job. Coworkers told her to be careful about living anywhere near the campus. But Walton had spent summers at her uncle's house on Mulberry in the Fruit Belt as a child. That was her community. She wasn't afraid and figured she could find a whole house with a yard for a rent of about five or six hundred dollars. But by 2015, the 'hood was already changing. Only after savvy negotiating was she able to rent a place for a still costly $1,200. In many ways, Walton's arrival signaled the problem on the horizon.

Walton quickly saw how the Fruit Belt—a patchwork of well-tended homes, aged dwellings, and empty-lot prairies of weeded concrete—didn't fit the typical narrative about the affordable-housing crisis. New York State had just passed a historic rent-stabilization ordinance, but Buffalo wasn't included because of its high vacancy rates. There were plenty of places to live. Local scholars and urban planners concluded there was no gentrification in Buffalo. "You live in Buffalo, not Brooklyn," they told her. But Walton said they missed the point: "There is such a high vacancy rate because nobody can afford to live in the expensive apartments they're putting online."

Residents really rang the alarm when Google Maps and realtors renamed the Fruit Belt "Medical Park."[12] Though not there yet, developers were slowly sniffing around the Fruit Belt to seize some of the empty lots owned by the city and capitalize on the growing medical campus market. But organizing groups like Open Buffalo and the Fruit Belt Neighborhood Advisory Council held their ground, finally coming together as the Community First Alliance around 2016.

Early on, the alliance tried to negotiate with the medical campus for some community benefits. And it was at that point when Walton realized

"Fruit Belt neighborhood," *Buffalo News*, March 24, 2019. Cartoon by Adam Zyglis.

that in the minds of the "meds and eds," the residents didn't even exist.[13] "We didn't have anything to negotiate with, and people don't usually do things just because it's right. We realized the land could be the leverage." In 2015 community organizers had already convinced Buffalo City Council President Darius Pridgen to place a two-and-a-half-year moratorium on the sale of two hundred city-owned lots. In 2017 Walton joined others on trips to the Dudley Street Neighborhood initiative in Boston and discussed housing-justice campaigns while traveling to Barcelona. She agreed that a community land trust could provide the leverage they needed.

The trust takes ownership of the land and then leases the lots to developers and home owners or secures financing to build homes for sale at an affordable rate. When houses are sold, the selling price is capped at a certain level of profit so that they remain affordable to the next buyer. The city council partially lifted the moratorium in May 2018 and transferred twenty lots to the Fruit Belt Land Trust.[14] By 2019, she said, many developers were already scrambling to work with them, and the trust was partnering with Habitat for Humanity on two single-family homes.

Walton admits that at first it was hard to get folks on board. A land trust is very technical, and some people don't want a cap on the selling price. But she explained how any owner who leases the land benefits from a regulated price on the front end, and the land trust believes that a regulated value should stay with the land. Above all, by controlling the land, residents could have some say in the direction of the neighborhood, instead of being given solutions: "We got Google to address this tiny little neighborhood in Buffalo. We had a political cartoon drawn by [Pulitzer prize–winner] Adam Zyglis. We are extremely proud."

I asked Walton about those who say rent caps actually make housing prices increase because they don't encourage developers to build more. "Fuck developers," she remarked in a flat tone. Walton explained that building more doesn't guarantee fair prices, and everything doesn't have to make money. It's time to prioritize people over profit: "We've squandered so much wealth doing the wrong thing; now it's time to invest in people's lives."

I walked away from Buffalo proud, too. And students, politicians, and residents across the country continue to affirm Walton's belief that we can have a say in the future of our cities. In 2012 the college-heavy city of Boston struck a deal asking nonprofits with more than $15 million worth of tax-exempt property to volunteer 25 percent of the property taxes they would owe if they were not exempt. It's a start, although many of the institutions have fallen short in their contributions.[15]

In May 2019 the AFL-CIO, National Nurses United, and the Coalition for a Humane Hopkins issued a scathing report revealing Johns Hopkins University Hospital's "shocking record" of hounding low-income, primarily African American patients living around the campus for medical debt by filing thousands of lawsuits to garnish wages and seize bank accounts. Many of those targeted had likely been eligible for reduced or charity care. Johns Hopkins spokesperson Kim Hoppe pointed to the hospital's community benefits program and charity-care policy as evidence of its priority to meet every patient's needs but also maintains that it reserves the right to "pursue reimbursements." Unfortunately, the coalition argues, Hopkins has not done enough to make public to every patient the hospital's charity-care obligations dictated by the state.[16] And in October 2019 Milwaukee students partnered with campus food service workers to launch Marquette

University Neighborhood Kitchen, which turns unused food from dining halls into healthy meals for community members in need.[17]

Urban citizens are calling out from the shadows, and universities are slowly starting to listen. Although it had been gouging patients, Hopkins Hospital also offered a humane response to the uprisings after the 2015 police killing of Freddie Gray. The medical center led a coalition of activists and other hospitals to propose a $40 million health employment program to support one thousand entry-level jobs for city residents, including the formerly incarcerated. In the summer of 2019, Boston-area schools began to work with the Dorchester nonprofit CommonWealth Kitchen to place food products from small, mostly minority-owned start-ups in the dining halls at local hospitals and universities. In October 2019, Wayne State University announced a free tuition scholarship for any resident who graduates from a Detroit public high school and is accepted to the college.[18]

I also remain inspired by the campaigns that engage with the socioeconomic impact of higher education on our cities. In August 2019 the Debt Collective rallied academics around the country for a "College for All" legislative package of student-debt relief and tuition-free college that was brought before Congress. It also notably called for at least 75 percent of classes to be taught by full-time tenured or tenure-track faculty at a time when most instructors are contingent workers. At the same time, Scholars for Social Justice continues to build out its Reparations in Higher Education project. This campaign works on demanding institutional recognition and compensation from the colleges and universities supported by slavery, indigenous land theft, Jim Crow segregation, residential displacement, exploited labor practices, and more.

Building on this work, I have created the Smart Cities Lab (SCL), which studies and consults on the best practices for building equitable urban communities, with a special focus on university-based urban development. The notion of smart cities normally references technological solutions for urban planning but tends to omit discussions of the city's residents who are subjected to any new infrastructure. SCL puts people first to explore how urban revitalization can benefit existing urban communities without regard to income, social background, criminal record, or citizenship status. The work is governed by a mantra that I heard all over the country: *development without displacement.*

At the lab we have come up with some recommendations for building a better urban future. They include the following:

City-Enforced Payment in Lieu of Taxes. Colleges and universities that remain tax-exempt should compensate cities for their use of public services (police, fire, trash, road maintenance, electric grid use, etc.) and contribute to public needs (the school district). Schools must work with cities to determine what percentage of buildings are used for strictly academic purposes versus research brought to market, and they must compensate the municipality accordingly.

Community Benefits Agreements. Colleges and universities should enter into CBAs that address the shared use of space, especially if any public funds are involved. Schools should abide by zip-code–specific guidelines for living-wage job opportunities, fairly resourced subcontracted work, local access to construction projects, etc. CBAs can also include affordable-housing trusts, job training, compensation for campus-expansion displacement, tuition-free education, use of campus facilities (e.g., child care, recreation, and library facilities), and any other discussions of resource allocation. CBAs must always be governed by a community advisory board that meets on a regular basis and includes members of university and community organizations.

Community-Based Planning and Zoning Board. Every municipality should create a citywide planning and zoning board with binding authority that includes residents. A standing subcommittee should focus on university-based development. This board would coordinate with all relevant community boards or neighborhood-level governing authorities to help craft and govern a binding community-based neighborhood plan for all campus-expansion or renovation projects. This board would also help oversee the transfer of city-owned property for community land trusts to help manage real estate speculation in campus neighborhoods.

Just and Equitable Public Safety. Campus police departments must be replaced with unarmed, anticarceral, and community-based public safety teams. But if not, these police forces must at least be subject to public records laws and the Freedom of Information Act. School police should be restricted to clear campus boundaries. If campus police are licensed to patrol and enforce the law beyond campus, they must be subject to a community oversight board with prosecution power. Within the realm of policing, all student and nonstudent residents must be subject to the same law. Profiling and harassment must be severely punished. Campus police should be required to undergo the same training as municipal police. They must also receive additional course-based certification on deescalation techniques and community policing in urban campus settings.

Labor Practices. All higher education labor, from low-wage workers and adjunct instructors to graduate workers and full-time faculty, must have the right to engage in collective bargaining. Colleges and universities must completely divest from any sweatshop or prison labor. Whether directly employed or subcontracted, all workers must be paid a living wage and receive the requisite benefits. Workers must be protected from discrimination based on past criminal and credit history. Workers should be paid on a twelve-month cycle to account for the summer months and to maintain insurance and health benefits. All students who work on research that develops intellectual property that is licensed to private industry should be fairly compensated in accordance with their labor.

Athletic Revenues. High-revenue-generating sports extract uncompensated labor from worker/athletes disproportionately of color and from underserved communities. A portion of athletic revenues, beyond overhead, should be distributed to the worker/athletes and community-based initiatives.

=

These recommendations will never fully rehabilitate a community from the substantial losses in an ongoing process of university-driven neighborhood surveillance, upscaling, and displacement. Still, these proposals can perhaps lead to more-robust ways of building not just a better higher education system but also more-democratic cities.

The stories in this book show us that the quaint notion of the ivory tower is dead. Higher education must be understood alongside governmental and financial institutions as one of the most dominant forces shaping today's cities. But as of yet, the expanding noneducational and profit-generating investments of colleges and universities are rarely subject to the same kinds of public scrutiny and oversight as other industries.

We must force a spotlight on the decline of government accountability and social inclusion when local neighborhoods are largely handed over to the for-profit arm of higher education. Once we reckon with higher education's increasing influence over America's cities as employers, real estate holders, policing agents, and health-care providers, it's clear that a new kind of city is emerging right before our eyes. Who will decide how these UniverCities take shape? Whose voices will be heard?

We are already starting to see new kinds of mobilization from the people living in the shadows of ivory towers. At the height of the global pandemic, the citizens of New Haven stormed the city's March 30, 2020, Zoom budget meeting to vent their annoyance and outrage at Yale University's continued strain on city finances. They specifically pointed to Yale's vast and tax-exempt property holdings compared to the deficit-ridden New Haven public schools hungry for property-tax dollars. On July 29 a new coalition of Yale union workers and residents followed up with a six-hundred-vehicle "respect caravan" that brought downtown traffic to a halt. With signs that read "Yale: Pay Your Fair Share," rally-goers acknowledged that although the university offers the city voluntary payments in lieu of taxes, these funds are "pocket change" compared to Yale's $30 billion endowment.[19] For the protestors, COVID-19 merely exacerbated long-standing disparities between the city and its largest economic entity.

In late March 2020, COVID-19 forced Harvard's facilities to shut down. The university initially decided to provide workers directly hired by the school with thirty days of paid leave and benefits while subcontracted dining service employees would get nothing. It was only after public pressure from workers' unions, student groups, and the law school that Harvard changed course and provided all of its employees—including contract workers—with regular pay and benefits through May 28.[20]

Social upheaval around police violence in June and July 2020 forced Johns Hopkins to delay establishing its controversial private police force for at least two years. The official statement pointed out that this "moment of national reckoning" required the university to reconsider its policing decision. In response, Baltimore community activist Joseph Kane exclaimed,

"The power of the people is greater than the people in power!" In Portland, meanwhile, as the city reached eighty days of nightly protests, Portland State University said on August 13 that it would disarm its campus police force two years after an officer from the department shot and killed Jason Washington.[21]

For so long, universities have been places that encourage the pursuit of knowledge; at the same time, school administrators don't want their actions known. But campus protests and community organizing are helping to build out a *higher* education in the streets. The campus is revealed to be the shop floor of city workers, the land baron of residents, the political boss of neighborhoods. Therefore, whoever controls the university will shape the fight for living wages, fair housing, intellectual property, democratic accountability, health care, and public safety for all.

Through struggle, students and faculty become citizens building new relationships with residents, relationships in which everyone is transformed. In the process, these relationships are building a broader campus community with a new, shared knowledge of the world. It is this reconstructed campus community that might just serve as the staging ground for building a different urban future for us all.

ACKNOWLEDGMENTS

The people that I met in cities all over the country opened up their lives and their homes to this complete stranger and in these small acts reaffirmed the goodness of the human spirit. These encounters not only provided me the stories that animate this book, but their generosity gave me life lessons that are perhaps the most important takeaway from this work. Thank you.

My editor, Katy O'Donnell, indulged my incessant intensity one day and my surprising slackness the next. Thank you, Katy, for your broad vision, deep analysis, and sincere care for this project. You stayed true and committed to the story all along and generously stewarded me through the process of trying to bring these ideas to their rightful place. I'd also like to thank everyone else at Bold Type/Hachette. Alessandra Bastagli expressed the initial excitement for the book, and Clive Priddle put his weight behind the project from the beginning. Thanks to production editor Melissa Veronesi and designer Amy Quinn, who offered sharp eyes to the book, sharing my belief that the design is almost as important as the words on the page. Carolyn Levin provided meticulous legal oversight. And Patti Isaacs was gracious enough to help bring these cities to life with her amazing map work. A big shout out to Jocelynn Pedro, Lindsay Fradkoff, Claire Zuo, and Miguel Cervantes for all of their sage counsel on publicity and marketing.

Zoë Pagnamenta, you are truly a change agent. It didn't even take a full conversation to see that I was with the right one. Thank you for your commitment to important ideas and stories no matter their fiscal returns. You and Alison at the Zoë Pagnamenta Agency fully embraced the project, pushed me along, gave tough love, and remained fearless in the face of any doubts, especially my own.

While writing this book, I have benefited enormously from colleagues and students at Trinity College. I want to thank Bishop John Selders, Seth Markle, Diana Paulin, Christina Heatherton, Scott Gac, Scott Tang, Cheryl Greenberg, Dario Eraque, Tom Wickman, Garth Myers, Hilary Wyss, Juliet Nebolon, Xiangming Chen, Donna Marcano, Stefanie Chambers, Zayde Antrim, Isaac Kamola, David Tatem, Pat Moody, Nancy Rossi, and Veronica Zuniga for their support. Deans Rena Fraden and Tim Cresswell and President Joanne Berger-Sweeney let me know, in many ways, that they believed in this work. Ambar Paulino, Chiarra Davis, and Samia Khoder served as unparalleled research assistants.

I began thinking about the ideas here more than fifteen years ago, and some colleagues, whom I consider friends, have been here through it all. Jonathan Scott Holloway, John Jackson, Mark Anthony Neal, Robin D. G. Kelley, Minkah Makalani, and Vijay Prashad never stopped helping me clarify my ideas, even when not directly about this book. When I brought the notion of "UniverCities" to Andrew Ross, he just calmly said, "You have to go to Phoenix." But then he went on to introduce me to people, push my thinking, and remain a critical but nurturing ear throughout. Paul Lawrie first brought me to Winnipeg and then found ways for me to return. He and Rosa served as the perfect hosts for me on multiple occasions, introducing me to Merchants Corner and forcing me to understand Canada on its own terms while making sure I always felt at home. I didn't know Craig Wilder well, beyond the genius of his writing. I am so blessed to have been able to share more attentive space with him. He is the epitome of an old-school race man. His depth and generosity know few bounds. I am sure it was largely because of his endorsement that Zoë even took me on.

All of my comrades with Scholars for Social Justice remind me that this work is not simply "academic" but must drive forward the righteous cause of liberation for us all . . . or else why are we doing it? I especially thank Barbara Ransby, Cathy Cohen, Adom Getachew, Dayo Gore, Sarah Haley, Leith Mullings, and Alvaro Huerta for their intellectual and political leadership. I also appreciate the critical collegiality of Abigail Boggs, Eli Meyerhoff, Nick Mitchell, Zach Schwartz-Weinstein, Neha Vora, Laura

Goldblatt, Vineeta Singh, Sharon Stein, and everyone else in the emergent Abolitionist University Studies community.

This book quite simply wouldn't have made it over the finish line without Liesl Olson, Llana Barber, and Emma Shaw Crane, who read every word, sometimes more than once, and offered detailed feedback and advice throughout. And Thabiti Lewis truly embodies the phrase "brother from another mother." He is that and more. Every time I hit the wall of procrastination and timidity, he pushed me to do better. VisionMerge Productions has served as an incredible steward for all of my photography and graphic design needs.

The growing community of thinkers, community experts, colleagues, and friends who set the stage include Raymond Stewart, Roderick Ferguson, Mabel Wilson, Donnette Francis, Jafari Allen, Ananya Roy, Stacey Champion, Jim McPherson, Babe and Arlene Sarver, Braden Kay, Dede Devine, Will Townes, Chaclyn Hunt, Brad Hunt, Marcia Chatelain, Destin Jenkins, Alexis Neumann, Andrew Berman, Nick Pinto, Daniella Zalcman, Safina Lewis, Melvyn Colon, Linda Torres, Jeremy Read, Jim Silver, Domonique Griffin, Dennice Barr, India Walton, Henry Louis Taylor Jr., Timothy Murphy, Nathan D. B. Connolly, Claudrena Harold, Andrew Kahrl, Richard Powell, Sylviane Diouf, Brianna Bibb, David Stradling, Alex Dwiar, Leslie Alexander, Russell Rickford, and Brandon Byrd. And I want to say Rest in Power to Sherman Kreiner and Debra Friedman, who were indefatigable stewards of this work but passed away before its completion.

Sarah Banet-Weiser and David Wescott offered insightful editorial assistance on article versions of this research. And I am grateful for the feedback from colleagues and audiences when the following institutions invited me to present this work: Schomburg Center for Research in Black Culture, Vernacular Architecture Forum, Center for Architecture, Northwestern University, University of Buffalo, Duke University, University of California San Diego, University of Winnipeg, University of Virginia, Vanderbilt University, Marquette University, Columbia University, Yale University, Tongji University, Parsons School of Design, University of Kansas, CUNY Graduate Center, Northeastern University, and the University of Pennsylvania.

I am also indebted to the journalists who helped guide my on-the-ground thinking in cities, especially at independent and student news outlets, including the *Village Voice, Baltimore Brew, Baltimore Beat, New Haven Independent, Indy Week, Amsterdam News, Chicago Defender, Phoenix New Times, South Side Weekly, Chicago Reader, Hyde Park Herald, Chicago Reporter, Block Club Chicago, Chicago Maroon, Downtown Devil, Trinity Tripod, NYU Local, Columbia Spectator,* and the *Daily Trojan.*

Finally, to the family, your love, support, and high standards mean everything to me. My mother, Mary Jo Baldwin, is one of the most insightful people I know and was always asking about the progress of "the book." Nylan, Noah, and Ellison, it has been my honor to help you grow and develop into strong, creative, and caring young Black men. You are all better writers and thinkers than me already, so thank you for letting me aspire to your greatness. And Bridgette, through it all you remain a beacon of grace, mercy, empathy, and brilliance. There are no words for the blessings you bring to our world.

NOTES

Introduction: Chess Moves on a Checkerboard

1. Rachel Levine, "Neighborhood Activists Protest Checkerboard Move," *Chicago Maroon*, January 13, 2004; Todd Spivak, "Checkerboard Proprietor Crashes U. of C. Protest," *Hyde Park Herald*, December 17, 2003.

2. Friends of the Checkerboard Lounge, "U of C Committing Act of Cultural Piracy: Open Letter to University of Chicago President Don Randel," *Hyde Park Herald*, November 19, 2003.

3. Paula Robinson, "This Tale of Two Cities Could Have a Happier Ending," *Hyde Park Herald*, January 7, 2004.

4. Sam Ackerman, "Checkerboard Tradition Will Continue on 53rd Street," *Hyde Park Herald*, December 17, 2003; Celeste Garrett, "Legendary Blues Club Runs Out of Encores," *Chicago Tribune*, May 26, 2003.

5. Curtis Lawrence, "Neighbors Fight to Keep Blues Club—Bronzeville Activists Say U. of C. 'Stealing' Famed Checkerboard," *Chicago Sun-Times*, December 11, 2003.

6. James Porter, "The Last Juke Joint," *Time Out Chicago*, June 9-16, 2005; Jim Sonnenberg, "Last Call at the Checkerboard Lounge," *Crain's Chicago Business*, February 15, 2003; Sonnenberg, "The Thrill Is Going," *Crain's Chicago Business*, February 17, 2003, 1; Jeff Heubner, "Whose Blues Will They Choose," *Chicago Reader*, December 1, 2000. See also David Grazian, *Blue Chicago: The Search for Authenticity in Urban Blues Clubs* (Chicago: University of Chicago Press, 2005). Racial heritage tourism in Bronzeville is the subject of Michelle Boyd, *Jim Crow Nostalgia: Reconstructing Race in Bronzeville* (Minneapolis: University of Minnesota Press, 2008).

7. Todd Spivak, "Competing Plans for the Checkerboard," *Hyde Park Herald*, October 15, 2003.

8. Jim Wagner, "Checkerboard Owner Asked for U of C's Help," *Hyde Park Herald*, December 17, 2003.

9. Davarian L. Baldwin, "When Universities Swallow Cities," *Chronicle of Higher Education*, August 4, 2017; Baldwin, "The '800-Pound Gargoyle': The Long History of Higher Education and Urban Development on Chicago's South Side," *American Quarterly* 67, no. 1 (March 2015).

10. Gabriel Sherman, "The School That Ate New York," *New York*, November 14, 2010; Carolyn Adams, "The Meds and Eds in Urban Economic Development," *Journal of Urban Affairs* 25, no. 5 (2003).

11. Sharon Haar, *The City as Campus: Urbanism and Higher Education in Chicago* (Minneapolis: University of Minnesota Press, 2011).

12. Richard Florida, *Cities and the Creative Class* (London: Routledge, 2004); Florida, *Rise of the Creative Class: And How It's Transforming Work, Leisure, Community, and Everyday Life* (New York: Basic Books, 2002); Mike Sharsky, "A Harmony of Purpose," *US Airways*, February 2009.

13. Alison Steinbach, "What to Expect for Downtown Mesa's ASU Campus and Plaza, Opening 2022," *Arizona Republic*, October 3, 2019; Lynn Trimble, "Here Are the Latest Plans to Bring an ASU Campus to Downtown Mesa," *Phoenix New Times*, June 6, 2018; Ry Rivard, "Private Colleges Go West for Students, Don't Find Them Yet," *Inside Higher Ed*, April 25, 2014; Sommer Mathis, "The Next Destination for Liberal-Arts Education Is . . . Arizona?," *Atlantic*, January 29, 2014.

14. Kevin Kiley, "Big City Dreams," *Inside Higher Ed*, September 1, 2011. See also Javier C. Hernandez, "Bloomberg's Push for an Applied Sciences School," *New York Times*, April 26, 2011. Some protested the selection because of Technicon's reported ties to the Israeli occupation of Palestine. See Rick Seltzer, "Cornell Tech Officially Opens Campus on New York City's Roosevelt Island," *Inside Higher Ed*, September 13, 2017; Adam Hudson, "Cornell NYC Tech's Alarming Ties to Israeli Occupation," *Nation*, March 1, 2013.

15. Lisa Prevost, "Colleges Invest So 'What's the Town Like?' Gets an Upbeat Answer," *New York Times*, February 25, 2020; John Hurdle, "New Jersey Town and University Bridge Their Divide, and Both Reap a Reward," *New York Times*, May 29, 2018.

16. Allen Dieterich-Ward, *Beyond Rust: Metropolitan Pittsburgh and the Fate of Industrial America* (Philadelphia: University of Pennsylvania Press, 2016); Michele Parrish, "SLU Home Ownership Plan to Spur Area Development," *University News*, February 6, 2003; Rosalind Early, "First View: Hotel Ignacio," *St. Louis*, March 21, 2013; "SLU Trades One Street for Another," *Vanishing STL*, April 30, 2010.

17. University officials celebrated how the renamed "USC Village" provided more on-campus housing to ease the pressure of housing inflation in the surrounding neighborhoods when students went out looking for rentals. But residents thought that although USC Village brought students back to live on campus, the housing was more expensive and cheaply made. Students were going to eventually return to the surrounding neighborhoods and drive rents back up. See Sarah Chan and Kylie Chung, "With the Rise of USC Village Comes a Community Left in Limbo," *Daily Trojan*, August 23, 2017; Lauren Herstik, "U.S.C. Expands in a 'Neglected' Neighborhood, Promising Jobs and More," *New York Times*, August 15, 2017; Hortensia Amaro, *USC State of the Neighborhood Report* (University of Southern California's State of the Neighborhood Project and Advancement Project, 2015). Discussions of the housing market didn't even address the impact that USC Village posed for local businesses and shoppers. See Sahra Sulaiman, "USC Poised to Displace Black-Owned Bike Repair Business . . . for the Second Time," *Streetsblog Los Angeles*, May 1, 2017; Danni Wang, "USC Village Rises," *Daily Trojan*, April 17, 2017; Burke Gibson, "USC Growth Forces Locals to Adapt," *Daily Trojan*, April 17, 2016; Julia Poe, "Village Displaces Local Businesses," *Daily Trojan*, April 17, 2016. On the village design, see Christopher Hawthorne, "Disneyland Meets Hogwarts at $700-Million USC Village," *LA Times*, August 21, 2017.

18. Gary Haber, "EBDI Biopark Project Not Creating Jobs, Residents Say," *Baltimore Business Journal*, November 10, 2011; Patrice Hutton, "Relocated Residents Speak

Out—Families Forcibly Moved Out of E. Baltimore Find JHU at Fault," *Johns Hopkins News-Letter*, November 3, 2005; Siddhartha Miller, "Gentrify or Die? Inside a University's Controversial Plan for Baltimore," *Guardian*, April 18, 2018; Lawrence T. Brown et al., "The Rise of Anchor Institutions and the Threat to Community Health: Protecting Community Health, Building Community Power," *Kalfou* 3, no. 1 (Spring 2016).

19. Claudrena N. Harold, "No Ordinary Sacrifice: The Struggle for Racial Justice at the University of Virginia in the Post–Civil Rights Era," in *Charlottesville: The Legacy of Race and Inequity*, ed. Louis Nelson and Claudrena N. Harold (Charlottesville: University of Virginia Press, 2018).

20. Cathie Anderson, "UC's Lowest Paid Workers Strike to Protest Outsourcing," *Sacramento Bee*, November 13, 2019; Max Abrams, "AFSCME Files Six New Unfair Labor Practice Complaints Against UC, Plan to Strike Nov. 13," *Daily Nexus*, November 6, 2019; Emily Deruy, "Workers at Some UC Campuses Say They Don't Earn Fair Wages," *Mercury News*, October 22, 2017.

21. Nathalie Baptiste, "Campus Cops: Authority Without Accountability," *American Prospect*, November 2, 2015; Anna Hess, "Penn Police Sensitivity Trainings Aim to Combat Excessive Use of Force," *Daily Pennsylvanian*, April 28, 2015.

22. Stephanie Addenbroke and Amaka Uchegbu, "Tahj Blow '16 Forced to Ground at Gunpoint by YPD," *Yale Daily News*, January 25, 2015; Marc Santora, "Yale Report Clears Police Officer in Encounter with Student," *New York Times*, March 4, 2015.

23. Elise Young, "Princeton Will Pay $18 Million to Settle Residents' Tax Case," *Bloomberg*, October 14, 2016.

24. University endowments have come under much scrutiny as of late. An endowment represents money or other financial assets, like property, donated to nonprofit organizations, including colleges and universities. These institutions use the resulting investment income to grow the principal and provide additional income. Endowments are exempt from corporate income tax because they are meant to serve the public (largely students) in the present and future. To retain tax-exempt status, philanthropies are required to spend at least 5 percent of their assets annually. Most universities look at endowments as long-term financial support and hence place them in money-market accounts with equity firms, rarely spending more than the required 5 percent. Critics argue that this fiscal approach presumes that schools won't receive tuition and additional resources annually and results in endowment hoarding. Some say higher education institutions could spend at least 8 percent, instead of presently spending more on their financial advisor fees rather than actually meeting their public mission by lowering tuition or serving the community. See Sandy Baum and Victoria Lee, *The Role of College and University Endowments* (Urban Institute, 2019); Victor Fleischer, "Stop Universities from Hoarding Money," *New York Times*, August 19, 2015.

25. Elise Young, "Princeton's Neighbors Say to Heck with Freebies—We Want Cash," *Bloomberg*, May 2, 2016.

26. Amit R. Paley and Valerie Strauss, "Student Loan Nonprofit a Boon for CEO," *Washington Post*, July 16, 2007; Andrew Ross, "Universities and the Urban Growth Machine," *Dissent*, October 4, 2012.

27. Neha Vora, *Teach for Arabia: American Universities, Liberalism, and Transnational Qatar* (Redwood City, CA: Stanford University Press, 2018); Issac Kamola, *Making the World Global: U.S. Universities and the Production of the Global Imaginary* (Durham, NC:

Duke University Press, 2019); Michelle Chen, "The Labor Abuse That Went into NYU's Abu Dhabi Campus," *Nation*, July 26, 2018.

28. As part of the larger scholarship, see, for example, Jeffrey Selingo, *College (Un) bound: The Future of Higher Education and What It Means for Students* (Seattle: Amazon, 2015); Goldie Blumenstyk, *American Higher Education in Crisis? What Everyone Needs to Know* (New York: Oxford, 2014); Sheila Slaughter and Gary Rhoades, *Academic Capitalism and the New Economy: Markets, State, and Higher Education* (Baltimore: Johns Hopkins University Press, 2009); Mark Bousquet, *How the University Works: Higher Education and the Low-Wage Nation* (New York: NYU Press, 2008); Henry Giroux, *The University in Chains: Confronting the Military-Industrial-Academic Complex* (Boulder, CO: Paradigm, 2007); Jennifer Washburn, *University Inc.: The Corporate Corruption of Higher Education* (New York: Basic Books, 2006); Derek Bok, *Universities in the Marketplace: The Commercialization of Higher Education* (Princeton, NJ: Princeton University Press, 2004).

29. LaDale Winling, *Building the Ivory Tower: Universities and Metropolitan Development in the Twentieth Century* (Philadelphia: University of Pennsylvania Press, 2018); Harley Etienne, *Pushing Back the Gates: Neighborhood Perspectives on University-Driven Revitalization in West Philadelphia* (Philadelphia: Temple University Press, 2012); Haar, *The City as Campus*; Margaret Pugh O'Mara, *Cities of Knowledge: Cold War Science and the Search for the Next Silicon Valley* (Princeton, NJ: Princeton University Press, 2005); David C. Perry and Wim Wiewel, *The University as Urban Developer* (Armonk, NY: M.E. Sharpe, 2005); John Gilderbloom and R. L. Mullins, *Promise and Betrayal: Universities and the Battle for Sustainable Urban Neighborhoods* (Albany: State University of New York Press, 2005). See also "Town Meets Gown: Special Issue," *Journal of Planning History* 10, no. 1 (February 2011); Brown et al., "The Rise of Anchor Institutions."

30. Florida, *Rise of the Creative Class*, 166.

31. Richard Florida, *The New Urban Crisis: How Our Cities Are Increasing Inequality, Deepening Segregation, and Failing the Middle Class—and What We Can Do About It* (New York: Basic Books, 2017). Even during the Great Recession, urban leaders across the country rushed to pay Florida's consulting firm Catalytix up to $250,000 for a "tactics and action plan" hoping to transform their cities. For a recent example of Florida continuing to capitalize on the "creative city" model, see Nancy Dahlberg, "Can Miami Rise from Being a Service Economy? There's Hope in the Numbers," *Miami Herald*, March 8, 2017. Critiques of Florida came fast and hard from the very beginning. See Susie Cagle, "Fallacy of the Creative Class: Why Richard Florida's 'Urban Renaissance' Won't Save U.S. Cities," *Grist*, February 11, 2013; Alec MacGillis, "The Ruse of the Creative Class," *American Prospect*, December 18, 2009; Murray Whyte, "Why Richard Florida's Honeymoon Is Over," *Toronto Star*, June 27, 2009.

32. Richard Florida, "The Extraordinary Value of Great Universities," *CityLab*, December 15, 2011.

Chapter 1: When Universities Swallow Cities

1. Markeshia Ricks, "Tax Yale Effort Revived," *New Haven Independent*, March 16, 2016; Martha Kessler, "Yale Property Tax Bill Dies in Connecticut," *Bloomberg*, May 6, 2016. See also Daphne A. Kenyon and Adam H. Langley, *Payments in Lieu of Taxes: Balancing Municipal and Nonprofit Interests* (Cambridge, MA: Lincoln Institute of Land Policy, 2010).

2. Ricks, "Tax Yale Effort Revived"; Elaine Povich, "Short on Cash, Cities and States Consider Taxing Nonprofits," *Pew Charitable Trusts/Research & Analysis/Stateline*, October 4, 2016; Ellen Wexler, "Yale Fights Tax Bill," *Inside Higher Ed*, May 3, 2016.

3. Roberto Mangabeira Unger, *The Knowledge Economy* (London: Verso, 2019); Slaughter and Rhoades, *Academic Capitalism and the New Economy*.

4. Ricks, "Tax Yale Effort Revived"; Gordon Lafer, "Land and Labor in the Post-industrial University Town: Remaking Social Geography," *Political Geography* 22 (2003); Michelle Liu, "Yale Properties Remain Under Tax Scrutiny," *Yale Daily News*, April 5, 2016. One of the earliest meditations on the cold war university and what management consultant Peter Drucker coined the "knowledge industry" comes from Clark Kerr, *The Uses of the University* (Cambridge, MA: Harvard University Press, 1963), 87–88.

5. "Who Pays?" *Yale Daily News*, February 21, 2014; Ed Stannard, "Yale's Tax-Exempt New Haven Property Worth $2.5 billion," *New Haven Register*, September 1, 2014.

6. J. Brian Charles, "For College Towns, Having a World-Famous University Is a Mixed Blessing," *Governing*, October 2018; Lafer, "Land and Labor in the Post-industrial University Town."

7. Jennifer Klein, "New Haven Rising," *Dissent*, Winter 2015; Michelle Chen, "When the Biggest Employer Isn't Employing the Town," *Nation*, February 5, 2016.

8. Camilla Brandfield-Harvey, "Gourmet Heaven to Close Both New Haven Locations," *Brown Daily Herald*, September 5, 2014; Elliot Lewis, "Wage War," *Yale Herald*, March 8, 2019; "Ex-owner of Gourmet Heaven in New Haven Has Multiple Wage Violations Dismissed," *New Haven Register*, December 7, 2016.

9. Thomas Breen, "Yale Unions Celebrate Jobs Pact," *New Haven Independent*, August 12, 2019; Henry Reichard, "The Jobs Yale Promised," *New Journal*, May 1, 2019; Christopher Peak, "Yale Slammed on Local Hiring Promise," *New Haven Independent*, February 22, 2019.

10. Ed Stannard, "Yale Grad Sues over Forced Withdrawal from School," *New Haven Register*, November 16, 2018.

11. Miriam Heyman, "The Ruderman White Paper on Mental Health in the Ivy League," *Ruderman Family Foundation*, December 2018; Jonathan Foiles, "Are Colleges Failing Students with Mental Illness?" *Psychology Today Australia*, January 28, 2019.

12. Andrew Giambrone, "When Mentally Ill Students Feel Alone," *Atlantic*, March 2, 2018; Esmé Weijun Wang, "Yale Will Not Save You," *Sewanee Review* (Winter 2019).

13. Eric Levenson, "Yale Police Shooting: Body Camera Footage Shows Moments Police Opened Fire," *CNN.com*, April 24, 2019; Bhvishya Patel and Matthew Wright, "Moment Cops Open Fire on Unarmed Black Couple Near Yale Campus as They Sat in Car Singing," *Daily Mail*, April 22, 2019; Sharon Otterman, "Police Shoot at a Black Couple Near Yale, Prompting a Week of Protests," *New York Times*, April 24, 2019.

14. Clare Dignan, "Hamden Fights Court Order That Halted Hearing for Officer Who Shot Woman," *CTInsider*, June 30, 2020; Sam Gurwitt, "Court Stalls Cop's Termination," *New Haven Independent*, December 6, 2019; Meera Shoaib, "Yale Concludes Pollock Review," *Yale Daily News*, December 26, 2019.

15. Nicholas Rondinone and Josh Kovner, "Protests Continue as New Haven Community Demands Swift Investigation of Police Shooting Involving Hamden, Yale Officers," *Hartford Courant*, April 18, 2019; Black Students for Disarmament at Yale, "Urgent Call to Disarm Yale Police Department," *Down*, April 20, 2019; Erik Ortiz, "Police Shooting

Near Yale Exposes Complex Racial Divide," *NBCnews.com*, April 24, 2019; Serena Lin, "Community Protests Officer-Involved Shooting," *Yale Daily News*, May 16, 2020. See also T. J. Grayson, "A Police Shooting at Yale Shows How Campus Police Have Fostered a Climate of Fear," *Slate*, April 29, 2019; Harry Zehner, "It's Time for Accountability and Disarmament at Yale," *Daily Campus*, April 24, 2019.

16. Craig Steven Wilder, *Ebony and Ivy: Race, Slavery, and the Troubled History of America's Universities* (New York: Bloomsbury, 2013); Caine Jordan, Guy Emerson Mount, and Kai Parker, "'A Disgrace to All Slaveholders': The University of Chicago's Founding Ties to Slavery and the Path to Reparations," *Journal of African American History* 103, nos. 1–2 (Winter/Spring 2018); John Boyer, *The University of Chicago: A History* (Chicago: University of Chicago Press, 2015).

17. John Thelin, *A History of American Higher Education* (Baltimore: Johns Hopkins University Press, 2004); Roger Williams, *The Origins of Federal Support for Higher Education: George W. Atherton and the Land-Grant College Movement* (University Park: Pennsylvania University Press, 1991).

18. Sharon Stein, "A Colonial History of Higher Education Present: Rethinking Land-Grant Institutions Through Processes of Accumulation and Relations of Conquest," *Critical Studies in Education*, December 2017, 4; Robert Lee and Tristan Ahtone, "Land Grab Universities," *High Country News*, March 30, 2020. See also Sharon Stein, "Confronting the Racial-Colonial Foundations of U.S. Higher Education," *Journal for the Study of Postsecondary and Tertiary Education* 3 (2018).

19. John Wennersten, "The Travail of Black Land-Grant Schools in the South, 1890-1917," *Agricultural History Society* 65, no. 2 (Spring 1991); Donald Spivey, *Schooling for the New Slavery: Black Industrial Education, 1868-1915* (Westport, CT: Greenwood, 1978).

20. Carol Severino, "Greenery vs. Concrete and Walls vs. Doors: Images and Metaphors Affecting an Urban Mission," *Metropolitan Universities* 6, no. 2 (Fall 1995); Peter Knapp, *Trinity College in the Twentieth Century: A History* (Hartford, CT: Trustees of Trinity College, 2000). See also Thomas Bender, *The University and the City: From Medieval Origins to the Present* (New York: Oxford University Press, 1991).

21. Glen Weaver, *The History of Trinity College*, vol. 1 (Hartford, CT: Trinity College Press, 1967).

22. Weaver, *The History of Trinity College*.

23. Robin Bachin, *Building the South Side: Urban Space and Civic Culture in Chicago, 1890-1919* (Chicago: University of Chicago Press, 2004), 53-57. The "Old University of Chicago" was located on land donated from Stephen Douglas's slave plantation wealth in what became the Black neighborhood of Bronzeville until the school faced a mortgage foreclosure in 1886. See John Boyer, *The University of Chicago: A History* (Chicago: University of Chicago Press, 2015).

24. Bachin, *Building the South Side*.

25. Susan Campbell, *Frog Hollow: Stories of an American Neighborhood* (Middletown, CT: Wesleyan University Press, 2018); Xiangming Chen and Nick Bacon, *Confronting Urban Legacy: Rediscovering Hartford and New England's Forgotten Cities* (Lanham, MD: Lexington Books, 2015).

26. Knapp, *Trinity College in the Twentieth Century*.

27. "A Supplement to the Catalogue of Trinity College, for the Year 1918-1919," *Trinity College Bulletin, 1918-1919 Necrology*; Knapp, *Trinity College in the Twentieth Century*.

28. "Building Ghettoes," *Chicago Defender*, October 7, 1937. On the Great Migration, see James Grossman, *Land of Hope: Chicago, Black Southerners and the Great Migration* (Chicago: University of Chicago Press, 1989); Davarian L. Baldwin, *Chicago's New Negroes: Modernity, the Great Migration, and Black Urban Life* (Chapel Hill: University of North Carolina Press, 2007). On the "Chicago School," see Davarian L. Baldwin, "Chicago's 'Concentric Zones': Thinking Through the Material History of an Iconic Map," in *Many Voices, One Nation: Material Culture Reflections on Race and Migration in the United States of America*, ed. Margaret Salazar-Porzio and Joan Fragaszy Troyano (Washington, DC: Smithsonian Institution Scholarly Press); Baldwin, "Black Belts and Ivory Towers: The Place of Race in US Social Thought," *Critical Sociology* 30, no. 2 (2004).

29. Web Behrens, "Raisin on the Run," *Time Out Chicago*, September 21-September 27, 2006; Drake and Cayton, *Black Metropolis*, 182-187.

30. Hirsch, *Making the Second Ghetto*, 148.

31. "The South East Chicago Commission," *Hyde Park Herald*, July 21, 2004. See also Muriel Beadle, *The Hyde Park-Kenwood Urban Renewal Years: A History to Date* (Chicago: 1965), 10-13; Bruce Sagan, "The Major Story of the Last 50 Years: Urban Renewal," *Hyde Park Herald*, July 21, 2004; Peter Rossi and Robert Dentler, *The Politics of Urban Renewal: The Chicago Findings* (New York: Free Press of Glencoe, 1961).

32. Hirsch, *Making the Second Ghetto*, 144.

33. See LaDale Winling, "Students and the Second Ghetto: Federal Legislation, Urban Politics, and Campus Planning at the University of Chicago," *Journal of Planning History* 10, no. 1 (2011). On commercial rezoning, see Beadle, *The Hyde Park-Kenwood Urban Renewal Years*, 19-21; Bruce Sagan, "Harper Court: It Takes Determination and $100 Bonds," *Hyde Park Herald*, July 24, 2004.

34. See Brentin Mock, "The Meaning of Blight," *CityLab*, February 16, 2017; Wendell Pritchett, "The 'Public Menace' of Blight: Urban Renewal and the Private Use of Eminent Domain," *Yale Law & Policy Review* 21, no. 1 (2003); Yale Rabin, "Expulsive Zoning: The Inequitable Legacy of Euclid," in *Zoning and the American Dream: Promises Still to Keep*, ed. Claire Smrekar and Ellen Goldring (Chicago: Planners, 1989).

35. See Christopher Loss, *Between Citizens and the State: The Politics of American Higher Education in the 20th Century* (Princeton, NJ: Princeton University Press, 2011). This concept is also discussed in Winling, *Building the Ivory Tower*, 5.

36. Margaret Pugh O'Mara, *Cities of Knowledge: Cold War Science and the Search for the Next Silicon Valley* (Princeton, NJ: Princeton University Press, 2005); Rebecca Lowen, *Creating the Cold War University: The Transformation of Stanford* (Berkeley: University of California Press, 1997); Stuart Leslie, *The Cold War and American Science: The Military Industrial Complex at MIT and Stanford* (New York: Columbia University Press, 1993).

37. "Defense Contracts Subvert University Services," *Stanford Daily*, January 31, 1968.

38. Arnold Hirsch, "'Containment' on the Home Front: Race and Federal Housing Policy from the New Deal to the Cold War," *Journal of Urban History* 26, no. 2 (January 2000).

39. Winling, *Building the Ivory Tower*, 82-90.

40. J. Martin Klotsche, *The Urban University and the Future of Our Cities* (New York: Harper and Row, 1966); Kenneth Ashworth, "Urban Renewal and the University: A Tool for Campus Expansion and Neighborhood Improvement," *Journal of Higher Education* 35, no. 9 (1964); David Boroff, "The Case for the Asphalt Campus," *New York Times*

Magazine, April 21, 1963; David Carson, "Town and Gown," *Architectural Forum* 118 (March 1963); Lawrence Hechinger, "Campus vs. Slums: Urban Universities Join Battle for Neighborhood Renewal," *New York Times*, October 1, 1961.

41. Winling, *Building the Ivory Tower*, 91; Julian Levi, "Slum Fighter Levi Tells What to Do," *Life*, April 11, 1955; "An Encroaching Menace," *Life*, April 11, 1955.

42. Winling, "Students and the Second Ghetto," 70. Two years later, hospitals were included in the program. See Guian A. McKee, "The Hospital City in an Ethnic Enclave: Tufts-New England Medical Center, Boston's Chinatown, and the Urban Political Economy of Health Care," *Journal of Urban History* 42, no. 2 (2016).

43. J. Mark Souther, "Acropolis of the Middle-West: Decay, Renewal, and Boosterism in Cleveland's University Circle," *Journal of Planning History* 10, no. 1 (2011); Catherine Conner, "Building Moderate Progress: Citizenship, Race, and Power in Downtown Birmingham, 1940-1992" (PhD diss., University of North Carolina at Chapel Hill, 2012), 43.

44. See McKee, "The Hospital City in an Ethnic Enclave."

45. Stefan M. Bradley, *Harlem vs. Columbia University: Black Student Power in the Late 1960s* (Urbana: University of Illinois Press, 2009); Paul Cronin, ed., *A Time to Stir: Columbia '68* (New York: Columbia University Press, 2018).

46. Clara Bingham, "'The Whole World Is Watching': An Oral History of the 1968 Columbia Uprising," *Vanity Fair*, March 26, 2018; Jennifer Shuessler, "At Columbia, Revisiting the Revolutionary Students of 1968," *New York Times*, March 21, 1968; Karen Matthews, "Former Students Recall 1968 Protest That Shut Down Columbia," Associated Press, April 22, 2018; Samantha Sokol, "NYC That Never Was: A Gym in Morningside Park Sparks 1968 Columbia University Protests and Shutdown," *Untapped Cities*, October 8, 2013.

47. Bradley, *Harlem vs. Columbia University*, 28.

48. Joseph Lelyveld, "35 Hotel Tenants Picket Court in a Protest Against Columbia," *New York Times*, December 18, 1964; "Columbia Action Stirs Community: Mrs. Motley Seeks to Know Why 350 Were Ousted," *New York Times*, November 21, 1965.

49. MacKenzie S. Carlson, "A History of the University City Science Center," exhibit, University of Pennsylvania University Archives, September 1999.

50. Brian Page and Eric Ross, "Legacies of Contested Campus: Urban Renewal, Community Resistance, and the Origins of Gentrification in Denver," *Urban Geography* 38, no. 9 (2017).

51. See Vineeta Singh, "'Which Neither Devils nor Tyrants Could Remove': The Racial-Spatial Pedagogies of Modern U.S. Higher Education" (PhD diss., University of California San Diego, 2018); Arthur Cohen and Florence Brawer, *The American Community College* (San Francisco: Jossey-Bass, 1982).

52. Cohen and Brawer, *The American Community College*.

53. See Donna Murch, *Living for the City: Migration, Education, and the Rise of the Black Panther Party in Oakland, California* (Chapel Hill: University of North Carolina Press, 2010); Singh, "'Which Neither Devils nor Tyrants Could Remove.'"

54. See Martha Biondi, "'Brooklyn College Belongs to Us': Black Students and the Transformation of Public Higher Education in New York City," in *Civil Rights in New York City: From World War II to the Giuliani Era*, ed. Clarence Taylor (New York: Fordham University Press, 2011). This community college model and the "open admissions" policy should also be placed alongside what became the Higher Education Act (HEA)

of 1965. The HEA made higher education more accessible and affordable, especially for women and students of color. But its focus on student grants, work study, and low-interest loans had the unintended consequence of turning higher education into a tuition-driven market. Instead of investing public aid directly into schools, with the intent of making higher education a tuition-free opportunity, the idea of "student assistance" opened the door to a massive student loan industry, and public schools suffered the most when federal and state resources were further concentrated in elite universities.

55. Peter Moskowitz, *How to Kill a City: Gentrification, Inequality, and the Fight for the Neighborhood* (New York: Nation Books, 2017); Richard Lloyd, *Neo-Bohemia: Art and Commerce in the Postindustrial City* (London: Routledge, 2005); Christopher Mele, *Selling the Lower East Side: Culture, Real Estate, and Resistance in New York City* (Minneapolis: University of Minnesota Press, 2000); Neil Smith, *The New Urban Frontier: Gentrification and the Revanchist City* (London: Routledge, 1996); Sharon Zukin, *Loft Living: Culture and Capitol in Urban Change* (New Brunswick, NJ: Rutgers University Press, 1989).

56. Initiative for a Competitive Inner City (ICIC) and CEOs for Cities, *Leveraging Colleges and Universities for Urban Revitalization: An Action Agenda* (Boston: CEOs for Cities, 2002), quoted in Haar, *The City as Campus*, 149. See also Karin Fischer, "The University as Economic Savior," *Chronicle of Higher Education*, July 14, 2006; Robert Campbell, "Universities Are the New City Planners," *Boston Globe*, March 20, 2005.

57. Lee Benson et al., *Knowledge for Social Change: Bacon, Dewey, and the Revolutionary Transformation of Research Universities in the Twenty-First Century* (Philadelphia: Temple University Press, 2017). For more on "anchor institutions," see Oscar Perry Abello, "How 6 Universities Are Keeping Promise of Being a Good Neighbor," *Next City*, October 11, 2017; Eugenie Birch, David C. Perry, and Henry Louis Taylor Jr., "Universities as Anchor Institutions," *Journal of Higher Education Outreach and Engagement* 17, no. 3 (2013); *Urban Universities as Anchor Institutions: A Report of National Data and Survey Findings* (Coalition of Urban Serving Universities, 2010); *How to Behave Like an Anchor Institution* (CEOs for Cities, 2010); *Town-Gown Collaboration in Land Use and Development* (Cambridge, MA: Lincoln Institute of Land Policy, 2009).

58. For a sense of Taylor's present-day thinking, see Henry Louis Taylor, D. Gavin Luter, and Camden Miller, "The University, Neighborhood Revitalization, and Civic Engagement: Toward Civic Engagement 3.0," *Societies*, October 30, 2018.

59. Etienne, *Pushing Back the Gates*, 9.

60. Emily Sladek, *Higher Education's Anchor Mission: Measuring Place-Based Engagement* (Anchor Dashboard Learning Cohort, 2017).

61. Mike Sheridan, "Amenities, Diversity Are Key Ingredients of Innovation Communities," *UrbanLand*, October 16, 2018; Bruce Katz and Julie Wagner, *The Rise of Innovation Districts: A New Geography of Innovation in America* (Brookings, May 2014).

62. Dave Merrill, Blacki Migliozzi, and Susan Decker, "Billions at Stake in University Patent Fights," *Bloomberg*, May 24, 2016; John Bringardner, "Should Universities Profit from Student Research?" *New Yorker*, February 21, 2014.

63. Jacob Rooksby, *The Branding of the American Mind* (Baltimore: Johns Hopkins University Press, 2016).

64. Edward Gately, "SkySong Set to Lease New Buildings," *Arizona Republic*, April 11, 2012; Mark Flatten, "Scottsdale's SkySong Avoids Property Taxes Without GPLET Lease," *Goldwater Institute*, February 18, 2010.

65. Jonathan Wander, "Cool Tech in Pittsburgh," *Pittsburgh*, January 25, 2011; Glenn Thrush, "The Robots That Saved Pittsburgh," *Politico*, February 4, 2014.

66. Steven Kurutz, "Pittsburgh Gets a Tech Makeover," *New York Times*, July 22, 2017; Thrush, "The Robots That Saved Pittsburgh"; Edward Helmore, "Pittsburgh's Thriving Tech Sector Brings New Life to Post-industrial City," *Guardian*, October 8, 2016.

67. Noah Brode, "CMU Settles Patent Lawsuit for $750M, to Be Shared with Inventors," *WESA.fm*, February 18, 2016; Mike Masnick, "Patent Trolling Carnegie Mellon Wins What Could Be Largest Patent Verdict Ever: $1.2 Billion," *Techdirt*, December 27, 2012.

68. Carnegie Mellon University, *Student Maternity Accommodation Protocol and Resources*, September 2015.

69. Shawn Gude and Rachel M. Cohen, "Baltimore Since Beth Steel: Hopkins Hospital Workers Fight for 15," *Dissent*, June 26, 2014.

70. Michael Sandler, "CEO Pay Soars at Top Not-for-Profits," *Modern Healthcare*, August 8, 2015.

71. Sandler, "CEO Pay Soars."

72. Jess Walsh, "Living Wage Campaigns Storm the Ivory Tower: Low Wage Workers on Campus," *New Labor Forum* 6 (Spring–Summer, 2000); Daphne T. Greenwood, *The Decision to Contract Out: Understanding the Full Economic and Social Impacts* (University of Colorado, Colorado Springs: Colorado Center for Policy Studies, 2014).

73. Danielle Douglas-Gabriel, "Harvard Dining Hall Workers End Strike," *Washington Post*, October 26, 2016; Luke O'Neil, "Harvard's Striking Workers Have a Secret Weapon," *Slate*, October 18, 2016; Brandon J. Dixon and Hannah Natanson, "Harvard Dining Services Picket in Historic Strike," *Harvard Crimson*, October 6, 2016. On Harvard's expansion, see Kyle Paoletta, "Is Harvard Destroying Allston or Saving It?" *Boston*, September 9, 2019; Hakeem Angulu, "How Harvard's Expansion Affects the Communities Around It," *Medium*, September 7, 2018; Michael Ryan, "Painting the Town Crimson," *Boston Globe*, October 24, 2004.

74. Max Graham, "Planning Commission Conditionally Approves Developments at Bakery Square," *Pittsburgh Post-Gazette*, June 12, 2018; Todd Bishop, "University of Pittsburgh Chancellor on Amazon, Growth and the Tension over the City's Nonprofits," *GeekWire*, February 7, 2018.

Chapter 2: Rural College in a Capital City

1. Jim Barr, "Car Chase Ends in Crash on Vernon," *Trinity Tripod*, April 19, 1994.

2. Barr, "Car Chase Ends in Crash."

3. Mike McIntire, "By Altering Traffic, City Aims to Combat Street Crime," *Hartford Courant*, August 10, 1994.

4. McIntire, "By Altering Traffic."

5. McIntire.

6. Letter to the Editor, "Closed Street—Closed Minds," *Trinity Tripod*, September 20, 1994, quoted in Hunter Drews, "In the Shadows 'Neath the Elms': Mapping the Racial and Spatial Dynamics of Trinity College" (B.A. thesis, Trinity College, 2016); Caroline Maguire, "City Votes to Close Vernon St.," *Trinity Tripod*, September 13, 1994.

7. "C.A. Doxiadis to Theorize on City Plans," *Trinity Tripod*, March 1, 1966.

8. "Doxiadis Stresses Man, Not Form in City Plans," *Trinity Tripod*, March 8, 1966; "Doxiadis Sees Entopia Centered Around Man," *Trinity Tripod*, March 15, 1966.

9. *The Trinity Community: Feasibility Studies for Area Improvement Prepared for Trinity College, the Hartford Hospital, and the Institute of Living* (Hartford, CT: Doxiadis Associates, March 1967).

10. Administrators argued that the property purchases were not efforts to expand the campus but to fill out the "natural limits of the campus." But the notion of natural limits was never clearly defined. "Administration Denies Charges of Expansion," *Trinity Tripod*, October 3, 1969.

11. Campbell, *Frog Hollow*.

12. Stacy Metzler, "Trinity Aids in Revitalization of Hartford," *Trinity Tripod*, September 6, 1994.

13. *25th Anniversary Annual Report* (Hartford, CT: Southside Institutions Neighborhood Alliance, 2003); Melvyn Colon, "SINA—An Enduring Multi-anchor Partnership in Hartford," *Journal on Anchor Institutions and Communities* 1 (2016).

14. Art Feltman, *Tax Exemption of Private Colleges and Hospitals: A Hartford Case Study* (University of Connecticut School of Law, 1986); Robert Frahm, "Study Fuels Criticism of Trinity College," *Hartford Courant*, May 9, 1987; "Misreading Trinity's Mission," *Hartford Courant*, May 13, 1987. On Backer, see also Marie Shanahan, "Longtime Hartford Community Activist Retiring," *MetroHartford*, September 4, 1995; Ivan Backer, *My Train to Freedom* (New York: Skyhorse, 2016).

15. Katherine Farrish, "Trinity Forges Ties in Frog Hollow," *Hartford Courant*, August 29, 1994; Andrew Crawford, "In Your Backyard," *University Business Journal*, June 2001.

16. Steve Metcalf, "Raising Hackles in Academe," *Hartford Courant*, December 8, 1996.

17. Metcalf, "Raising Hackles in Academe."

18. Stacy Metzler, "Student/Hartford Resident Comments on Community," *Trinity Tripod*, September 13, 1994.

19. "Tito Puente to Star in Free Concert at Trinity," *Hartford Courant*, August 30, 1996.

20. Mike Swift and Rick Green, "A Grand Vision for Frog Hollow," *Hartford Courant*, January 14, 1996; "No Pie-in-the-Sky Fantasy," *Hartford Courant*, April 29, 1996.

21. Evan S. Dobelle, "A Bold Plan to Rescue a City Neighborhood," *Hartford Courant*, January 21, 1996; "Trinity Neighborhood Initiative to Create Community of Learning," *Trinity Reporter*, February 1996.

22. Swift and Green, "A Grand Vision for Frog Hollow"; "Boys and Girls Club Dedication Signals Momentum for Neighborhood Initiative," *Trinity Reporter*, Spring–Summer, 1998); Michael Kuczkowski, "Changing the Face of Frog Hollow," *Hartford Advocate*, March 20, 1997; Jane Gross, "Trinity College Leads Effort to Create Hartford Renewal," *New York Times*, April 4, 1997.

23. Farrish, "Trinity Forges Ties in Frog Hollow"; Gross, "Trinity College Leads Effort to Create Hartford Renewal." See also "Make the Undesirable Desirable," *Hartford Courant*, April 30, 1996.

24. Kuczkowski, "Changing the Face of Frog Hollow"; Swift and Green, "A Grand Vision for Frog Hollow."

25. Jack Dougherty, Jesse Wanzer, and Christina Ramsay, "*Sheff v. O'Neill*: Weak Desegregation Remedies and Strong Disincentives in Connecticut, 1996-2008," in *From the Courtroom to the Classroom: The Shifting Landscape of School Desegregation*, ed. Claire Smrekar and Ellen Goldring (Cambridge, MA: Harvard Education Press, 2009).

26. Hartford Areas Rally Together (HART), *People's History: The Story of Hartford Areas Rally Together* (Hartford, CT: HART, 1995); Farrish, "Trinity Forges Ties in Frog Hollow."

27. *Urban Engagement at Trinity College*, report to the board of trustees, May 2004.

28. James A. Trostle and Kevin B. Sullivan, "Trinity College and the Learning Corridor: A Small, Urban Liberal Arts College Launches a Public Magnet School Campus," *Open Access Journals at IUPUI*, journals.iupui.edu/index.php/muj/article/download/20176/19787.

29. Kathleen Megan, "After Trinity, Dobelle's Grand Ideas, Spending Land Him in Trouble," *Hartford Courant*, October 20, 2013.

30. Lizabeth Hall, "Private Grant Boosts Trinity's Efforts," *Hartford Courant*, June 5, 1998.

31. Kelly Ballantyne, "Neighbors Get High-Tech: Nonprofits Near Trinity Can Learn to Use Computers," *Hartford Courant*, January 24, 2001; Eric Goldscheider, "College Initiates Programs to Give Back to Its Neighbors," *New York Times*, November 1, 2000.

32. Meir Rhinde, "Trinity Pulls Back: After Years of Spending Money to Community Projects in the Neighborhood," *Hartford Advocate*, August 10, 2005.

33. President's Cornerstone Planning Group, *The Cornerstone Plan of Trinity College* (Trinity College, 2005); "President-Elect James F. Jones, Jr.," *Trinity Reporter* (Spring 2004); Jane Gordon, "Easy-Going, but Hands-On, at Trinity," *New York Times*, May 23, 2004.

34. Ashley Battle, "Coalition Protests Trinity Project," *Hartford Courant*, August 2, 2005.

35. Robert Frahm, "Trinity, Civic Groups Plan Sports Complex," *Hartford Courant*, June 5, 2004; "Ice Skating on Broad Street," *Hartford Courant*, June 4, 2004.

36. "Memorandum of Understanding Community Sports Complex," Southside Institutions Neighborhood Alliance (SINA) and Trinity College, November 1, 2005.

37. Greg Bordonaro, "$25 Million Plan to Add New Housing at Trinity," *Hartford Business*, September 10, 2012.

38. Kevin McClure, "Examining the 'Amenities Arms Race' in Higher Education: Shifting from Rhetoric to Research," *College Student Affairs Journal* 37, no. 2 (Fall 2019); Lindsay Corsino, "Colleges Have Entered an Amenities Arms Race to Attract New Students," *Phase Zero Design*, August 23, 2017.

39. Drews, "In the Shadows 'Neath the Elms.'"

40. Jorge Lugo, interview by Edosa Onaiwu, November 20, 2018.

41. Steven Goode, "Trinity College Residents Make Way for Student Housing," *Hartford Courant*, July 2, 2010. See also Kerri Provost, "Demolition Planned to Clear Street for New Student Housing," *Real Hartford*, May 28, 2013.

42. Goode, "Trinity College Residents Make Way."

43. Nicholas Rondinone and David Owens, "Two Arrested in 2012 Assault on Student That Shook Trinity," *Hartford Courant*, February 27, 2015. See also Hillary Federico, "Trinity Pressed to Boost Safety," *Hartford Courant*, March 6, 2012.

44. Josh Kovner, "Internal Trinity College Report: 'Preppy Looking White Males' Assaulted Student," *Hartford Courant*, May 15, 2012.

45. Rondinone and Owens, "Two Arrested in 2012 Assault."

46. Brittany Viola and Nick Auerbach, "Students Rally for Safety, Receive Feedback from Administration," *Trinity Tripod*, March 13, 2012; Christopher Brown and Kerri

Provost, "Trinity Students Rally," *RealHartford*, March 9, 2012. A Trinity professor supplied me with a collection of emails and other digital documents related to the Kenny controversy. It contains emails from the administration and students, including the student letter calling for a "Trinity Pass." See also Drews, "In the Shadows 'Neath the Elms.'"

47. Rondinone and Owens, "Two Arrested in 2012 Assault."

48. Kelly Glista, "Suspect Talked to Help Friend," *Hartford Courant*, February 28, 2015; David Owens, "Trinity Student's Attacker Sentenced," *Hartford Courant*, March 5, 2016.

49. Chiarra Davis, "The Longest Walk: Rape, Drugs, and Racial Aggression at Trinity College" (B.A. thesis, Trinity College, 2017).

50. Jill Konopka, "Three Sex Assaults Reported Within Two Weeks at Trinity College," *NBC Connecticut*, March 8, 2016.

51. Davis, "The Longest Walk," 13.

52. Davis, 6.

53. Davis, 6.

54. Interviewee 3, interview by Chiarra Davis, September 30, 2016; Interviewee 5, interview by Chiarra Davis, November 3, 2016; and Interviewee 4, interview by Chiarra Davis, October 31, 2016, all in Davis, "The Longest Walk."

55. Interviewee 18, interview by Chiarra Davis, October 6, 2016, in Davis, "The Longest Walk."

56. Kenneth Gosselin, "Trinity College Closes Deal for Downtown Hartford Campus," *Hartford Courant*, January 5, 2015; Gregory Seay, "Berger-Sweeney Looks to Strengthen Trinity's Ties to CT Inc.," *HartfordBusiness*, January 5, 2015; Kathleen Megan, "Trinity to Lease Downtown Space; Has a Buyer for 200 Constitution Plaza," *Hartford Courant*, November 21, 2016; Rick Seltzer, "Trinity College in Connecticut Sells Building and Changes Enrollment Strategy," *Inside Higher Ed*, December 1, 2016.

57. Kenneth Gosselin, "Teaming Up Downtown," *Hartford Courant*, December 4, 2009; Kenneth Gosselin, "Downtown: UConn Back in Hartford," *Hartford Courant*, October 30, 2016; Kenneth Gosselin and Jena Carlesso, "UConn Downtown Hartford Campus Makes Its Debut During Ceremonial Event," *Hartford Courant*, August 23, 2017.

58. "Trinity Preps for Downtown Hartford Campus in Fall '17," *HartfordBusiness*, December 22, 2016; David Holahan, "Strengthening Ties: Trinity College and the City: New Action Lab Downtown," *Hartford Courant*, March 1, 2018.

59. Matt Pilon, "Tech Giant Infosys to Tap Trinity College's Liberal Arts Talent," *Hartford Business Journal*, September 20, 2018; Ravi Kumar, "The Liberal Arts Degree Is Alive and Well—and Critically Important to the Future of Tech," *CNBC.com*, August 28, 2019; "Infosys and Trinity College Launch Catalytic Partnership," *PRnewswire*, September 20, 2018; Sean Teehan, "To Assert Relevance, Liberal-Arts Colleges Lean into Skills Training, Business Partnerships," *HartfordBusiness*, February 4, 2019.

60. Michelle Layser, "Opportunity Zones," *Crain's Chicago Business*, April 15, 2019; William Fulton, "Opportunity Zones: Gentrification on Steroids?" *Kinder Institute for Urban Research*, February 20, 2019; Jenna Nicholas and Eutiquio Chapa, "An Opportunity for Higher Ed," *US News*, February 14, 2019; Samantha Jacoby, "Potential Flaws of Opportunity Zones Loom, as Do Risks of Large-Scale Tax Avoidance," *Center on Budget and Policy Priorities*, January 11, 2019; Timothy Weaver, "The Problem with Opportunity Zones," *CityLab*, May 16, 2018; Adam Looney, "Will Opportunity Zones Help Distressed Residents or Be a Tax Cut for Gentrification?" *Brookings*, February 26, 2018.

61. Stephen Singer, "Four Cities Win First Innovation Places Funding to High-Tech Growth," *Hartford Courant*, June 7, 2017; *Hartford/East Hartford Innovation Places Strategic Plan*, April 1, 2017.

Chapter 3: The Schools That Ate New York

1. Sherman, "The School That Ate New York."

2. John Sexton, "Global Network University Reflection," December 21, 2010, www .nyu.edu/about/leadership-university-administration/office-of-the-president-emeritus /communications/global-network-university-reflection.html. See also Rachel Aviv, "The Imperial Presidency," *New Yorker*, September 2, 2013.

3. John Sexton, "Fire and Ice: The Knowledge Century and the Urban University," August 10, 2007, www.nyu.edu/about/leadership-university-administration/office -of-the-president-emeritus/communications/fire-and-ice-the-knowledge-century-and-the -urban-university.html.

4. Nick Pinto, "As Growth Shifts into Overdrive, NYU Faces a Rebellion from Within," *Village Voice*, February 20, 2013.

5. Sherman, "The School That Ate New York."

6. J. Alex Tarquinio, "New Campus Buildings Take Shape," *Wall Street Journal*, December 30, 2013. See also Gary Stern, "The Colleges That Ate New York," *Commercial Observer*, January 21, 2015.

7. Richard Florida, "The Reality of America's College Towns," *CityLab*, September 8, 2016; Laura Kusisto, "The World's Biggest College Town," *Observer*, February 2, 2011.

8. Leslie Casimir, "Protest Targets Landlord in Low-Income Evicts," *New York Daily News*, June 11, 2006; Sarah Hines, "The Struggle for Housing," *Socialist Worker*, June 19, 2006.

9. Steven Gregory, "The Radiant University: Space, Urban Redevelopment, and the Public Good," *City & Society* 25, no. 1 (April 2013).

10. Gregory, "The Radiant University."

11. Casimir, "Protest Targets Landlord." For a sample of the Juan Gonzalez investigative series in the *New York Daily News*, see "Renters in Crisis: Reform Needed Now," July 26, 2006; "Phony Repairs Add to Abuse," May 15, 2006; "Full-Court Press vs. Poor Tenants," May 7, 2006. See also Hines, "The Struggle for Housing." For an updated story, see Juliana Kim, "Inside Manhattanville Tenants' Fight Against Predatory Landlords," *Columbia Spectator*, February 21, 2018.

12. Charles Bagli, "Columbia Buys Sites and Assures Neighbors," *New York Times*, April 21, 2004; Charles Bagli, "Columbia, in a Growth Spurt, Is Buying a Swath of Harlem," *New York Times*, July 30, 2003.

13. Bagli, "Columbia Buys Sites."

14. "West Harlem Renaissance: Court Okay for Columbia Development Big Win," *New York Daily News*, June 26, 2010.

15. Daphne Eviatar, "The Manhattanville Project," *New York Times*, May 21, 2006.

16. Bagli, "Columbia Buys Sites."

17. Bagli.

18. New York City is divided into fifty-nine community boards with fifty members appointed by each borough president. In 1989 the city charter empowered boards to submit plans for adoption by the city planning commission and city council, but their role is

merely advisory. But CB 9's plan remains notable because it proposed development based on the existing fabric of the neighborhood while respecting the university's need for expansion. Also, 197-a would allow Columbia to build around a mixed-use landscape of manufacturing, affordable housing in historic buildings, and current property owners. On the area's potential, see Allen Salkin, "Vital Signs Under the Viaduct," *New York Times*, October 19, 2008; Gregory, "The Radiant University."

19. *Community Board 9 Manhattan 197-a Plan*, September 24, 2007; Student Coalition on Expansion and Gentrification, *Columbia's West Harlem Expansion: A Look at the Issues*, 2014.

20. "Bollinger Speaks Out on Campus Environment," *Columbia Spectator*, October 12, 2007; *Tuck-It-Away et al. v. New York State Urban Development Corporation*, 2009, New York Supreme Court, Appellate Division.

21. *The Civil Rights Implications of Eminent Domain Abuse* (Washington, DC: U.S. Commission on Civil Rights, 2014); Justin Kamen, "A Standardless Standard: How a Misapplication of *Kelo* Enabled Columbia University to Benefit from Eminent Domain Abuse," *Brooklyn Law Review* 1217 (Spring 2012); Keith Hirokawa and Patricia Salkin, "Can Urban University Expansion and Sustainable Development Co-exist? A Case Study in Progress on Columbia University," *Fordham Urban Law Journal* 637 (April 2010); Katherine Mirett, "Columbia University's Big Bite out of the Big Apple: The Problem of Unrestricted Eminent Domain in New York and the Need for More Active Courts," *Seton Hall Law Review* 423 (2012).

22. Lee Bollinger, interview by Brian Lehrer, *The Brian Lehrer Show*, March 8, 2006, transcript.

23. Abigail Daniel, interview by Ambar Paulino, March 11, 2015.

24. Eviatar, "The Manhattanville Project."

25. Gregory, "The Radiant University."

26. Jimmy Vielkind and Erin Durkin, "CU Paving Way for Eminent Domain Use," *Columbia Spectator*, April 15, 2005.

27. See Brentin Mock, "The Meaning of Blight," *CityLab*, February 16, 2017; Wendell Pritchett, "The 'Public Menace' of Blight: Urban Renewal and the Private Use of Eminent Domain," *Yale Law & Policy Review* 21, no. 1 (2003); Rabin, "Expulsive Zoning."

28. Empire State Development Corporation (Allee, King, Rosen, and Fleming), *Manhattanville Neighborhoods Condition Study*, 2007. See also Duncan Currie, "Why Columbia's Proposed Expansion Has Met Resistance," *Weekly Standard*, August 8, 2007; Matthew Pickel, "Standing Pat in a Post-*Kelo* World: Preservation of Broad Eminent Domain Power in *Knaur v. New York State Development Corporation*," *Boston College Law Review* 52 (2011).

29. Gregory, "The Radiant University," 60.

30. Trymaine Lee, "Bracing the Lion," *New York Times*, July 22, 2007.

31. Kenny Nuñez, interview by Ambar Paulino, March 18, 2015.

32. Sam Levin, "Was Manhattanville Blighted?" *Columbia Spectator*, October 12, 2016.

33. Thomas Lopez-Pierre, interview by Ambar Paulino, March 4, 2015.

34. Anemona Hartocollis, "Neutrality in Expansion at Columbia Questioned," *New York Times*, June 30, 2007; *Tuck-It-Away Associates, L.P., Petitioner-Respondent v. Empire State Development Corporation, Respondent-Appellant*, Supreme Court, Appellate Division, July 15, 2008.

35. Timothy Williams, "Harlem Area Is Blighted, State Agency Declares," *New York Times*, July 18, 2008.

36. CB 9 Hearing Testimony Transcript, August 15, 2007, 99. See also Sewell Chan, "Panel Rejects Columbia's Expansion Plan," *New York Times*, August 16, 2007; Anna Phillips, "Key Committee Rejects Expansion Plan," *Columbia Spectator*, August 16, 2007.

37. "Statement of Mayor Bloomberg and Governor Paterson on Final Public Approval of General Project Plan for Columbia University Expansion," www1.nyc.gov, May 20, 2009.

38. Betsy Morais, "Singh Family Gas Station Continues Holdout," *Columbia Spectator*, August 23, 2013.

39. Eliot Brown, "Storage Mogul Is an Obstacle to Columbia's Expansion," *New York Sun*, July 19, 2007; Adam Sieff, "The Clever Capitalism of Nicholas Sprayregen," *Columbia Spectator*, September 17, 2010.

40. *Tuck-It-Away Associates, L.P., Petitioner-Respondent v. Empire State Development Corporation*; Julio Vitullo-Martin, "Columbia Gets a Lesson in Property Rights," *Wall Street Journal*, January 1, 2010; Elizabeth Dwoskin, "Court Deals Blow to Columbia's $6.3 Billion Harlem Land Grab," *Village Voice*, December 3, 2009; Charles Bagli, "Court Bars New York's Takeover of Land for Columbia Campus," *New York Times*, December 3, 2009.

41. Charles Bagli, "Court Upholds Columbia Campus Expansion Plan," *New York Times*, June 24, 2010.

42. Megan McArdle, "Columbia Eminent Domain Case Will Not Be Heard," *Atlantic*, December 14, 2010.

43. *West Harlem Community Benefits Agreement*, May 18, 2009, https://gca.columbia.edu/sites/default/files/2016-11/CBAAgreement.pdf, quoted in Ambar Paulino, "Weaving Ebony and Ivy: Columbia University's Role in Transforming West Harlem" (B.A. thesis, Trinity College, 2015), 46. See also Maggie Astor, "Where Have All the Benefits Gone?" *The Eye: Magazine of the Columbia Spectator*, February 17, 2011.

44. Jeff Mays, "Group Handling Columbia Cash Spent $300K on Consultants with Political Ties," *DNAInfo*, December 8, 2011; Jeff Mays, "Group Distributing Columbia Cash Did Nothing Illegal, Investigators Say," *DNAInfo*, December 19, 2012; Avantika Kumar, "Attorney General Investigation Shows No Misuse of Funds at WHLDC," *Columbia Spectator*, October 20, 2014.

45. Kenny Nuñez, interview by Ambar Paulino, March 18, 2015.

46. Jeff Mays, "CB9 Calls for Audit of Columbia's Promises to West Harlem Community," *DNAInfo*, March 22, 2013; Jeff Mays, "Black Architects Say Columbia Shut Them Out of $6.3 Billion Harlem Campus," *DNAInfo*, December 18, 2012.

47. Jeff Mays, "State to Review Minority Hiring at Columbia Expansion Project," *DNAInfo*, February 4, 2013; Mays, "State Reviewing Columbia's Minority Hiring at West Harlem Campus Expansion," *DNAInfo*, June 5, 2013.

48. Abigail Daniel, interview by Ambar Paulino, March 11, 2015.

49. John Caulfield, "Columbia University Dedicates Its New Campus with Great Fanfare," *Building Design + Construction*, October 25, 2016.

50. James Russell, "The Architecture Behind Columbia's Manhattanville Ambitions," *CityLab*, May 2, 2019.

51. Justin Davidson, "Columbia University Tries to Welcome the Neighbors In—and Keeps Them at Arm's Length," *New York*, November 12, 2018. See also Nathan

Kensinger, "As Columbia Moves into Manhattanville, Its Industrial Past Is Erased," *Curbed NY*, March 8, 2018.

52. Kensinger, "As Columbia Moves into Manhattanville"; Clay Anderson and Stephanie Lai's three-part series, "Upscaled: The Cost of Columbia Construction for Struggling 12th Avenue Businesses," *Columbia Daily Spectator*, March 13, 2020 (all three parts). See also Elizabeth Kim, "Harlem Residents Deride Columbia's Plan for a Residential Tower as a 'Bait and Switch,'" *Gothamist*, December 11, 2019.

53. Russell, "The Architecture Behind Columbia's Manhattanville Ambitions."

54. Davidson, "Columbia University Tries to Welcome the Neighbors In."

55. Flores Alexander Forbes, *Will You Die with Me? My Life and the Black Panther Party* (New York: Altria, 2006).

56. "Racial Demographics of the Manhattanville Area," *NYC Planning* (2000-2010), Center for Urban Research, the Graduate Center, CUNY, May 23, 2011; Leah Hochbaum Rosner, "What to Know if You're Looking to Live in West Harlem/Manhattanville," *Brick Underground*, July 19, 2008; Kim, "Inside Manhattanville Tenants' Fight."

57. Michael Orry, "West Harlem's Real Estate Roars amid Columbia University's Expansion & Energized Factory District," *Insights: Ariel Property Advisors*, July 18, 2018. See also Anderson and Lai, "Upscaled."

58. Mike Longman, "Is the Market or Manhattanville Driving Hamilton Heights Development?" *City Limits*, February 9, 2015.

59. "Looking to the Future: NYU Aims for a Profound—and Necessary—Expansion Throughout Its Home City," *NYU Alumni Magazine*, Fall 2010.

60. Issac Kamola, *Making the World Global: U.S. Universities and the Production of the Global Imaginary* (New York: New York University Press, 2019); Monika Krause, Mary Nolan, Michael Palm, and Andrew Ross, eds., *The University Against Itself: The NYU Strike and the Future of the Academic Workplace* (Philadelphia: Temple University Press, 2008).

61. "Looking to the Future"; Nancy Scola, "N.Y.U.'s Alicia Hurley Takes on Intransigent Neighbors, Explains How They Will Sell Faculty on the Big 2031 Expansion Plan," *Politico*, April 23, 2012. See also Henry Grabar, "A Brief History of NYU Land Battles," *CityLab*, July 17, 2012.

62. Tim Teeman, "How Jane Jacobs Fought to Save New York," *Daily Beast*, November 7, 2016; James Nevius, "Jane Jacobs, Robert Moses, and the Battle Over LOMEX," *Curbed*, May 4, 2016; Chris Pomorski, "Power Couple: The Feud Between Jane Jacobs and Robert Moses Becomes Operatic," *Observer*, May 29, 2015.

63. Rebecca Bengal, "Living on an NYU Superblock," *Curbed NY*, August 15, 2018.

64. Sherman, "The School That Ate New York."

65. Mark Levine, "Ivy Envy," *New York Times Magazine*, June 8, 2003.

66. Aviv, "The Imperial Presidency"; Sherman, "The School That Ate New York."

67. Jake Scobey-Thal, "Town-Gown Relations 101: When the University Overtakes the Town," *Next City*, July 25, 2012.

68. Ernest Patrick, Patrick Deer, and Mark Crispin Miller, "Expand Minds, Not the NYU Campus," *New York Times*, April 25, 2012.

69. John Del Signore, "NYU to Build *Around* Provincetown Playhouse," *Gothamist*, May 16, 2008.

70. Sherman, "The School That Ate New York"; Andrew Berman, "N.Y.U. Is Really Growing on Us, Not in a Good Way," *Villager*, September 24-30, 2008. See also Felicia R. Lee, "N.Y.U. Plan Threatens Historic Theater," *New York Times*, April 30, 2008; Sarah

Bean Apmann, "The Birth of the Provincetown Playhouse," *Off the Grid: Blog of the Green-wich Village Society for Historic Preservation*, November 3, 2017.

71. Eli Rosenberg, "After a Long War, Can NYU and the Village Ever Make Peace," *Curbed NY*, March 19, 2014.

72. Lisa Foderaro, "N.Y.U. Expansion Plans Meet Neighborhood Critics," *New York Times*, April 14, 2010.

73. Charlie Eisenhood, "How NYU Plans to Expand in the Village & Why Residents Are So Mad," *NYU Local*, November 8, 2010.

74. Rebecca Spitz, "Enthusiasm for NYU 2031 Expansion Plan Not Uniform in Village," *NY1.com*, April 15, 2010; Sherman, "The School That Ate New York."

75. Joseph Berger, "Key Official Would Trim N.Y.U. Plan to Expand," *New York Times*, March 29, 2012; Amanda Fung, "NYU Loses First Round in Expansion Battle," *Crain's New York Business*, February 24, 2012; Nicole Breskin, "NYU Task Force Disbanded After Four Years," *DNAInfo*, July 9, 2010; Editorial, "NYU Begins Public Review of Expansion," *Downtown Express*, July 21–27, 2010; Editorial, "Stringer Was Right," *Villager*, July 22–28, 2010.

76. Gabriel Sherman, "I. M. Pei Scuttles Plans for NYU Tower," *New York*, November 18, 2010; Joey Arak, "Breaking: NYU Drops 40-Story Tower, but Here Comes Plan B!" *Curbed NY*, November 18, 2010.

77. Tom Acitelli, "Andrew Berman, the Village Crier," *New York Observer*, September 11, 2007.

78. Nancy Scola, "At NYU, Faculty Form a Group to Protest Big 2031 Expansion, and the Sexton Administration Stays Mum About It," *Politico*, March 13, 2012.

79. Ariel Kaminer, "NYU's Global Leader Is Tested by Faculty at Home," *New York Times*, March 9, 2013; Zoe Schlanger, "NYU Professors Sue Government Over 2031 Expansion," *Nation*, September 27, 2012.

80. Patrick, Deer, and Miller, "Expand Minds, Not the NYU Campus." On the plan's cost and NYU endowment, see Schlanger, "NYU Professors Sue Government Over 2031 Expansion"; Eisenhood, "How NYU Plans to Expand in the Village."

81. Jimmy Chin, "Why the 2031 Plan Is Untenable," *NYU Local*, April 24, 2015; Lynn O'Shaughnessy, "Look Who Doesn't Deserve Financial Aid at NYU," *CBS News*, June 19, 2013; Jake Flanagin, "The Expensive Romance of NYU," *Atlantic*, August 21, 2013; Pinto, "As Growth Shifts into Overdrive"; Claudia Dreifus, "NYU Eats World: An Alumna Laments the Rise of an Imperial University," *Chronicle of Higher Education*, September 29, 2014.

82. Rosenberg, "After a Long War"; Kaminer, "NYU's Global Leader Is Tested."

83. Lincoln Anderson, "C.B. 2 Votes Unanimous No! on NYU's Superblocks Plan," *Villager*, March 1, 2012; Letter, "C.B. 2 to Amanda Burden, Chair, NYC Department of Planning," March 11, 2012. See also Bengal, "Living on an NYU Superblock."

84. Lincoln Anderson, "Chamber Chief: NYU Plan Will Help Village Keep Its Character," *Villager*, March 15, 2012.

85. "Stringer-ing NYU Along," *New York Post*, March 28, 2012; Ed Koch, "NYU, Spread Your Wings," *New York Daily News*, March 14, 2012.

86. Andrea Swalec, "Scott Stringer Approves Modified NYU Expansion Plan," *DNAInfo*, April 11, 2012; Katherine Clarke, "NYU Expansion Detractors Rally at Public Hearing," *Real Deal*, April 25, 2012.

87. Maya Shwayder, "Matthew Broderick Testifies at Council Hearing on NYU Expansion," *DNAInfo*, June 29, 2012; "Statement from NYU Faculty Against the Sexton Plan @ City Council Hearing," June 29, 2012; Maya Shwayder, "NYU Professors Accuse President of Exaggerating Need for Expansion," *DNAInfo*, July 9, 2012.

88. Sherman, "The School That Ate New York"; Georgette Fleischer, "Lesson of the NYU Vote: City Hall Is Unreachable," *Villager*, August 2, 2012.

89. "Testimony of Matthew Broderick Before the City Council Subcommittee on Zoning and Franchises re: NYU 2031 Expansion Plan," June 29, 2012 (in author's possession).

90. Jeremiah Budin, "City Council Passes NYU's Village Expansion Plan," *Curbed NY*, July 25, 2012.

91. Joseph Berger, "NYU's Plan to Expand Is Approved by Council," *New York Times*, July 25, 2012.

92. Ariel Kaminer and Alain Delaqueriere, "NYU Gives Its Stars Loans for Summer Homes," *New York Times*, June 17, 2013; Jen Chung, "Congrats, NYU Students: You're Paying for Your Faculty's Million-Dollar Vacation Homes," *Gothamist*, June 18, 2013; James Covert, "NYU Gave President's Aspiring Actor Son Agreement on Campus," *New York Post*, April 16, 2014.

93. Arial Kaminer, "NYU Impending Compensation Inquiry, Senator Says," *New York Times*, July 10, 2013.

94. No-confidence votes were long considered a last-ditch, Hail Mary statement of faculty dissent that were rarely used. They could easily backfire when trustees more fervently circle the wagons behind an embattled president pushing their economic agenda. But in arguably the most high-profile case, Harvard's 2005 no-confidence vote against Larry Summers is argued to have led to his ultimate resignation. See Connor Durkin, "Let's Review: No Confidence at NYU," *NYU Local*, September 6, 2013; Kevin Kiley, "New York University Vote of No Confidence Raises Debate About Ambitions and Governance Models," *Inside Higher Ed*, March 18, 2013; Kaminer, "NYU's Global Leader Is Tested."

95. Virginia K. Smith, "Now That It's Really Happening, Here's What You Need to Know About That NYU Expansion," *Brick Underground*, July 9, 2015; Lincoln Anderson, "NYU Expansion Plan OK'd by State's Highest Court," *Villager*, June 30, 2015.

96. Eddie Small, "Cracking the University Real Estate Code," *Real Deal*, May 1, 2018; Stern, "The College That Ate New York"; Tarquinio, "New Campus Buildings Take Shape."

97. Longman, "Is the Market or Manhattanville Driving Hamilton Heights Development?"; Sylvia Morse, "NYU Controversy Shows It's Time to Rethink City Planning Process," *City Limits*, July 22, 2015.

Chapter 4: The "800-Pound Gargoyle"

1. Alia Shahzad, "The Bill That Would Have Subjected UCPD to FOIA," *Chicago Maroon*, May 28, 2018.

2. Lydialyle Gibson, "Due South," *University of Chicago Magazine*, February 2006.

3. Mike Stevens, "Learning from the 'Terrible Mistakes' of Urban Renewal," *Hyde Park Herald*, April 14, 2004.

4. Deanna Issacs, "Hyde Park & Kenwood Issue: The 800-Pound Gargoyle," *Chicago Reader*, March 4, 2010; Baldwin, "The '800-Pound Gargoyle.'"

5. Friends of the Checkerboard Lounge, "Checkerboard Move Recalls Urban Renewal Days," *Hyde Park Herald*, February 4, 2004; Paula Robinson, "This Tale of Two Cities Could Have Happier Ending," *Hyde Park Herald*, January 7, 2004.

6. Web Behrens, "A Savior for Bronzeville," *Crain's Chicago Business*, June 15, 2017.

7. Mindy Fullilove, *Root Shock: How Tearing Up City Neighborhoods Hurts America, and What We Can Do About It* (New York: One World/Ballantine, 2004).

8. Andrea Walker, "Chicago, Where Fun Comes to Die," *New Yorker*, June 24, 2009. See also Dennis Rodkin, "College Comeback: The University of Chicago Finds Its Groove," *Chicago*, March 16, 2011.

9. Robert Sharoff, "University of Chicago Works on Its Neighborhood," *New York Times*, October 23, 2012.

10. Sherry Tierney, "Rezoning Chicago's Modernisms: Ludwig Mies Van Der Rohe, Remment Koolhaus, the ITT Campus and Its Bronzeville Prehistory, 1914-2003" (M.A. thesis, Arizona State University, 2008); Phyllis Lambert, ed., *Mies in America* (New York: Harry N. Abrams, 2001); Linda Lutton, "Racial Change in Pilsen: Mi Casa? Tu Casa?" *WBEZ*, August 30, 2012; Kaaren Fehsenfeld, "Zoning in on Pilsen: As Development Moves In, Old-Timers Move Out," *ChicagoTalks*, May 26, 2010; Haar, *The City as Campus*, 155-160.

11. Jim Wagner, "Checkerboard Owner Asked for U of C's Help," *Hyde Park Herald*, December 17, 2003. On "leakage," see "Pair of Publications Spotlight Hyde Park Retail Development," *Hyde Park Herald*, July 26, 2008.

12. Michael Lipkin, "U of C Buys Harper Court for $6.5 Million," *Chicago Maroon*, May 16, 2008.

13. "University of Chicago Purchases Harper Court, Partners with City to Revitalize 53rd Street," *UChicago News*, May 13, 2008; Kadesha Thomas, "What's up with Harper Theater," *53rd Street Blog*, http://fiftythird.uchicago.edu, accessed February 12, 2010.

14. Kate Hawley, "Harper Court Developer Selected," *Hyde Park Herald*, January 20, 2010.

15. As part of an extensive series of *Chicago Reader* TIF articles by Joravsky, "A TIF Under the Microscope," July 15, 2010; "Shedding Light on the Shadow Budget," December 10, 2009; "October Surprise," November 5, 2009; "Mr. Big Spender," August 5, 2009; "University Village: The Story's Not Finished," May 28, 2009; "Show Us the Money," March 19, 2009.

16. Jordan Larson, "Hyde Park Hotel Construction Draws Protest," *Chicago Reader*, August 10, 2012; Chuck Sudo, "Penny Pritzker Resigns from Board of Education," *Chicagoist*, March 14, 2013; Curtis Black, "Chicago School Board Member Benefits from District Budget Cut," *Truthout*, August 12, 2012.

17. Hawley, "Harper Court Developer Selected"; Steve Kloehn, "Community Hears the Latest Ideas for Harper Court," *53rd Street Blog*, http://fiftythird.uchicago.edu, accessed February 17, 2010.

18. Kadesha Thomas, "Harper Court Moving Forward—Three Contenders," *53rd Street Blog*, http://fiftythird.uchicago.edu, accessed September 17, 2009.

19. John Slania, "Hyde Park's Big Test," *Time Out Chicago*, February 17, 2010; Lisa Grant, "U of C Needs to Work in Partnership with Community," *Hyde Park Herald*, August 27, 2008.

20. See Joel Hood, "Hyde Park Eatery's Luck Goes South," *Chicago Tribune*, May 29, 2009. See also Deva Woodley, "Growing Pains: Dixie Kitchen Closing June 7th," *53rd*

Street Blog, http://fiftythird.uchicago.edu, accessed January 1, 2009; Nolan, "Hyde Park's Big Test"; Johnathon Briggs, "Hyde Park Haircut Hub on the Move," *Chicago Tribune*, December 27, 2006.

21. "Black Restaurants to Be Displaced by Redevelopment Project," *Chicago Defender*, May 27, 2008.

22. Michael Sorkin, ed., *Variations on a Theme Park: The New American City and the End of Public Space* (New York: Hill and Wang, 1992).

23. This insight is reinforced by Sharoff, "University of Chicago Works."

24. Jason Grotto, "We Can't Do Everything for Everyone; U of C to Close Clinic but Says It Is Not Abandoning Poor Patients," *Chicago Tribune*, May 19, 2009, 1.

25. Claire Bushey and Kristen Schorsch, "The Fight for a University of Chicago Adult Trauma Center: The Rumble and the Reversal," *Crain's Chicago Business*, April 15, 2016.

26. Bruce Japsen, "U of C Goes Forward with New Facility; Despite Economy, Financing in Works for Hospital Pavilion," *Chicago Tribune*, July 23, 2009, 29; Jason Grotto, "We Can't Do Everything"; Carlos Ballesteros, "'No Trauma, No-Bama,' Activists Tell University of Chicago," *In These Times*, July 17, 2014; Bushey, "The Fight for a University of Chicago Adult Trauma Center."

27. Daniel Gross, "Chicago's South Side Finally Has an Adult Trauma Center Again," *New Yorker*, May 1, 2018; Lisa Schencker and Ese Olumhense, "University of Chicago's New Trauma Center Opens, with Cautious Optimism," *Chicago Tribune*, April 30, 2018.

28. Leah Hope and Laura Podesta, "Construction Begins on New South Side Trauma Center," *ABC 7 Chicago*, September 15, 2016.

29. Madhu Srikantha, "Undercover UCPD Detective Infiltrates Protest," *Chicago Maroon*, March 1, 2013; aaroncynic, "Two University of Chicago Police Employees Put on Leave After Infiltrating Protest," *Chicagoist*, March 6, 2013.

30. Lee Harris, "Jury Sides with Cop Allegedly Scapegoated by UCPD's 'Old Boy's Club,'" *Chicago Maroon*, May 17, 2018.

31. *Milton Owens, Plaintiff-Appellee v. University of Chicago*, 2019 Ill. App. 181439 (Ill. App. Ct 2019).

32. John Sloan, "The Modern Campus Police: An Analysis of Their Evolution, Structure, and Function," *American Journal of Police* 11, no. 2 (January 1992); Jared E. Knowles, *Policing the American University* (Civilytics Consulting, 2020).

33. Dan Bauman, "Campus Police Acquire Military Weapons," *New York Times*, September 21, 2014; Dante Barry and Pete Haviland-Eduah, "The Danger of Militarizing Campus Police Forces," *Ebony*, October 19, 2015; Nathalie Baptiste, "Campus Cops: Authority Without Accountability," *American Prospect*, November 2, 2015; Christopher Moraff, "Campus Cops Are Shadowy, Militarized, and More Powerful Than Ever," *Washington Post*, July 9, 2015. For a story of internal conflict within a campus police force, see Ema Schumer, "The Old Boys' Network: Racism, Sexism, and Alleged Favoritism in Harvard's Police Force," *Harvard Crimson*, January 31, 2020.

34. Jonah Newman, "More Than Half of Chicago Area Universities Have Armed Police Departments," *Chicago Reporter*, July 30, 2015; Baptiste, "Campus Cops: Authority Without Accountability."

35. Sharon Coolidge et al., "Prosecutor: UC Officer 'Purposefully Killed' DuBose," *Cincinnati Enquirer*, July 30, 2015.

36. Richard Pérez-Peña, "Fatal Police Shootings: Accounts Since Ferguson," *New York Times*, April 8, 2015; Jess Bidgood and Richard Pérez-Peña, "Mistrial in Cincinnati

Shooting as Officer Is Latest Not to Be Convicted," *New York Times*, June 23, 2017. See also David Graham, "How One Campus Cop Undid a City's Police Reforms," *Atlantic*, July 30, 2015.

37. Brandon Harris, "One Week in Cincinnati," *New Yorker*, August 10, 2015.

38. Scott Eric Kaufman, "'This Is Without Question, a Murder': Prosecutor Indicts 'Asinine' White Cop in Shooting Death of Unarmed Black Motorist," *Salon*, July 29, 2015; Robinson Meyer, "Body-Camera Footage Gets an Officer Indicted for Murder," *Atlantic*, July 29, 2015; Graham, "How One Campus Cop Undid a City's Police Reforms."

39. John Minchillo, "'It's Not a Good Situation': Cincinnati Officials React to Body Cam Footage in Police Shooting of Unarmed Black Motorist," *Vice*, July 28, 2015.

40. Marianne Kirby, "How #theIRATE8 Turned Sam DuBose's Death into a Local Revolution," *Daily Dot*, September 21, 2015; Chris Graves, "Irate 8 a New Generation of Activist," *Cincinnati Enquirer*, September 19, 2015.

41. John Mura and Sheryl Gay Stolberg, "Samuel DuBose's Death in Cincinnati Points to Off-Campus Power of Campus Police," *New York Times*, July 31, 2015. David Stradling offers a very detailed institutional account of the University of Cincinnati's varied means of expanding into the surrounding area. See Stradling, *In Service to the City: A History of the University of Cincinnati* (Cincinnati, OH: University of Cincinnati Press, 2018).

42. Max Kutner, "Indictment of Cincinnati Campus Cop Raises Fears About Armed Police at Schools," *Newsweek*, August 5, 2015; Salvador Hernandez, "Three Other Black Men Have Died in Altercations with University of Cincinnati Police," *BuzzFeedNews*, July 30, 2015; Ryan Felton and Oliver Laughland, "Officers at Sam DuBose Scene Involved in Death of Another Unarmed Black Man," *Guardian*, July 30, 2015.

43. James Leggate, "Report: Ex-UCPD Chief Skipped 'Basic Steps,'" *WCPO.com*, April 14, 2016; *Final Report for the Comprehensive Review of the University of Cincinnati Police Department* (EXIGER, 2016).

44. Hannah Gold, "Why Does a Campus Police Department Have Jurisdiction Over 65,000 Chicago Residents?" *Vice*, November 12, 2014.

45. Shahzad, "The Bill That Would Have Subjected UCPD to FOIA."

46. Jonah Newman, "University of Chicago to Release Data on Stops and Arrests by Campus Police," *Chicago Reporter*, April 13, 2015; "New Data Supports Old Accusations of Racial Profiling by University of Chicago Police Department," *Chicago Reporter*, April 5, 2016.

47. Ashvini Katrik-Narayan, "The Fight Over Chicago's Largest Private Police Force," *South Side Weekly*, July 16, 2018; Jonah Newman, "U. of C. Police Shooting Came at Time of Increased Stops, Continued Disparities," *Chicago Reporter*, April 6, 2018. See also Aaron Gettinger, "UCPD Pedestrian, Traffic Stops Involve Disproportionate Number of Blacks, Minorities," *Hyde Park Herald*, July 3, 2018.

48. Luke Broadwater, "Despite Intensive Lobbying Effort, Johns Hopkins Private Police Legislation Faces Uncertain Future," *Baltimore Sun*, February 8, 2019; Rollin Hu, "The Winding and Contested Path to a Johns Hopkins Police Force," *Baltimore Beat*, March 21, 2019.

49. Brandon Soderberg, "What a Private Police Force Would Mean for Johns Hopkins University and Baltimore," *Real News Network*, March 13, 2018; "Opposition Grows to Hopkins Armed, Private Police Force Proposal," *Real News Network*, February 21, 2019.

50. Newman, "U. of C. Police Shooting Came at Time of Increased Stops"; University Faculty and Staff, "Open Letter Regarding the UCPD Shooting," April 5, 2018.

51. Bruce DePuyt, "Senator on Hopkins Bill: 'It's Akin to Establishing a Vatican City Within Baltimore,'" *Maryland Matters*, February 21, 2019.

52. Bruce DePuyt, "Bloomberg Wades into Hopkins Police Controversy," *Maryland Matters*, January 22, 2019; Michelle Evans, "Bloomberg Donates $5 million to Baltimore Police to Combat Violence," *Baltimore*, December 4, 2017.

53. Mark Reutter, "On a Single Day, Johns Hopkins Officials Gave Baltimore's Mayor $16,000," *Baltimore Brew*, March 4, 2019.

54. Luke Broadwater, "Johns Hopkins Spent $581,000 on Lobbying During Push for Armed Police Force," *Baltimore Sun*, July 10, 2019.

55. Fern Shen, "Citing School Officials' Contribution to Pugh, Hopkins Students Protest Private Police Plan," *Baltimore Brew*, April 9, 2019; Larry Smith, "Johns Hopkins University's Private Police Force Would Bring More Cops to an Overpoliced Baltimore," *Appeal*, May 16, 2019; Abdallah Fayyad, "The Criminalization of Gentrifying Neighborhoods," *Atlantic*, December 20, 2017; Soderberg, "How to Protest Campus Cops."

56. It should be noted that organizing pressure did force Maryland lawmakers to alter the original proposal. The approved law includes requirements for activated body cameras, Baltimore residency for at least 25 percent of the officers, and a ban on using surplus military equipment. Unlike in other states, the Hopkins police force will be subject to Maryland's Public Information Act. But still, Hopkins appoints thirteen of the fifteen members of an accountability board that has no power to discipline officers. See Laura Pugh, "Johns Hopkins Police Bill Signed into Law, Despite Student and Community Objections," *Biomedical Odyssey*, April 28, 2019.

57. Jonah Charlton and Kylie Cooper, "'Fire Rush, Defund UPPD, Pay PILOTs': Over 100 Gather to Protest Police Violence," *Daily Pennsylvanian*, July 24, 2020; Genesis Qu, "UCLA Faculty Criticize Decision to Let LAPD Use Jackie Robinson Stadium," *Daily Bruin*, August 14, 2020. See also Julia Barajas, "At Some U.S. Universities, a Time to Rethink Cops on Campus," *Los Angeles Times*, July 9, 2020; Michael Sainato, "US Students Call on Universities to Dismantle and Defund Campus Policing," *Guardian*, June 24, 2020.

58. Darcy Kuang, "RAUC Hosts Reparations Summit with Activists," *Chicago Maroon*, April 29, 2019; Grace Del Veccho, "Inside the 19-Hour Occupation of the University of Chicago Police Headquarters," *Chicago Reader*, June 18, 2020.

59. "The University Must Disband Its Private Police Force," *Chicago Maroon*, June 28, 2020.

60. Kathy Bergen, Blair Kamin, and Katherine Skiba, "Obama Chooses Historic Jackson Park as Library Site," *Chicago Tribune*, July 27, 2016; Julie Bosman and Mitch Smith, "Chicago Wins Bid to Host Obama Library," *New York Times*, May 12, 2015. See also Rick Perlstein, "There Goes the Neighborhood," *Baffler*, July 2015.

61. Dahleen Glanton, "Obama Library Plan Is Reminder of Bad Blood Between Community, U. of C.," *Chicago Tribune*, January 23, 2015.

62. Maya Rhodan, "Barack Obama Is Beloved in Chicago, but Activists Are Divided Over His Future Presidential Center," *Time*, July 19, 2018; Curtis Lawrence, "Hope and Change Collide on the South Side," *CityLab*, November 7, 2017; Sam Cholke, "Obama Library Will Give $3.1 Billion Boost to Cook County, New Report Says," *DNAInfo*, May 12, 2017.

63. Lolly Bowean and Blair Kamin, "Obama Makes Pitch for His Center in Jackson Park," *Chicago Tribune*, February 28, 2018.

64. Sam Cholke, "Woodlawn Home Values Soar as Obama Library Draws New Interest to Area," *DNAInfo*, September 12, 2017; *Protect-Preserve-Produce: Affordable Housing & the*

Obama Center (Nathalie P. Voorhees Center for Neighborhood and Community Improvement, 2019); Curtis Black, "Obama Center Community Benefits Agreement Gains Traction as Jackson Park Site Controversy Continues," *Chicago Reporter*, November 21, 2019.

65. Audrey Henderson, "Will Obama's Presidential Center Invigorate or Gentrify Chicago's South Side," *Next City*, March 18, 2019; Ariel Zibler, "Obama Presidential Center Will Pay $10 for 99-Year Lease Set to Approve Building Plans," *Daily Mail*, September 19, 2018; Benjamin Schneider, "The Obama Center," *CityLab*, June 8, 2018; Edward McClelland, "Meet the Community Organizers Fighting Against . . . Barack Obama," *Politico*, February 28, 2018. On the unions, see Rachel Hinton, "Unions Join Push for Obama Center Benefits Agreement," *Chicago Sun-Times*, October 11, 2017. On Jackson Park and the lawsuit, see Richard Epstein and Michael Rachlis, "The Obama Presidential Center in Jackson Park Is Not a Done Deal," *Crain's Chicago Business*, December 4, 2019; Josh McGhee, "Obama Presidential Center Can Begin Construction in Jackson Park, Judge Rules," *Chicago Reporter*, June 11, 2019; Kristin Capps, "Chicago Gets the Obama Presidential Library, But at What Cost to the City's Parks?" *CityLab*, May 12, 2015. See also Camille Kirsch, "Professors Sign Letter in Support of Obama Center Benefits Agreement," *Chicago Maroon*, January 8, 2018.

66. Sofia Tareen, "Obama Library Brings Elation but Also Fear of Displacement," Associated Press, August 4, 2019; Benjamin Schneider, "The Obama Center: Caught in an Old David vs. Goliath Drama," *CityLab*, June 8, 2018; McClelland, "Meet the Community Organizers."

67. Brad Subramaniam, "City Allocates $4.5 Million to Housing Plan for Woodlawn," *Chicago Maroon*, March 3, 2020; Sara Freund, "How City Officials Propose to Preserve Woodlawn's Affordable Housing," *Curbed Chicago*, February 26, 2020; Christian Belanger, "Lightfoot Unveils Proposed Affordable Housing Ordinance in Letter to Woodlawn Residents," *Hyde Park Herald*, February 25, 2020; A. D. Quig, "City Grabbing Land Near Obama Library," *Crain's Chicago Business*, January 6, 2020.

68. Aaron Gettinger, "Goldenberg Says CBA Fight with City and U. of C.—Not the Obama Foundation," *Hyde Park Herald*, January 29, 2019.

69. Yao Xen Tan, "New Hotel to Be Built on 60th Street and Dorchester Avenue," May 15, 2017; Jay Koziarz, "Hyde Park Boutique Hotel Project Inches Closer Towards Breaking Ground," *Curbed Chicago*, March 1, 2017; "University of Chicago to Continue Expansion of College Housing," *news.uchicago.edu*, January 23, 2018. See also Allison Maytus, "U. of C. Presents Development Plans for South of 61st Street," *Hyde Park Herald*, May 26, 2016.

70. Max Budovitch, "The Fight to Remain, the Woodlawn Story," *South Side Weekly*, January 23, 2019; Matyus, "U. of C. Presents Development Plans"; Gibson, "Due South."

71. Budovitch, "The Fight to Remain"; Alana Semuels, "Should Urban Universities Help Their Neighbors?" *Atlantic*, January 19, 2015. See also Rosalyn Deutsche and Cara Gendel Ryan, "The Fine Art of Gentrification," *October* 31 (Winter 1984).

72. Chuck Sudo, "U of C Bought Tons of Property Around Washington Park for Obama Library Bid," *Chicagoist*, March 2, 2015.

73. Sam Cholke, "U. of C. Buys 26 Properties on South Side Ahead of Obama Library Decision," *DNAInfo*, December 10, 2014.

74. John Colapinto, "The Real-Estate Artist," *New Yorker*, January 20, 2014.

75. Stephanie Lane Sutton, "First It Was the Artists: The Myth of 'Nice' Gentrification in Art," *Chicago Literati*, July 2, 2014; Anne Gadwa Nicodemus, "Artists and

Gentrification: Sticky Myths, Slippery Realities," *Createquity*, April 5, 2013; David Lepeska, "The Accidental DIY Developer," *CityLab*, March 26, 2012.

76. Deanna Isaacs, "Theaster Gates Is Reopening a Slicker Arts Bank This Weekend," *Bleader*, April 25, 2018; Alex Greenberger, "Theaster Gates's Ambitious New Chicago Arts Center Will Open in October," *ARTnews*, August 11, 2015; Larne Abse Gogarty, "Art & Gentrification," *Art Monthly*, February 2014; Natalie Moore, "How Theaster Gates Is Revitalizing Chicago's South Side, One Vacant Building at a Time," *Smithsonian*, December 2015.

77. Joe Gose, "To Theaster Gates, Art and Redevelopment Are One and the Same," *Forbes*, December 4, 2018; Kathy Bergen, "U. of C. to Further Sculpt Arts Block on Garfield Boulevard," *Chicago Tribune*, June 3, 2016; Eleonora Edreva, "Gates to Open Bookstore in Washington Park," *South Side Weekly*, May 5, 2015; Harrison Smith, "The Art of Development," *South Side Weekly*, April 17, 2014; Catey Sullivan, "Will the Green Line Arts Center Help Turn the South Side into 'Florence During the Renaissance'?" *Chicago Reader*, November 13, 2018.

78. "Theaster Gates on the Real Meaning of Gentrification," *Phaidon*, January 5, 2016; Edreva, "Gates to Open Bookstore"; Colapinto, "The Real-Estate Artist"; Gogarty, "Art & Gentrification."

79. I have screenshots of the posts when workers took control of the Rebuild Twitter account, which pulled liberally from Gogarty, "Art & Gentrification." See also Mari Cohen and Christian Belanger, "Cracks in Theaster Gates's Rebuild Foundation," *South Side Weekly*, May 23, 2017.

80. Wake, "The Art of Social Work," *Medium*, April 27, 2017.

81. Lawrence, "Hope and Change Collide on the South Side."

82. Max Budovitch, "Where Are You Going Woodlawn?" *South Side Weekly*, October 30, 2018.

Chapter 5: A "Phoenix Rising"?

1. Marshall Terrill, *Downtown Phoenix Campus—Arizona State University: The First 5 Years* (Tempe: Arizona State University Press, 2011), 13, 15.

2. Rachel Leingang, "How Michael Crow Took ASU from a Party School to the Nation's 'Most Innovative' University," *Arizona Republic*, April 3, 2019.

3. Terrill, *Downtown Phoenix Campus*, 13.

4. Andrew Ross, *Bird on Fire: Lessons from the World's Least Sustainable City* (New York: Oxford University Press, 2011).

5. Talton moved on to the *Seattle Times*. He also wrote Arizona-themed essays for his blog, *Rogue Columnist*. For example, see his three-part 2013 series, "Phoenix 101: What Killed Downtown?" (March 11, March 18, and March 25).

6. Elizabeth Tandy Shermer, *Sunbelt Capitalism: Phoenix and the Transformation of American Politics* (Philadelphia: University of Pennsylvania Press, 2015); Andrew Needham, *Power Lines: Phoenix and the Making of the Modern Southwest* (Princeton, NJ: Princeton University Press, 2014). See also Kenneth Jackson, *Crabgrass Frontier: The Suburbanization of the United States* (New York: Oxford University Press, 1985); Carl Abbott, *The New Urban America: Growth and Politics in Sunbelt Cities* (New York: Oxford University Press, 1981).

7. Carol Heim, "Leapfrogging, Urban Sprawl, and Growth Management: Phoenix, 1950-2000," *American Journal of Economics and Sociology* 60 (January 2011); Grady

Gammage Jr., *Phoenix in Perspective* (Tempe: Herberger Center for Design, 2003); Rob Melnick, ed., *Urban Growth in Arizona* (Phoenix: Morrison Institute for Public Policy, ASU, 1988).

8. Bob Christie, "Arizona Sets Another Foreclosure Record in 2010," *Arizona Republic*, December 31, 2010; Doug MacEachern, "A Strategy to Grow Jobs," *Arizona Republic*, January 31, 2010; Ruth Simon and James Hagerty, "One in Four Borrowers Is Underwater," *Wall Street Journal*, November 24, 2009. See also Jonathan Laing, "Phoenix Descending: Is Boomtown U.S.A. Going Bust?" *Barron's*, December 19, 1988.

9. Ross, *Bird on Fire*, 81-88.

10. Dustin Gardiner, "'Bad Neighbor': Phoenix Struggles to Manage Its Vacant City-Owned Lots," *Arizona Republic*, November 24, 2016.

11. Jerod MacDonald-Evoy and Angel Phillip, "Arizona Cities Give Tax Breaks to Developers. Here's How You Help Pay for It," *Arizona Republic*, October 11, 2018; Antonia Noori Farzan, "Dirt Wars: The Battle over the Future of Downtown Phoenix," *Phoenix New Times*, May 31, 2017; John Washington, "Some Truths About Phoenix's Property Tax Deals," *Scottsdale Citizen*, June 23, 2016.

12. Nigel Duara, "Arizona's Once-Feared Immigration Law, SB 1070, Loses Most of Its Power in Settlement," *Los Angeles Times*, September 15, 2016; Stephen Lemons, "SB 1070's Third Anniversary: Arizona's War on the Brown Continues," *Phoenix New Times*, July 29, 2013; Marisa Demarco, "What SB 1070 Means to People Living in the Grand Canyon State," *Alibi*, May 20-26, 2010.

13. John Dougherty, "Un-Urban Development," *Phoenix New Times*, January 31, 2002; *Downtown Voices: Creating a Sustainable Downtown* (Phoenix, 2004).

14. *Downtown Phoenix: A Strategic Vision and Blueprint for the Future* (City of Phoenix, 2004).

15. One of these efforts took shape in the form of the innovation district PHX Core. See *PHX Core* (City of Phoenix, 2018); "Phoenix Launches New Innovation District—PHX Core," *AZ Big Media*, May 18, 2018. See also Farah Illich, "Downtown Phoenix's Tech Office Boom: How the City Created 'An Innovation Core,'" *DTPHX*, September 16, 2019.

16. Matt Bevilacqua, "Shannon Scutari on What Phoenix Is and What It Wants to Be," *Next City*, May 1, 2013.

17. "Phoenix Biomedical Campus," phoenix.gov, March 22, 2011.

18. Angela Gonzales, "Trent Provided Foundation for Bioscience Hub," *Phoenix Business Journal*, March 31, 2010; Yuri Artibise, "Arizona Biomedical Collaborative," *Downtown Phoenix Journal*, November 17, 2009. See also Anne Ryman, "$1.4 Bil Campus-Construction Plan Gains Backers," *Arizona Republic*, April 8, 2008.

19. "TGen Provides Arizona with $77 Million in Annual Economic Impact," tgen.org, September 29, 2009.

20. *BioIndustry in Phoenix: Collaborating for Success* (City of Phoenix, www.phoenix.gov/econdevsite/documents/066778.pdf).

21. "Duke Reiter and ASU's University City Exchange: Driven by a Sense of Urgency," *ASU Now*, February 27, 2019; Deanna Isaacs, "Hello, I Must Be Going," *Chicago Reader*, April 29, 2010; Jesse Stein, "Interview with SAIC's New President Wellington 'Duke' Reiter," *F Newsmagazine*, August 25, 2008.

22. Wellington Reiter, "The Big Three: New Orleans, Detroit, Phoenix" (Washington, DC: American Institute of Architects, May 2012). Reiter would also consult on the

University of Central Florida's downtown Orlando campus. See Gabrielle Russon, "Downtown Phoenix Campus Inspires UCF," *Orlando Sentinel*, October 16, 2016.

23. "A Visionary Blueprint Worthy of a 'Yes,'" *Arizona Republic*, March 1, 2006.

24. Nan Ellin, "Canalscape: Practicing Integral Urbanism in Metropolitan Phoenix," *Journal of Urban Design* 15, no. 4 (August 2010); Nan Ellin, *Phoenix: 21st Century City* (London: Booth-Clibborn, 2006); Si Robins, "ASU Students Design Temp Use Project for Vacant Land in Downtown Phoenix," *Downtown Phoenix Journal*, November 27, 2009.

25. Jonathan Dee, "Oasis," *New York Times*, May 18, 2003; Taz Loomans, "The Renaissance of Will Bruder Architect . . . ," *azarchitecture jarson&jarson*, February 21, 2012.

26. Summer Sorg, "Michael Levine and the Warehouse Area," *Arizona News*, October 19, 2017; Molly Bilker, "Warehouse Renovator Supports Local Art and Businesses While Preserving Downtown History," *Downtown Devil*, December 14, 2012.

27. Ross, *Bird on Fire*, 95; Susan Copeland, "From the Mag: Creating Downtown," *Downtown Phoenix Journal*, November/December 2011.

28. Lauren Loftus, "Queen of the Market: Cindy Gentry Campaigns for Local, Affordable Food for All," *Phoenix New Times*, May 23, 2016.

29. Susan Copeland, "A Realistic Downtown Assessment," *Arizona Republic*, January 29, 2011.

30. Debra Friedman, "An Extraordinary Partnership Between Arizona State University and the City of Phoenix," *Journal of Higher Education Outreach and Engagement* 13, no. 3 (2009).

31. She shared with me the agenda for *The Barrett Urban Experience 2010*.

32. Brenna Goth, "Arizona State University Now Ground-Floor Tenant of Westward Ho," *Arizona Republic*, September 17, 2016.

33. A sample of Hillyard's *Downtown Devil* articles includes "Together, We're Bringing Downtown Phoenix to Life," December 8, 2011; "It's Time to Close Downtown Divide," April 21, 2011. See also Brandon Kutzler, "Discussion Addresses Mistakes, Successes on ASU Downtown Campus Since 2006 Opening," *Downtown Devil*, February 1, 2012.

34. Connor Radnovich, "Downtown ASU Policy Limits Use of University Buildings to Only ASU-Affiliated Individuals," *Downtown Devil*, March 12, 2012.

35. Molly Bilker, "Downtown Students, Community Members Enjoy New Sun Devil Fitness Complex," *Downtown Devil*, April 22, 2013.

36. Brandi Porter, "Phoenix Public Market Café Opens, Aims to Become a Hub for Downtown Community," *Downtown Devil*, May 9, 2013; Daniel Zayas, "Phoenix Public Market Announces Closure after Months of Financial Hardship," *Downtown Devil*, May 8, 2012. On the art school, see Lynn Trimble, "ASU School of Art to Expand Program in Phoenix's Warehouse District," *Phoenix New Times*, November 11, 2016; Sophia Kunthara, "ASU School of Art to Move Half of Graduate Programs to Downtown Warehouse Space," *Downtown Devil*, November 19, 2013.

37. "Downtown Phoenix," *ASU Now*, September 17, 2018; Mackenzie Shuman, "ASU's Downtown Phoenix Campus Has Brought Innovation to the City," *State Press*, September 9, 2018. See also Brenda Richardson, "A Development Boom Aims to Transform Downtown Phoenix into an Urban Mecca," *Forbes*, October 27, 2019.

38. Robert Pela, "Roosevelt Row: The Fight to Keep Downtown Phoenix 'Authentic' Is a Fight to Let It Become Something It's Never Been," *Phoenix New Times*, February 25, 2015; Lynn Trimble, "Roosevelt Row Developments Inspire Protest in Phoenix," *Phoenix New Times*, January 21, 2015. See also Farzan, "Dirt Wars."

39. Lynn Trimble, "Why Artist Pete Petrisko Wants You to Stop Calling Roosevelt Row an Arts District," *Phoenix New Times*, January 9, 2017.

40. Tynin Fries, "Downtown Phoenix Struggles with Affordable Housing in Midst of Development," *AZ Big Media*, May 2, 2017. There has been some community push to include more-affordable units in new developments. See Lynn Trimble, "Phoenix Approves $231 Million Mixed-Use Development for Downtown Transit Hub," *Phoenix New Times*, April 18, 2019; Daniel Perle and Kevin Lane, "City Council Reduces Some Rents on Micro-apartment Project," *Downtown Devil*, March 3, 2016; Daniel Perle, "Community Petitions for Affordable Housing on Micro-apartment Project," *Downtown Devil*, March 2, 2016.

41. Daniel Perle, "Lawsuit Could Threaten Future of GPLET Tax Incentives," *Downtown Devil*, March 13, 2017; Angel Philips, "GPLET Tax Incentive Draws Developers but May Also Hurt Small Businesses," *Downtown Devil*, May 2, 2014.

42. Rebecca Spiess, "Amended GPLET Reform Bill Passes Through Legislature," *Downtown Devil*, April 12, 2018.

43. "Groundbreaking Celebrates New PBC Innovation Center," *ASU Now*, March 14, 2019; Angela Gonzales, "How Wexford's $77M Research Facility in Downtown Phoenix Came to Fruition," *Phoenix Business Journal*, March 7, 2019; Thomas Triolo, "ASU Partners with Wexford for Phoenix Biomedical Campus Expansion," *Downtown Devil*, January 24, 2018.

44. Mia Armstrong, "New Council-Approved Developments Set to Change Student Life in Tempe," *State Press*, January 18, 2018; Jerod MacDonald-Evoy, "Tempe Approves $21 Million Tax Break for Hotel and Conference Center," *Arizona Republic*, January 11, 2018; Mike Sunnucks, "ASU Plans $72M Greek Housing Development, Omni Hotel Lease," *Phoenix Business Journal*, November 17, 2016. ASU is also following a growing trend of generating revenue by building a luxury retirement community on the university campus. See Teresa Ghilarducci, "Dorm Life for Seniors: Sex, Drugs and Real Estate," *Forbes*, January 20, 2020; Ray Stern, "Demand Soaring for 62-and-Over High-Rise on ASU's Tempe Campus, Company Says," *Phoenix New Times*, April 18, 2017.

45. Laurie Roberts, "Arizona's Largest Office Complex Pays No Taxes (But You and I Sure Do)," *Arizona Republic*, December 18, 2017; Michael Crow, "No, Universities Aren't 'Doing Fine' on Needed Funding," *Arizona Republic*, February 10, 2019.

46. Sean McCarthy, "ABOR Tax Free Zones," *ATRA Special Report*, 2017. See also McCarthy, "When a University Helps a Business Avoid Property Taxes," *James G. Martin Center for Academic Renewal*, November 7, 2018; MacDonald-Envoy and Philips, "Arizona Cities Give Tax Breaks to Developers"; Mark Flatten, "Shifting the Burden: Cities Waive Property Taxes for Favored Businesses," *Goldwater Institute*, February 18, 2010.

47. Kevin Stone, "State of Arizona Ordered to Pay Nearly $1M Over Dismissed ASU Hotel Lawsuit," *KTAR News*, February 11, 2020; Michael Crow, "For the Last Time: Our ASU-Omni Hotel Deal Is Not a Dishonest Scheme," *Arizona Republic*, November 19, 2019; Stephen Lemons, "Experts: ASU's $140 Return on $28M 'Investment' in Omni Deal Screws K–12," *Phoenix New Times*, April 12, 2019; Stephen Lemons, "Mark Brnovich Aims to End Michael Crow's Crony Capitalism, and That's a Good Thing," *Phoenix New Times*, April 4, 2019; Laurie Roberts, "Mark Brnovich Targets ASU Tax Dodge: 'Michael Crow Has Become the Most Powerful Person in Arizona,'" *Arizona Republic*, January 11, 2019.

48. Lauren Adams, "Voices from the Field: Culturally Appropriate Services to Support Healthy Mind, Body, Spirit," *AcademyHealth*, August 2, 2018.

49. "Phoenix on the Verge," *Local Initiatives Support Corporation*, April 5, 2016; Bob McClay, "Native American Group Opens Affordable Apartment Complex in Downtown Phoenix," *KTAR News*, December 17, 2013.

50. Carianne Payton Scally, Amanda Gold, and Nicole DuBois, "The Low-Income Housing Tax Credit: How It Works and Who It Serves," *Urban Institute*, July 2018; Jacqueline Salmon, "Low-Income Tax Credits Draw Criticism," *Washington Post*, June 13, 1992.

Epilogue: The Ivory Tower Is Dead!

1. Valerie Shantz, "Shared Futures: Big Institutions and Their Inner-City Neighbours," *Canadian Centre for Policy Alternatives*, March 2012.

2. It's also important to note that Axworthy was a local boy who graduated from the school when it was still United College. After getting his PhD at Princeton he came back to UWinnipeg to teach, and he founded the Institute of Urban Studies there.

3. Edward T. Jackson, *Catalyst for Sustainability: The Achievements, Challenges, Lessons, and Prospects of the University of Winnipeg Community Renewal Corporation* (Montreal: J. W. McConnell Family Foundation, 2018); Diane Peters, "Universities Are Helping to Shape City Development," *University Affairs*, October 24, 2017.

4. Carol Sanders, "Unique Housing Weaves Mosaic in Core," *Winnipeg Free Press*, October 3, 2016.

5. The UWCRC sustainability model has been universally celebrated. But UWinnipeg alum and employee James Patterson believes that university officials continue to bury the student origins of Diversity Foods. In 2004 he and two other students who had also worked in the food industry coordinated with Jim Silver on a fourth-year student-engagement project around food services as a social enterprise to break down barriers between campus and community. According to Patterson, the student government got wind of the idea and helped fund a more developed vision plan ("Food Cubed") just as the university sent out a request for proposals for its food service contract. He understood that it was probably right to think students couldn't service such a large university contract. But Patterson said that Kreiner did have lunch with his team and asked to put the student proposal under the UWCRC banner. He pointed out that there are a number of similarities between Food Cubed and what ultimately became Diversity Foods. But Patterson says Diversity didn't go far enough with the social-engagement goals, including a kitchen incubator for neighborhood restaurants that had been pushed out of the city. See *The Food Cubed Plan* (Winnipeg: University of Winnipeg Students' Association, 2004).

6. Jim Silver, *Solving Poverty: Innovative Strategies from Winnipeg's Inner City* (Winnipeg: Fernwood, 2016).

7. Ligia Braidotti, "Housing to Make Successful University Students," *Winnipeg Free Press*, January 8, 2018.

8. Mahmood told me that community concessions such as the RecPlex charter came only after community outrage over what residents felt were past university transgressions. UWinnipeg had built the Duckworth Center with its back facing the neighborhood across Ellice Avenue. He said that even with the new university developments, the Spence neighborhood continues to face a significant housing crisis. See *Spence Neighbourhood Five-Year Plan: 2016-2021* (Winnipeg: Spence Neighbourhood Association, 2016).

9. Robert Silverman et al., "Perceptions of Residential Displacement and Grassroots Resistance to Anchor Driven Encroachment in Buffalo, NY," *Urbanities* 8, no. 2

(November 2018); Robert Mark Silverman, Jade Lewis, and Kelly Patterson, "William Worthy's Concept of 'Institutional Rape' Revisited: Anchor Institutions and Residential Displacement in Buffalo, NY," *Humanity & Society* I–24 (2014).

10. Oscar Perry Abello, "Buffalo Neighborhood Takes Control of Fight Against Displacement," *Next City*, July 26, 2016.

11. Susan Schulman, "Battle over Fruit Belt Parking Ends in Residents' Favor," *Buffalo News*, June 17, 2016.

12. "Editorial: Fruit Belt's Map Quest Shows Residents' Pride," *Buffalo News*, March 27, 2019.

13. *Rising Tide: A Blueprint for Community Benefits from the Buffalo Niagara Medical Campus* (Buffalo: Community First Alliance, 2016).

14. Susan Schulman, "City Lifts Fruit Belt Moratorium After Adopting Strategic Development Plan," *Buffalo News*, May 29, 2018; Karen Robinson, "First Land Trust Effort in Fruit Belt Is Growing, but So Is Skepticism," *Buffalo News*, March 8, 2018; Harper S. E. Bishop, "Fruit Belt: Take It Back Before It's Gone," *Public*, August 10, 2016; "A Plan That Bears Fruit: A Community Land Trust and Other Tools for Neighborhood Revitalization in the Fruit Belt," *Partnership for the Public Good*, June 22, 2016.

15. Matt Rocheleau, "Many Colleges Missing Mark on Voluntary Payments to City," *Boston Globe*, July 21, 2015; "After Criticism, Northeastern Pays Boston for Municipal Services, but Less Than City Wanted," *Boston Globe*, March 2, 2015.

16. *Taking Neighbors to Court: Johns Hopkins Medical Debt Lawsuits* (AFL-CIO/National Nurses United/Coalition for a Humane Hopkins, 2019); Meredith Cohn and Lorraine Mirabella, "Johns Hopkins Hospital Sues Patients, Many Low Income, for Medical Debt," *Baltimore Sun*, May 17, 2019.

17. Mary Schmitt and Tracy Staedter, "Sharing Hope," *Marquette*, April 30, 2020.

18. Guian McKee, "Race, Place, and the Social Responsibilities of UVA in the Aftermath of August 11 and 12," in *Charlottesville 2017: The Legacy of Race and Inequity*, ed. Louis P. Nelson and Claudrena N. Harold (Charlottesville: University of Virginia Press, 2018); Janelle Nanos, "Diverse, Locally Owned Food Start-Ups Make the Menus at Harvard, UMass, and BC," *Boston Globe*, January 24, 2020; David Jesse, "Wayne State Offers Free Tuition to Detroit Teens Who Graduate High School," *Detroit Free Press*, October 23, 2019.

19. Thomas Breen, "Rally Demands Yale, YNHH Pay 'Fair Share,'" *New Haven Independent*, May 26, 2020; Ko Lyn Cheang, "Respect Caravan Clogs Downtown Streets," *New Haven Independent*, July 29, 2020.

20. Jazz Shaw, "Harvard Realizes People Noticed Their Hypocrisy," *hotair.com*, April 1, 2020; Terrence Doyle, "Harvard Will Compensate Its Furloughed Contract Dining and Catering Workers," *Eater Boston*, March 27, 2020. See also Danielle Douglas-Gabriel, "Students Are Pressing Colleges to Keep Paying Campus Workers," *Washington Post*, April 17, 2020.

21. Kate Ryan, "Johns Hopkins University Delays Plans for Campus Police Force," *WTOP News*, June 12, 2020; "Full Statement Here: Hopkins to Put Off Establishment of Police Force for at Least 2 Years," *Maryland Matters*, June 12, 2020; Jacob Took, "Abolish, Not Delay: Opposition to Proposed 'Pause' on Johns Hopkins Private Police Force Grows," *Baltimore Beat*, June 13, 2020. See also Gillian Flaccus, "Portland State Disarms Campus Police After Black Man's Death," *Yahoo.com*, August 12, 2020; Meerah Powell, "PSU to Disarm Campus Police Officers This Fall," *OPB*, August 13, 2020.

INDEX

Credit: VisionMerge Productions

Davarian L. Baldwin is a leading urbanist, historian, and cultural critic. The Paul E. Raether Distinguished Professor of American Studies and founding director of the Smart Cities Lab at Trinity College, Baldwin is the author of *Chicago's New Negroes: Modernity, the Great Migration, and Black Urban Life* and coeditor, with Minkah Makalani, of the essay collection *Escape from New York! The New Negro Renaissance Beyond Harlem*. He has received grants and fellowships from Harvard University, the University of Virginia, the University of Notre Dame, and the Logan Nonfiction Writing Fellowship from the Carey Institute for the Global Good. He lives with his wife and children in Springfield, Massachusetts.